MICROSOFT WORD

FOR WINDOWS® 95

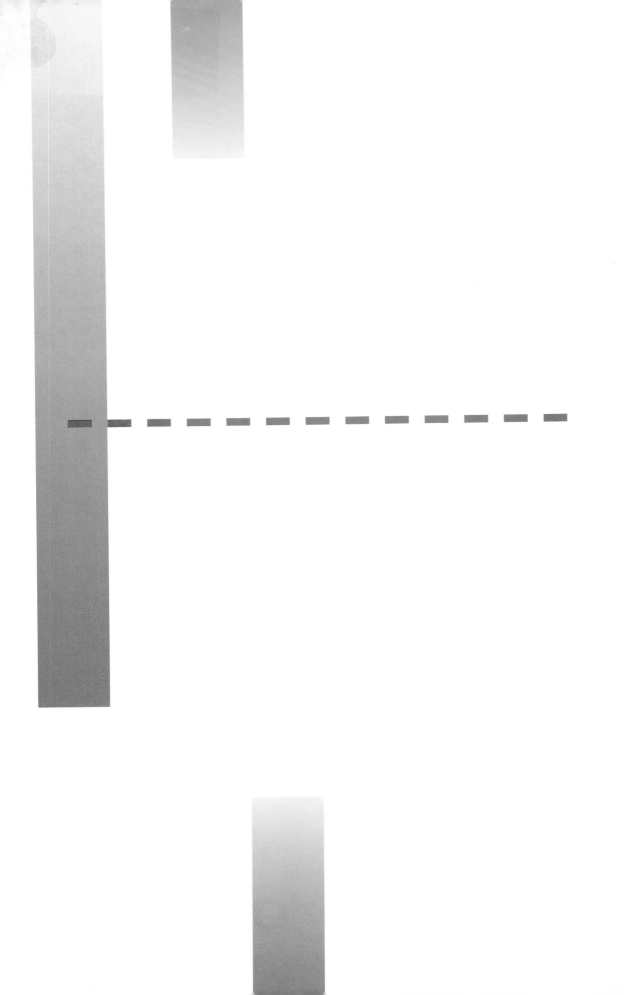

MICROSOFT® WORD

FOR WINDOWS® 95

PATRICIA MURPHY
St. Thomas Aquinas College
Sparkill, New York

SOUTH-WESTERN EDUCATIONAL PUBLISHING

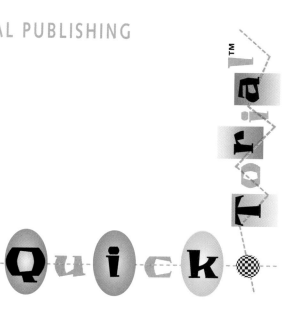

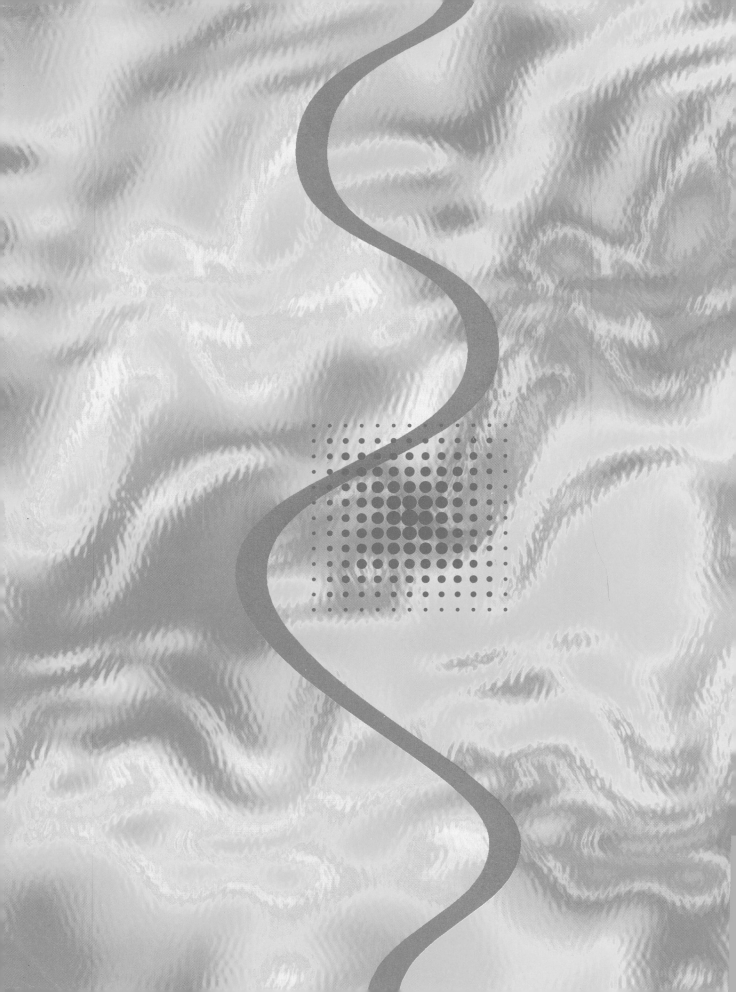

International Thomson Publishing

*South-Western Educational Publishing is
an ITP company. The ITP trademark
is used under license.*

ISBN: 0-538-71469-7

1 2 3 4 5 6 7 8 9 PR 02 01 00 99 98 97 96

Printed in the United States
of America

Credits

Managing Editor:	Janie F. Schwark
Developmental Editor:	Dave Lafferty
Marketing Manager:	Kent Christensen
Art Director:	John Robb
Cover and Book Design:	Willow Design
Development and Production:	Jennings & Keefe Media Development
Consulting Editor:	Cynthia Putnam
Copy Editor:	Virginia Rich
Page Makeup:	Rad Proctor

Microsoft Word for Windows 95: QuickTorial is designed to be an instructor-led or a self-paced learning tool for those using Word on an IBM-compatible personal computer. It is appropriate for high school students, college students, and adult learners in the nontraditional classroom.

This book may be used both in the classroom and by those in the workforce who need to learn Word. When this book is used in a self-paced environment by an individual not familiar with other word processing software, we suggest that there be someone nearby who can help the student if he or she has a problem with the exercises.

The estimated completion time is the time the average learner with some previous word processing experience would need to work through the learning materials and the exercises at the end of each lesson.

❖ Lesson Features

Each lesson contains the following:

- ✚ Learning objectives
- ✚ Estimated completion time
- ✚ Explanations of Word features
- ✚ Step-by-step exercises to reinforce learning through hands-on practice
- ✚ Written activities and review exercises to reinforce student understanding
- ✚ Exercises that use Word documentation and the online Help feature
- ✚ On Your Own problems that allow students to develop critical thinking skills

Exercises are strategically placed to give the student an opportunity to reinforce skills already learned before going on to learn new features.

❖ System Requirements

To use Word 7.0, you need:

- ✚ An IBM-compatible machine with an 80386DX or higher processor
- ✚ A 3.5-inch floppy disk drive
- ✚ A hard disk large enough to support all your applications and to store student materials
- ✚ A VGA video display
- ✚ At least 8 megabytes memory
- ✚ A mouse
- ✚ Windows 95

❖ Student Disk

The Student Disk contains files used in the exercises. Microsoft recommends the floppy drives not be used for working with files. It is a very slow process when you work from a floppy drive, and files can be corrupted and lost easily. We suggest each student create a folder with his or her own name on the hard drive and copy the exercise files to that folder. If you use another folder, you will have to substitute it when the folder is mentioned in this book.

❖ Supplements

The Teacher's Manual is designed to ensure a successful teaching experience. It includes the following:

✚ Helpful course planning suggestions and objectives as well as general teaching tips from the author

✚ Teaching suggestions specific to each lesson

✚ Reproducible production tests and solutions

✚ Solutions to activities and exercises

A Solutions Disk provides solutions to activities and exercises in electronic form.

❖ To the Student

Word 7.0 is one of Microsoft's word processing programs and a component of the Microsoft Office for Windows 95 suite of applications. This book assumes that you have already learned to use your computer and that you have learned to use Windows 95, Microsoft's operating system for the personal computer. With Windows 95 the user can navigate through applications on the computer by clicking the mouse pointer on icons or pictures instead of entering commands on a blank screen as earlier computer programs required. This book also assumes that Word is installed on your computer and is set to work with your printer.

It is very important that you watch your screen carefully as you go through the exercises in this book. If you click the mouse or press keys without understanding what is happening, you will miss a great deal. It is also important that you work through this book in the order presented. Each lesson builds on what you learned in previous lessons, so you may find yourself missing a lot if you skip through a lesson.

Every effort is made throughout this book to use Microsoft Word terminology when working with the program. This will help you to access online information about any of the procedures or features used.

You can do as many or as few of the exercises at the end of the lesson as you like or are assigned in class. The exercises concentrate on main points covered in the lesson and provide good practice.

Once you work through this book, you will be able to use many of Word's features to create professional-looking documents quickly and easily. The first few times you use a feature, you may have to use this book or the online Help to refresh your memory about the steps involved. For features you seldom use, you might always need to use online Help.

Conventions Used in This Book

Each topic includes brief explanatory text on using the particular Word feature and includes screen captures to help students understand what should happen on their screens.

Whenever a toolbar button is mentioned for the first time, the tool appears beside the text.

Information useful to the student but not appropriate in the explanatory text is entered in a Note in the margin.

The exercises that follow each small group of topics allow the student to use the features just covered.

Each of the numbered steps in the exercises begins by telling the student what is to be accomplished in that step.

Menus, commands, file names, and tool buttons the student is to click and short entries the student is to type are shown in boldface type.

Paragraphs the student is to type are shown in monospaced type.

Keys the student is to press are displayed within a keycap, for example "press **Enter**"

When more than one key is to be pressed at one time, the student will be asked to hold one key and press the second.

The word *mouse* is used to refer to any pointing device students may be using (trackball, pen). You will use the mouse rather than keystrokes whenever possible to accomplish tasks.

Definitions you need to know for using the mouse:

✤ *Point* means to move the mouse until the pointer is in the appropriate position on the screen.

✤ *Click* means to press the left mouse button with a quick motion. Always click the left mouse button unless you are directed to click another button.

✤ *Double-click* means to click twice without hesitating between clicks.

✤ *Drag* means to hold down the mouse button while you are moving the mouse. You can move some items on the screen by dragging them to a new position and dropping them.

The mouse pointer assumes different shapes as you move it around the screen. The shapes are shown in the following table.

Mouse Pointer Shapes	Used To
↖	Choose commands.
↗	Select text in selection bar.
I	Position insertion point.
↙ ↘	Size windows or graphics.
⧗	Signal Word is busy processing a command and you cannot access other commands.

❖ Acknowledgments

Many thanks to Dave Lafferty at South-Western for his patience and support throughout the entire Office project and to Cindy Putnam and Janet Andrews at Jennings & Keefe. Thanks also to my husband and children and many relatives and friends who have been so supportive not only during this project but over many years. Thanks to The Berkeley Colleges where I was teaching when first introduced to computers back in 1980. Once again, the big thank you goes to all the corporate employees who came to **Abbott Institute** when they needed to learn computer programs. It was their insistence on top-quality training that shaped my ability to develop instructional materials for computer applications.

Patricia Murphy

St. Thomas Aquinas College, Sparkill, New York

contents

contents

contents

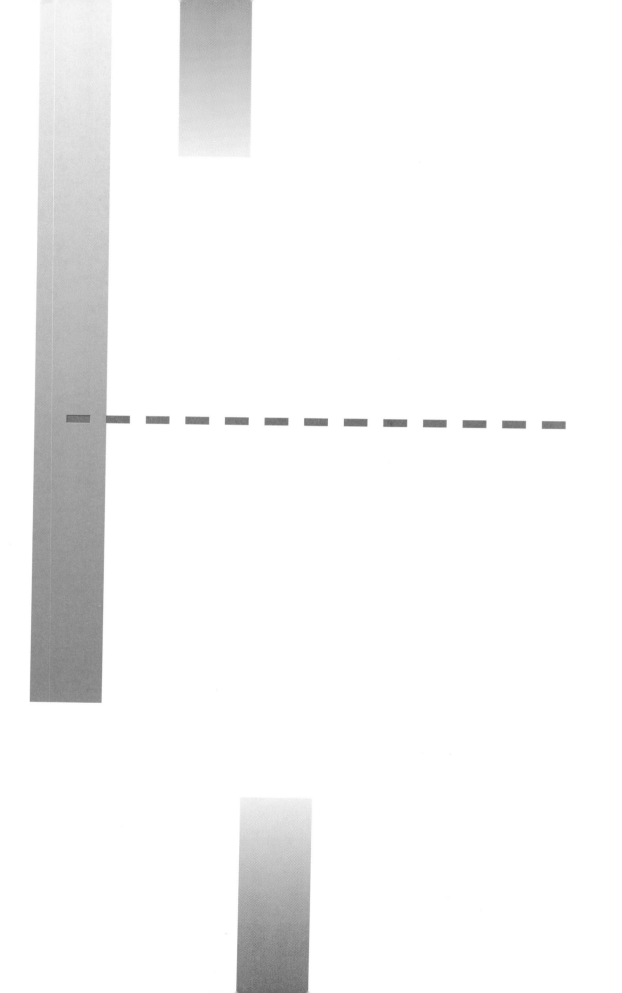

GETTING STARTED WITH WORD

FOR WINDOWS® 95

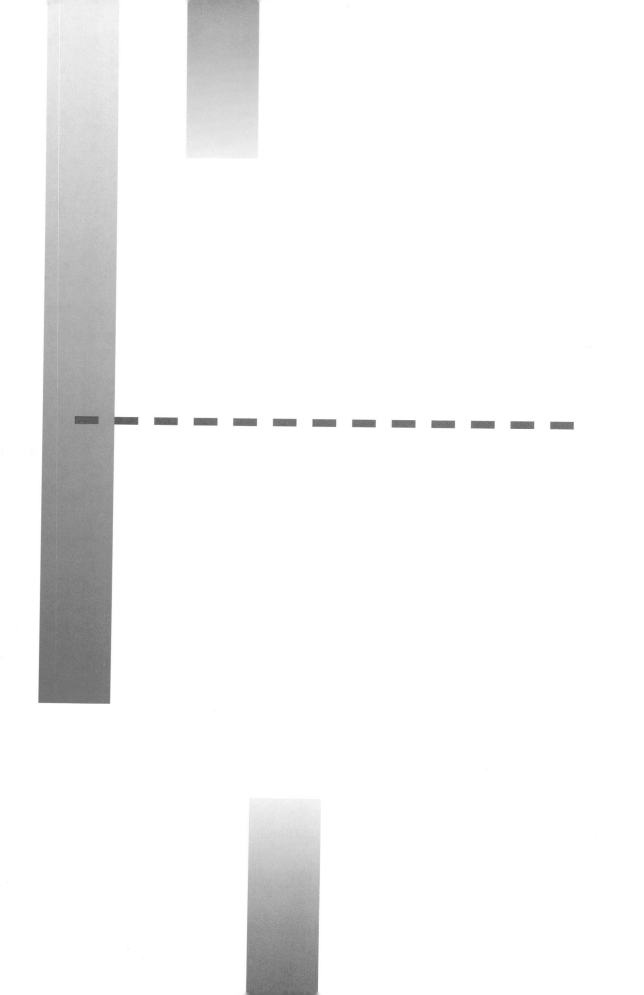

Getting Started with Word

❖ OBJECTIVES

When you complete this lesson, you will be able to:

1. Start Word and exit from Word.

2. Identify parts of the Word screen.

3. Work with dialog boxes, menus, and toolbars.

4. Customize Word.

5. Use Help.

6. Find, open, save, and close documents.

7. Work with multiple documents.

Estimated Time: $1\frac{1}{2}$ hours

❖ INTRODUCTION

Word is a word processing program that you can use on its own or as part of the Microsoft Office suite of applications. You can prepare letters, reports, memos, invoices, and even newsletters, because Word now includes many desktop publishing features. If you are using Word with other Microsoft Office applications, you can use information or graphics from Excel (spreadsheet), PowerPoint (presentation package), and Access (database) files as well as files from non-Microsoft applications in your Word documents.

In this lesson you will reset your Word software to match the settings in this book and learn the basics to get started using word processing features.

❖ STARTING WORD

If your Word software was installed using the basic installation, Windows 95 should have a Microsoft Word command on the Programs menu. If you have Office for Windows 95 installed on your computer, there should be a New Office Document command on the Start menu. There should also be a Start a New Document button on the Office Shortcut Bar (see Figure GS-1).

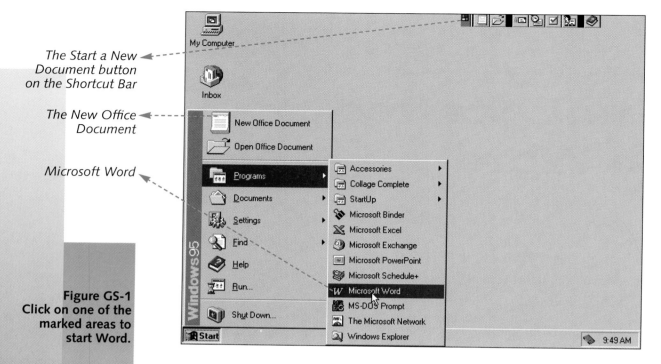

The Start a New Document button on the Shortcut Bar

The New Office Document

Microsoft Word

Figure GS-1
Click on one of the marked areas to start Word.

You can start Word by doing one of the following:

❖ Clicking the Start button, clicking Programs, and then clicking Microsoft Word.

   or

❖ Clicking the Start button, clicking New Office Document, and clicking the Blank Word Document icon.

   or

❖ Clicking the Start a New Document button on the Office Shortcut Bar (if you have Microsoft Office).

❖ IDENTIFYING THE PARTS OF THE WORD SCREEN

To work with Word, you need to know the parts of the Word screen shown in Figure GS-2.

Application control menu icon—lets you click to open a menu to move, size, or close the application window.

Title bar—shows you the name of the application and the document in use.

I-beam—click it where you want to position the insertion point.

Minimize buttons—let you click to shrink the window to an icon.

Word Restore button—appears when a window has been maximized and lets you restore the Word window to its original smaller size.

Document Restore button—appears when a window has been maximized and lets you restore the document window to its original smaller size.

Application Close button—lets you close the application.

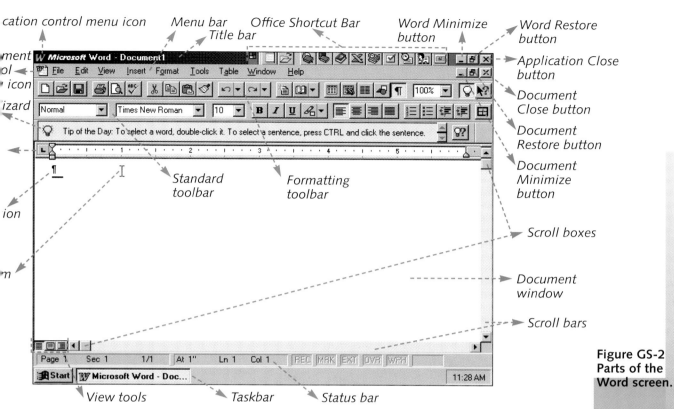

cation control menu icon   Menu bar   Office Shortcut Bar   Word Minimize button   Word Restore button

Title bar

Application Close button

Document Close button

Document Restore button

Document Minimize button

Standard toolbar   Formatting toolbar

Scroll boxes

Document window

Scroll bars

View tools   Taskbar   Status bar

**Figure GS-2
Parts of the
Word screen.**

Document Close button—lets you close the document.

Document control menu icon—lets you move, size, or close the document window.

Insertion point—blinking vertical bar displaying the position where information you enter appears.

Menu bar—shows the names of drop-down menus.

Scroll bar—lets you click above or below or to the left or right of the scroll box to move a full screen up, down, left, or right.

Scroll box—lets you move to a position by dragging the scroll box until Word displays the page you want.

Status bar—displays messages to help you use Word.

Standard toolbar—contains shortcut buttons for commonly used menu commands.

Formatting toolbar—lets you format without using menus.

Ruler—lets you set margins, tabs, and indents.

Taskbar—lets you quickly switch between open applications.

Office Shortcut Bar—lets you quickly switch between Office 95 applications.

Document window—where you enter and edit text.

TipWizard Box—watches the way you work and displays tips that can help you work more efficiently.

View tools—let you switch views for the document.

note

You should leave the TipWizard Box turned on while working with Word because it provides information about easier ways of accomplishing your tasks.

❖ EXITING FROM WORD

You can exit from and close the Word application by:

❖ Choosing the Exit command on the File menu.

or

❖ Clicking the Close button on the title bar.

or

❖ Double-clicking the Word control menu icon.

When you exit from the Word program, Word prompts you to save any unsaved changes in documents and closes open documents. You will learn to save documents later in this lesson.

Exercise GS-1

1. To start Word, click the **Start** button, click **Programs,** and click **Microsoft Word.** Read the TipWizard tip if it is displayed.

2. To familiarize yourself with the names of various parts of the Word window, carefully look over your screen and Figure GS-2 with the parts of the Word window identified. If your Word window does not look like the one shown in Figure GS-2, you will be able to adjust it in the next exercise in this lesson.

3. To exit from Word, click the application **Close** button.

4. To start Word again, click the **Start** button, click **Programs** and click **Microsoft Word.**

❖ WORKING WITH MENUS AND DIALOG BOXES

Drop-down menus display commands (see Figure GS-3). You click the name of the menu on the menu bar to see its commands.

When menu commands are dimmed like Cut and Copy are in Figure GS-3, Word knows there is nothing selected to cut or copy. When there is no possibility of using a command, the command is not available and Word dims it.

When you point to menu commands, you can see a short description of the selected command on the status bar.

You can close a menu without selecting a command by clicking on a blank part of the document window or by pressing (Esc).

Some menu commands display shortcut keys—keystrokes you can use instead of opening the menu (see Figure GS-3). If you find you often use a menu and would prefer to use keystrokes, check the menu to find the shortcut keys. You will not use them in this book.

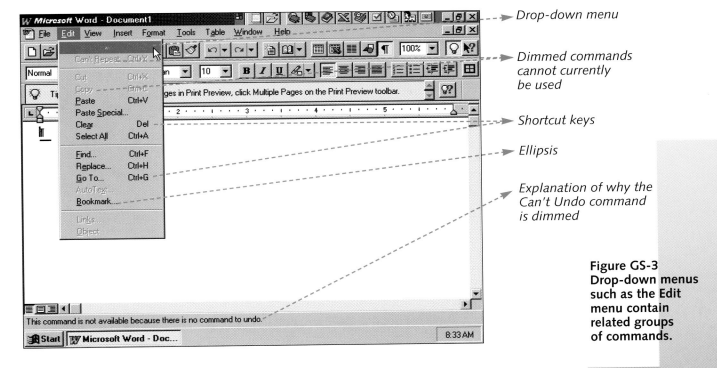

- Drop-down menu
- Dimmed commands cannot currently be used
- Shortcut keys
- Ellipsis
- Explanation of why the Can't Undo command is dimmed

Figure GS-3
Drop-down menus such as the Edit menu contain related groups of commands.

When you select a command that has an ellipsis (…) after it, you will see a dialog box such as the one shown in Figure GS-4, where you can enter information for the system.

When Word needs more information to carry out a command, you make choices in a dialog box. Table GS-1 describes how to work with various parts of dialog boxes.

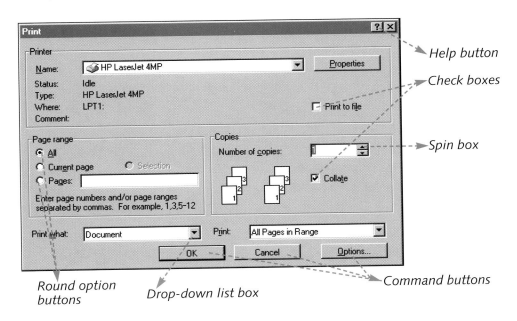

- Help button
- Check boxes
- Spin box
- Round option buttons
- Drop-down list box
- Command buttons

Figure GS-4
A menu command followed by an ellipsis leads to a dialog box such as the Print dialog box.

To Select	Click
A file tab in a dialog box	File tab
Or clear options in round option buttons or in check boxes	The button or the box
Number in a spin box	Up arrow or down arrow to the right of the box until the number you want appears
Item in a drop-down list	Down arrow to display the list and click the item you want

Table GS-1

Dialog boxes also contain command buttons (see Figure GS-4). The command buttons you will see most often are OK and Close or Cancel.

❖ Click OK to carry out choices you make in the dialog boxes.

❖ Click Cancel or Close to close a dialog box without making changes.

When you want to see a brief explanation for a part of a dialog box, click the question mark (Help) button to display a ScreenTip. ScreenTips are available for commands, various parts of dialog boxes, and other screen areas.

Some menu commands display check marks to the left of the command (see Figure GS-5). If the check mark is displayed, these commands are turned on. You can toggle them on or off by clicking them or sometimes by making another selection.

Some commands shown in Figure GS-5 (Normal, Outline, Page Layout, or Master Document) display a bullet to the left of the command. Choosing another of the options moves the bullet to the new selection.

Figure GS-5
Commands with check marks can be toggled on and off; those with bullets are options that are turned off when you make another selection.

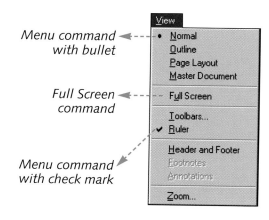

Menu command with bullet

Full Screen command

Menu command with check mark

Shortcut menus are available for many of the commands you use (see Figure GS-6). To display a shortcut menu:

❖ Point at the area with which you want to work.

❖ Click the right mouse button.

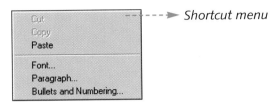
➤ *Shortcut menu*

Figure GS-6
This shortcut menu appears when you click the right mouse button near the insertion point in a blank document.

❖ CUSTOMIZING WORD

Because Word makes it easy to set up the program to suit your own needs, your screen may not look exactly like the one shown in this book. Whenever you start Word, it opens with the settings that were used during the last session.

If others are using your computer, you may have to change these settings each time you start a lesson so that your display matches the one used in this book. Even if your screen display matches, you should go through the exercises so you become familiar with the various options and commands available to you.

USING THE FULL SCREEN COMMAND

If the last user turned on the Full Screen command on the View menu (see Figure GS-5), you may not see the title bar, toolbars, scroll bars, or status bar on your screen. The Full Screen command lets you display as much as possible of your document without the other parts of the window that are usually displayed.

 If you do not see anything but your document and the Full Screen button, you can click the Full Screen button to return to a different view. You can also press (Esc) to leave Full Screen view.

MAXIMIZING YOUR WINDOWS

When you start Word the first time, the Word window does not fill the screen. Also if Word used less than the full screen to display documents during the last session, you may have to click the Maximize button for both the application and document windows. You can find the Maximize button at the top right of each window.

USING THE ZOOM COMMAND

You can use the Zoom command on the View menu (see Figure GS-7) or the Zoom button to view greater or lesser degrees of magnification on your screen. Word displays a preview of the character size that will display. You can also opt to see the entire width of the page, the whole page, or more than one page.

If the last user changed the Zoom settings and did not return to the 100% view, your document may appear to be smaller or larger than those in the figures in this book.

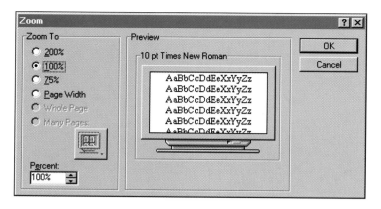

Figure GS-7
The Zoom dialog
box displays
options for viewing
the document.

USING NORMAL VIEW AND THE RULER

When you select normal view, you see a bullet next to the Normal command on the menu (see Figure GS-8). You can also use the View buttons on the left side of the horizontal scroll bar to change views.

When you display the ruler, you see a check mark next to the Ruler command.

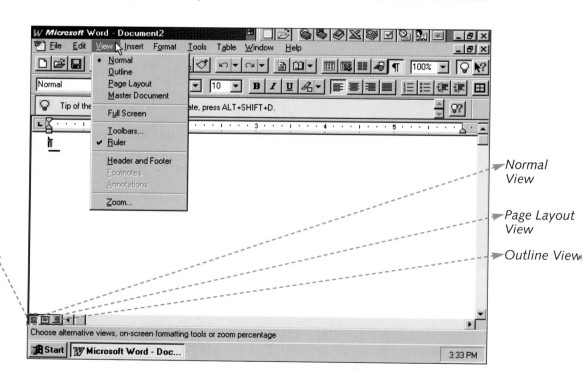

View buttons

Figure GS-8
Bullets and
check marks on
menus show
currently selected
commands.

USING THE TOOLBARS

You can click a toolbar button to use a menu command without having to open the menu. The Standard and Formatting toolbars are toggled on in the dialog box shown in Figure GS-9. Those toolbars contain buttons for the commands used most often in Word. You can customize toolbars to display buttons for commands you most often need.

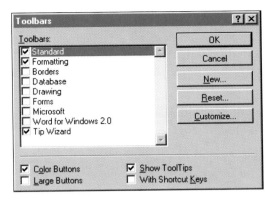

Figure GS-9
Use the Toolbars dialog box to select, show, and customize the various toolbars.

Exercise GS-2

1. To open the File menu, click **File** on the menu bar.

2. To close the menu without making a selection, click on white space in the document.

3. To return to a different view if your screen has a Full Screen tool (pictured earlier) on the right side of the window, click the **Full Screen** tool.

4. To maximize your display if your Word window and document do not fill the entire screen, look for the Maximize buttons (pictured earlier) and click them.

5. To check the settings in the Zoom dialog box, click the **View** menu and click **Zoom.** If 100% is not selected, select it. Then click the **OK** command button. If 100% is selected when the Zoom dialog box opens, you can click **OK** or **Cancel.**

6. To be sure you are using normal view, click the **View** menu and click **Normal.**

7. To be sure the Ruler is displayed, click the **View** menu and click **Ruler.**

8. To display the Standard, Formatting, and TipWizard toolbars, click the **View** menu and click **Toolbars.** If you do not see check marks in the Standard, Formatting, and TipWizard toolbars boxes, click **Standard, Formatting,** and **TipWizard.** If you see check marks in any of the other boxes, click them to turn them off. Click **OK** when finished.

USING THE OPTIONS COMMAND

The Options command on the Tools menu lets you change the default settings for many of Word's features.

You will use the Options command to match your system's setup to the one used in this book. Many of the selections in the Options dialog boxes will be covered in later lessons.

You can use the Customize command on the Tools menu to customize toolbars, menus, and shortcut keys. If you find your menus or shortcut keys are different from the ones used in this book, you can return to the original settings by choosing Reset all in their Customize dialog boxes.

In the following exercise you will look at each of the tabs in the Options dialog box to be sure the settings match those in Figures GS-10 through GS-21.

Exercise GS-3

1. To display the Options dialog box, click the **Tools** menu and click **Options.**

2. To check the settings on the View tab, compare them to those in Figure GS-10 and make any necessary changes. In the Show box, Highlight should be turned on. In the Window box, Status Bar, Horizontal Scroll Bar, and Vertical Scroll Bar should be turned on. In the Nonprinting Characters box, All should be turned on.

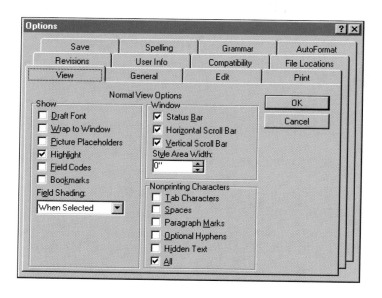

**Figure GS-10
View options affect
how Word displays
your document.**

3. To check the settings on the General tab, click the **General** tab, compare the settings to those in Figure GS-11 and make any necessary changes. Background Repagination, Beep on Error Actions, Update Automatic Links at Open, Mail as Attachment, Recently Used File List 4 Entries, and TipWizard Active should all be turned on. The Measurement Units box should display Inches.

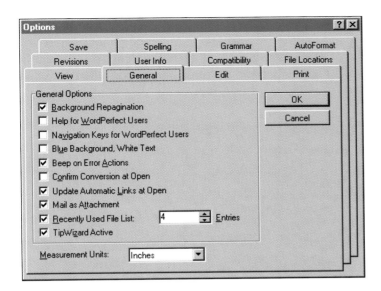

Figure GS-11
General options
cover miscellaneous
settings.

4. To check the settings on the Edit tab, click the **Edit** tab, compare the settings to those in Figure GS-12, and make any necessary changes. Typing Replaces Selection, Drag-and-Drop Text Editing, Automatic Word Selection, Use Smart Cut and Paste, and Use Tab and Backspace Keys to Set Left Indent should be turned on.

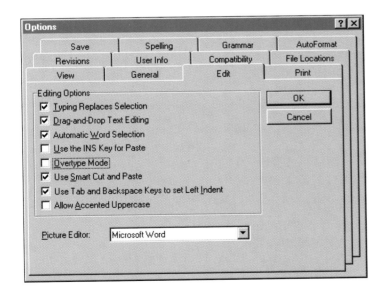

Figure GS-12
Edit options affect
how you enter and
edit text.

5. To check the settings on the Print tab, click the **Print** tab, compare the settings to those in Figure GS-13, and make any necessary changes. Background Printing and Drawing Objects should be checked. If you find you are always having to reverse the order of pages from the printer, click **Reverse Print Order.**

Figure GS-13
Print options control various elements of your printouts.

6. To check the settings on the Revisions tab, click the **Revisions** tab, compare the settings to those in Figure GS-14, and make any necessary changes. The legal community often uses revision marking, and you will use it if you are routing documents via a network.

Figure GS-14
Revisions options let you track changes in a document.

7. To check the settings on the User Info tab, click the **User Info** tab (see Figure GS-15). If you are using your own computer and would like to change the user information, do so. If you are using a classroom computer, the settings should probably not be changed.

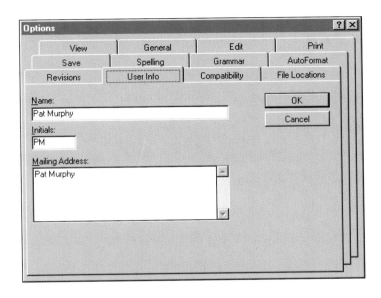

Figure GS-15
Word will sometimes use information on the User Info tab to save you time.

8. To check the settings on the Compatibility tab, click the **Compatibility** tab, compare the settings to those in Figure GS-16, and make any necessary changes. None of the options should be turned on now, but if you regularly exchange documents with other applications, use the drop-down box to find the application you need.

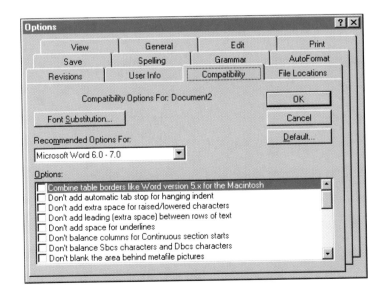

Figure GS-16
Compatibility options affect how your document translates to other word processing programs.

9. To check the settings on the File Locations tab, click the **File Locations** tab, compare the settings to those in Figure GS-17, and make any necessary changes. If your instructor followed the suggestions for this book, the location for your documents should be a folder with your name. Click **Documents** and then click the **Modify** button if you want Word to default to looking for documents in your folder. You can also create a new folder by clicking the Create New Folder button in the Modify Location dialog box.

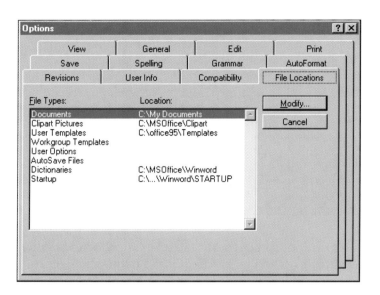

Figure GS-17
File Locations options tell Word where to look for documents.

10. To check the settings on the Save tab, click the **Save** tab, compare the settings to those in Figure GS-18, and make any necessary changes. Allow Fast Saves and Automatic Save Every 10 Minutes should be turned on.

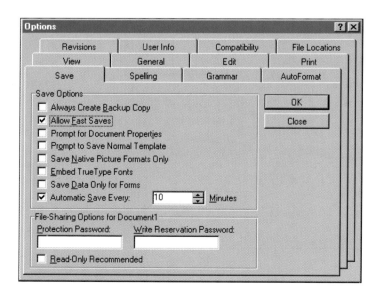

Figure GS-18
Save options affect how you save, back up, and protect documents.

11. To check the settings on the Spelling tab, click the **Spelling** tab, compare the settings to those in Figure GS-19, and make any necessary changes. Automatic Spell Checking, Always Suggest, Ignore Words in Uppercase, and Words with Numbers should be toggled on.

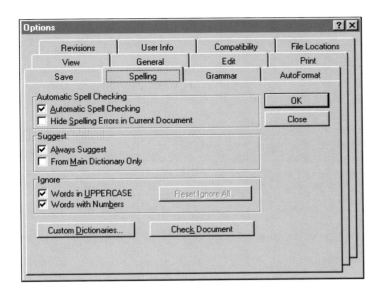

Figure GS-19
Spelling options affect how the spelling checker works.

12. To check the settings on the AutoFormat tab, compare the settings to those in Figure GS-20 and make any necessary changes. Show Options For AutoFormat As You Type, Apply Borders, Automatic Bulleted Lists, and Automatic Numbered Lists, and all options in the Replace As You Type box should be toggled on.

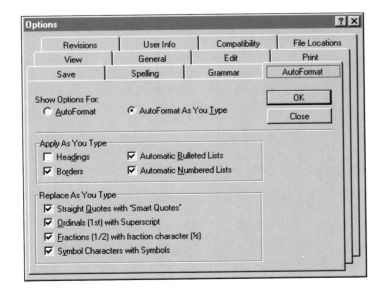

Figure GS-20
AutoFormat options give you easy ways to apply formatting as you type.

13. To carry out any changes you made and close the dialog box, click **OK.**

❖ USING HELP

You can use Word's online Help to get information about using any of the Word features or dialog boxes.

THE HELP MENU

Use the Microsoft Word Help Topics command on the Help menu to display the Help window.

❖ Use the Contents tab to display topics organized by category (see Figure GS-21). To see a list of topics in a category, double-click the book icon. To see a topic, double-click it.

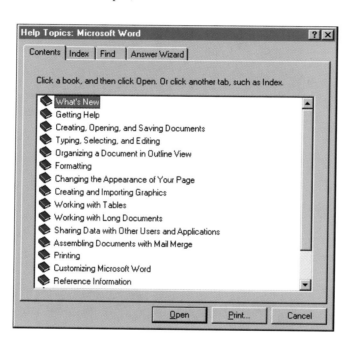

Figure GS-21
The Help Contents tab displays topics organized by category.

❖ Use the Index tab to enter a topic you want to find or to scroll through the list of entries. To display information about an entry, click the entry and then click the Display button (see Figure GS-22).

❖ Use the Find tab to search for words or phrases in help topics. Windows must create a database containing every word in the help files before you can use Find.

 ❖ Use the Answer Wizard tab to type a request for help in your own words (see Figure GS-23). Windows uses IntelliSense to list online help topics that might assist you with your work. You can also access the Answer Wizard by double-clicking the Help button on the Standard toolbar or by choosing Answer Wizard on the Help menu. You might need to rephrase your question to find the topic you need.

The Microsoft Network command on the Help menu connects you to forum on The Microsoft Network. You can find out how to connect to Microsoft technical resources, including online support forums.

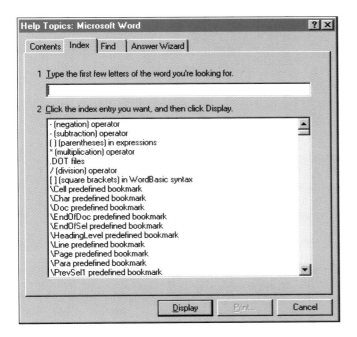

Figure GS-22
You can use the scroll bar or you can type to move to an index entry.

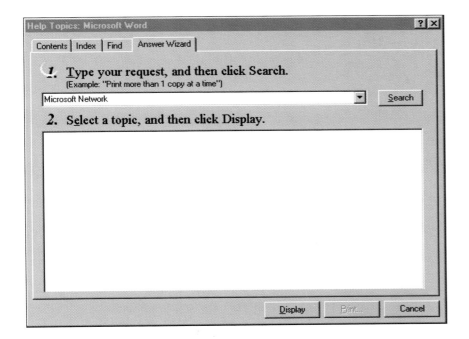

Figure GS-23
Type a request for help in your own words with Answer Wizard.

WordPerfect Help is available for users who are switching to Word from WordPerfect.

About Microsoft Word displays information about the Word program.

SCREENTIPS

ScreenTips offer brief explanations for commands, parts of dialog boxes, and items you see on the screen.

 To use the ScreenTips feature, click the Help button.

 When the question mark appears on the mouse pointer, click the item for which you want information.

 To use the ScreenTips feature while a dialog box is displayed, click the question mark button at the top right of the dialog box.

To remove a ScreenTip from the screen or remove the question mark from the mouse pointer, press **Esc** or click the Help button or question mark button again.

TOOLTIPS

 Word's ToolTips display the name of a tool when you point to the tool with the mouse. They are especially helpful when you are just beginning to use Word and cannot remember what command a tool represents.

Exercise GS-4

1. To open the Help menu, click **Help** on the menu bar. Click **Microsoft Word Help Topics.**

2. To see the Contents tab if it is not already displayed, click the **Contents** tab.

3. To see the list of new features in Word 7.0, double-click **What's New.**

4. To display the Index tab, click the **Index** tab.

5. To move quickly to IntelliSense, type **Intel.** Notice IntelliSense is selected.

6. To display information about IntelliSense, click the **Display** button. Word displays a list of topics.

7. To display information about the Working smarter topic, click **Working smarter with new IntelliSense features** and click **Display.**

8. To see help for the **Format text while you type** box, click it.

9. To remove the explanation box from the screen, click on a blank space in the Help window.

10. To return to the Contents dialog box, click **Help Topics.**

11. To display the Answer Wizard, click the **Answer Wizard** tab.

12. To enter a question, type **How do you print more than one copy** and click **Search.**

13. To display the Help window, click **Print more than one copy** and click **Display.**

14. To print a copy of the Help window, click **Options,** click **Print Topic,** and click **OK** in the Print dialog box.

15. To return to the Answer Wizard window, click **Help Topics.**

16. To close Help, click the **Close** button.

❖ OPENING, SAVING, AND CLOSING DOCUMENTS

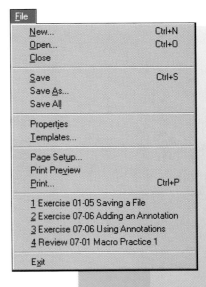

You can use the New, Open, Close, Save, Save As, and Save All commands on the File menu to create, open, save, and close documents. You can use the Properties command on the File menu to see a lot of system statistics and information about a document.

STARTING NEW DOCUMENTS

When you start Word, you see a new document on the screen. The new document is the equivalent of a blank piece of paper where you can begin entering your text.

The first document of any session is called Document1. Each new document you open during a session will have a consecutive number.

You can have as many documents open at one time as the memory in your system allows. That means you can work with more than one document at a time.

To create a new document, you can:

❖ Click the New button on the toolbar.

or

❖ Open the File menu and choose the New command.

The quickest way to create a new document is to click on the New button.

When you want to create a new document based on a template other than the Normal one, use the Open command on the File menu to display the New dialog box shown in Figure GS-24. (You will learn more about templates in Lesson 3.)

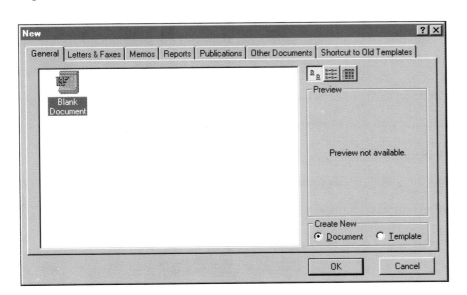

If you or your instructor used the instructions that came with the practice disk for this book, the system should look at a folder with your name that contains the practice files.

Figure GS-24
You create new documents in the New dialog box.

FINDING, OPENING, AND MANAGING DOCUMENTS

To open an existing document, you can:

 ❖ Click the Open button on the toolbar.

or

❖ Click Open on the File menu.

or

❖ Click the name of the file if it shows on the bottom of the File menu.

The fastest way to display the Open dialog box shown in Figure GS-25 is to click the Open button on the toolbar.

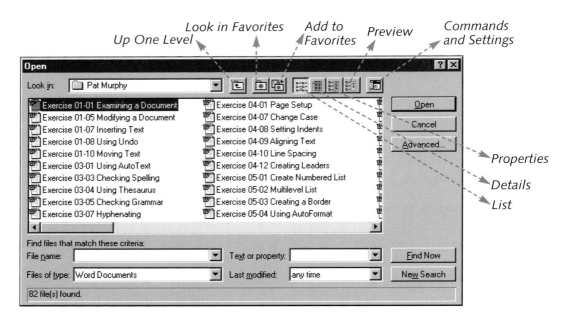

Figure GS-25
Select the file
you want to
open in the Open
dialog box.

You can also open one of the last four files used by clicking on its file name displayed at the bottom of the File menu.

You can use the Open dialog box to open, find, and manage your files.

To open a document on a different drive or in a different folder, click the location you want in the Look In box. Word displays the contents of the selected drive or folder below the Look In box.

To see the contents of a document before opening it, select the document and then click the Preview button (see Figure GS-25). You can also use the List, Details, or Properties buttons to change the information displayed for a selected document.

To move one folder level higher, you can click the Up One Level button.

To display Favorite folders, click the Look in Favorites button. The Favorites folder stores shortcuts to files and folders. You can use the Favorites for quick access to a file without having to remember where the file is located.

To add a file to a favorite folder, click the Add to Favorites button.

To open a specific document, you can type its name in the File Name box.

To open a specific type of file (i.e., a file created in another application), click the file type in the Files of Type box.

To find all files containing certain text in either the title or the body of the document , enter the text enclosed in quotation marks in the Text or Property box. For instance, to find all files containing the words Microsoft Office, type "Microsoft Office."

To find all files saved in a specific time period, click the time period in the Last Modified box.

To find documents that match the specified criteria, click the Find Now button. The Find Now button changes to a Stop button during a search so you can cancel a search.

To clear all of the criteria you entered in the boxes at the bottom of the Open dialog box and return to the default values, click the New Search button.

To further narrow a search or to save, rename, or delete searches, click Advanced.

To open the menu to manage files, select a file and point to it while clicking the right mouse button.

SAVING DOCUMENTS

To save a document, you can use the Save or Save As commands on the File menu. To save all open documents, you can use the Save All command. If you have not saved a file before, the Save As dialog box shown in Figure GS-26 appears whether you select Save or Save As.

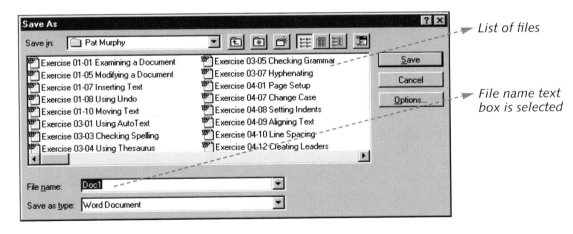

List of files

File name text box is selected

Figure GS-26 The Save As command lets you save a new file or save an existing file with a new name or location.

You can use the Save As command to save an already saved file with a new name or file location. You might, for instance, want to keep the document you opened as one file and have another file containing the changes you just made to the original file.

You can use the Save tool on the Standard toolbar to display the Save As dialog box if your document has not been saved before. If the document has been saved already, the Save tool will save it to its original file without displaying a dialog box.

When Word displays the Save As dialog box, the File name text box is selected. As soon as you begin typing the new file name, the first character you enter overwrites the default name (typing replaces selection). Notice the file will be saved in the default folder you designated a few minutes ago in the Options dialog box. You can change the folder.

A file name can contain up to 255 characters and can be uppercase or lowercase. File names can contain spaces but cannot contain a period or any of the following characters: * / : [ ] + = ^ | < >.

If you share your documents with others who use different word processing programs, you can save a Word document in another file format by clicking the drop-down button on the Save as Type box and clicking the type of file you want.

You can also change the drive or folder to which your Word document is to be saved in the Save As dialog box.

The Options button in the Save As dialog box displays the Options dialog box shown in Figure GS-27.

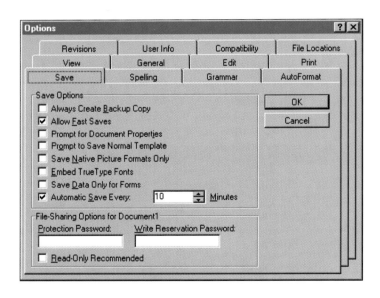

Figure GS-27
The Options dialog box displays various save options.

note

Backup copies can clutter your hard drive with almost duplicate files. Do not turn this option on if space is limited on your system.

You can set options to have Word save the previous version as a backup every time you save a document. If there is a power failure or other problem with your computer, you can restore the document to its last saved version by opening its backup copy.

In the Options exercise, you set the Automatic Save command to save your document every ten minutes. You also allowed fast saves, which save only new material during each save. Fast saves require more disk space, and you should save long documents without the fast save option when you are finished working on them.

You can also protect documents with passwords so others cannot open or change your documents. You will learn more about password protection in a later lesson.

CLOSING DOCUMENTS

When you save a Word document to a disk, the document stays open on your screen so you can continue working with it. To close documents, you can use the Close or Close All command on the File menu or the Close button on the right side of the menu bar. If you want to close all open documents, hold (Shift) while you click the File menu. You will see Close All instead of Close on the menu.

When you choose the Close command, Word prompts you to save the document if you made any changes since it was last saved. When you choose the Close command and there are no more open documents, you see the screen shown in Figure GS-28. Notice the only menus available are File and Help. When you open a document or create a new one, the full menu reappears.

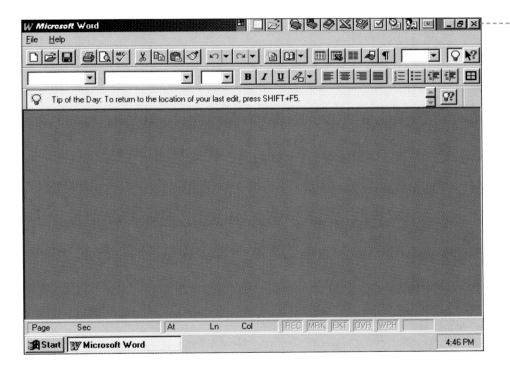

Close button

**Figure GS-28
Only the File and Help menus appear when there are no open documents in Word.**

WORKING WITH MULTIPLE DOCUMENTS

You can open the Window menu to see a list of all open Word documents. The check mark signals the active document—the document on top. You simply click the document you want to move to the top of the pile when you want to work with it.

You can use the Arrange All command to display all of your open documents (see Figure GS-29). The document with the colored title bar is the active document. Any commands you select or text you enter will affect the active document. If you want to return to a window that displays only the active document, click on that document's Maximize button.

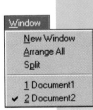

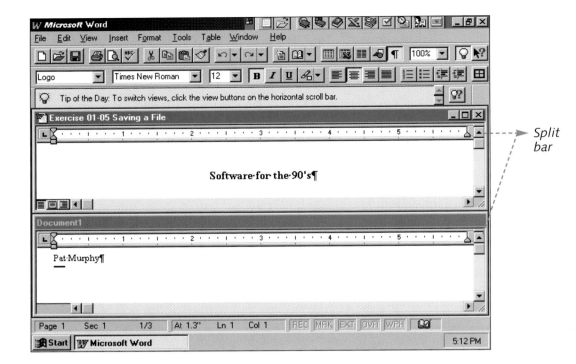

Figure GS-29
You can use
Arrange All to
display all open
documents.

 You can use the Split command or the Split bar on the vertical scroll bar (shown on the left) to split the window in two parts if you want to see different parts of the same document at the same time.

You can make another open document active by clicking it on the Window menu.

Exercise GS-5

1. To enter some text in the document on your screen, type **your name.**

2. To open an existing document, click the **Open** tool, scroll down the list of files until you see **Exercise GS-05 Saving a File,** and double-click it.

3. To display the original document Word created when you started the program, click the **Window** menu and click **Document1.**

4. To return to the Exercise GS-05 Saving a File document, click the **Window** menu and click **Exercise GS-05 Saving a File.**

5. To see both documents on the screen, click the **Window** menu and click **Arrange All.**

6. To see the properties of this file, click **File** and click **Properties.** Click each of the tabs to see the kind of information available. Click **Close.**

7. To make Document1 active, click somewhere in the white space in that document.

8. To save the unsaved Document1, click the **Save** tool, type **Exercise GS-05 Practice 1,** and click **Save.**

9. To save the Exercise GS-05 Saving a File document with a new name so you have a second copy of it, click somewhere in the white space in the document to activate it, click the **File** menu, and click **Save As.** Type **Exercise GS-05 Practice 2** and click **Save.**

10. To close both documents, hold (Shift) and click the **File** menu. Click **Close All.** Notice how the Word window looks when there are no documents open (see Figure GS-28).

11. To open a new document, click the **New** tool.

❖ S U M M A R Y

You have now learned how to start Word, customize the program to work with this book, work with the Word window, create and open documents, use Help, save and close documents, and exit from Word.

Try the exercises on the following pages to test how well you remember what you learned. Don't be afraid to go back and look up the answers, because that will help to reinforce what you learned.

activities

❖ TRUE/FALSE

On the blank line before each sentence, place a **T** if the statement is true or an **F** if it is false.

_____ 1. You can open only three documents at a time.

_____ 2. You should leave documents open when you know you will not use them again during the Word session.

_____ 3. It is faster to use menu commands than to use toolbar buttons.

_____ 4. The shortcut keys for many commands are listed on the menus.

_____ 5. Word opens with the settings used in the previous session.

_____ 6. There is a Help button in every dialog box.

_____ 7. When you save a document, it is automatically closed.

_____ 8. You can use the Properties command to see information about the active document.

_____ 9. You must always have the written documentation that comes with your software nearby to be able to find information about using a Word feature.

_____ 10. You can print any of the Help windows that you access with the Search command.

❖ COMPLETION

Fill in the blanks in the following statements.

1. The _____ command on the _____ menu is the command to use when you want to save all of your open documents.

2. You can use the _____ button to make your document fill the screen.

3. You can open the _____ menu to see a list of files that are open.

4. You can open the _____ menu to see a list of the last four files used in Word.

5. You can use the _____ command on the Window menu to display all of your open documents.

6. The part of a window that shows a document's name is the _____.

7. You can use the _____ bar at the bottom of the screen to switch from one opened application to another.

8. The File Locations tab in the _____ dialog box is where you specify where files will be stored.

9. The _____ dialog box is where you specify the name you want to assign to a document.

10. If you want to close a dialog box without selecting any of its options, click _____.

review

Review Exercise GS-1

1. Use online Help to get information for closing a document.

2. Print the Help window.

If you are not sure about how to proceed, return to the Help section and check how you searched for a topic during the lesson.

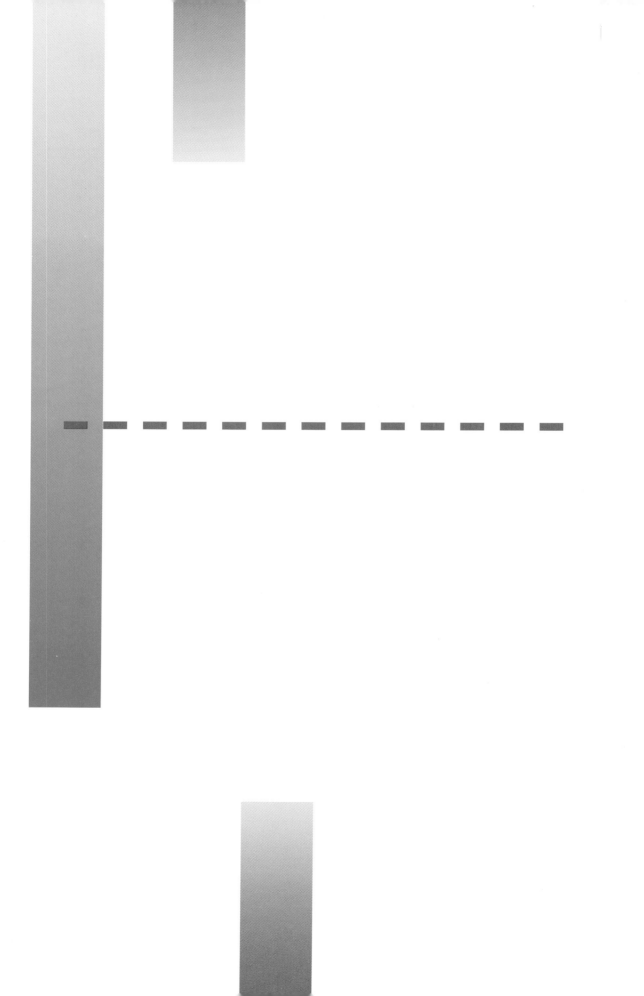

MICROSOFT® WORD

FOR WINDOWS® 95

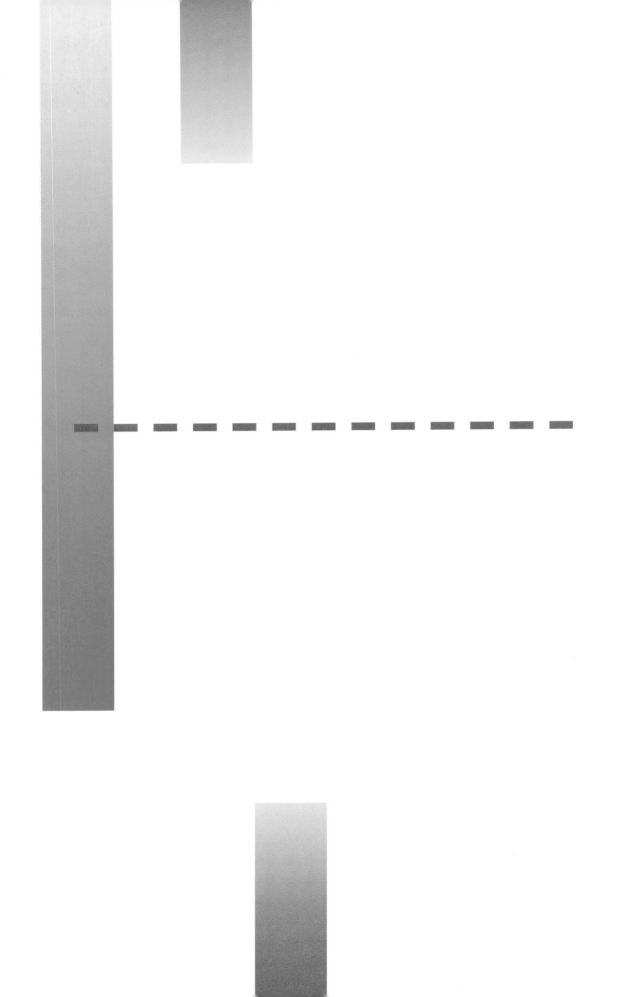

lesson 1

Entering and Editing Text

❖ OBJECTIVES

When you complete this lesson, you will be able to:

1. Use the mouse or keyboard to move around within a document.

2. Enter and select text.

3. Insert and delete text.

4. Use Undo, Redo, and Show/Hide tools.

5. Cut, copy, and paste.

Estimated Time: $1\frac{1}{2}$ hours

❖ INTRODUCTION

In this lesson you will learn a good many Word basics. If you have been using other Windows applications, you may already be familiar with the basics. If you are new to Windows applications, however, it may seem you accomplish tasks in the reverse order from older DOS programs. Don't be concerned. Within a few days you will be comfortable with the Word and Windows 95 approach to basics.

❖ MOVING AROUND THE WORD DOCUMENT

Before you can work with an existing document, you have to know how to move your insertion point from place to place within the document. The insertion point is where any text you type is entered.

You can move the insertion point:

✛ With the mouse.

✛ With the arrow keys (⬆ ⬇ ➡ ⬅).

✛ With menu commands.

MOVING WITH THE MOUSE

The easiest way to move the insertion point is to use the mouse to position the I-beam where you want it and click. The insertion point always stays within margins. If you click outside a margin, the insertion point moves to the text closest to where you clicked.

Exercise 01-01 Examining a Document, as shown in Figure 1-1, is a three-page document that contains information about Microsoft Office. Watch the document closely as you do the following exercise. If you move just a little to the left of the margin, the selection pointer appears instead of the I-beam. If you click while the selection pointer is displayed, you select the line instead of positioning the insertion point.

Selection pointer ◄-------

Selection bar ◄-------

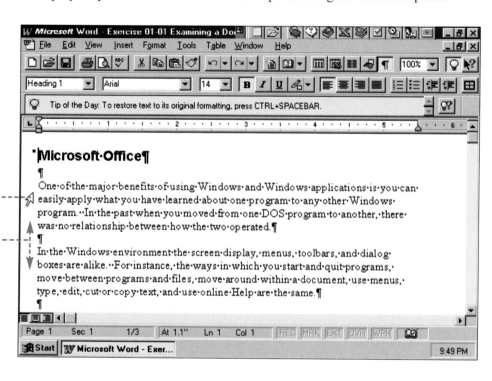

Figure 1-1
The selection pointer appears when the I-beam is moved into the left margin.

Exercise 1-1

1. To open a document, click the **Open** tool and double-click **Exercise 01-01 Examining a Document** in the box below the Look In box.

2. To move the insertion point to the position before *In the past* on the third line of the first paragraph, click the I-beam before the **I** in *In the past*.

3. To move the insertion point to the position before *In the Windows* at the beginning of the second paragraph, click the I-beam before the **I** in *In the Windows*.

4. To see how the insertion point returns to the closest text or nonprinting character when you click in white space, click the I-beam in white space to the right of the text.

5. Continue clicking the I-beam until you are comfortable positioning the insertion point.

If you want to move to a position not displayed in the document window, use the scroll bars (see Figure 1-2). When you use the scroll bars to move through a document, you must click the I-beam where you want the insertion point.

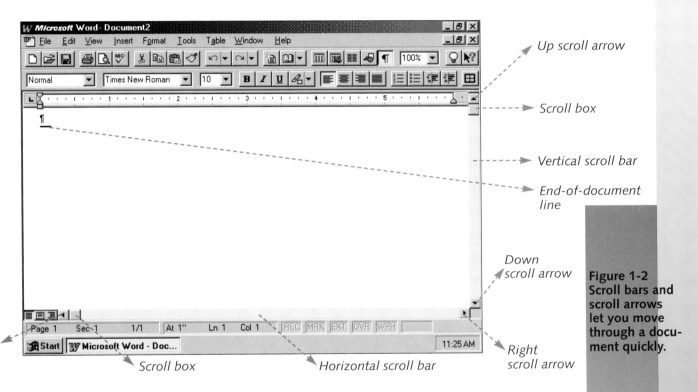

Figure 1-2
Scroll bars and scroll arrows let you move through a document quickly.

Table 1-1 contains directions for using the scroll bars.

Do This	To
Click the up or down scroll arrow	Scroll up or down one line
Click above or below scroll box in vertical bar	Scroll up or down one screen
Drag scroll box (page numbers display)	Move to a new location
Click page up or page down scroll arrow in page layout view	Move to same position on previous or next page
Hold **Shift**, click left scroll arrow	Move into left margin beyond text
Click left or right scroll arrow	Scroll left or right

Table 1-1

Exercise 1-2

1. To be sure that you are in normal view, click the **View** menu and click **Normal.**

2. To move to the end of the document using the mouse, point to the **down scroll arrow,** and click and hold the mouse button until you scroll to the end of the document. You should see what appears to be a partially filled sheet with the end-of-document line at the upper left. Notice the status bar shows you are on Page 3, Section 1, Page 3 of 3. Notice you do not see the insertion point. Because the insertion point is not in any position, the status bar is blank in the At, Line, and Column spaces.

3. To position the insertion point at the end of the document, click the insertion point at the end-of-document line.

4. To enter text, type *your name.*

5. To move to page 2, drag the **scroll box** until you see Page 2 next to the scroll box.

6. To return to the beginning of the document, drag the **scroll box** in the vertical scroll bar to the top of the scroll bar.

7. To position the insertion point at the beginning of the document, click the I-beam before Microsoft Office.

MOVING WITH KEYSTROKES

You can use the keystrokes in Table 1-2 to move the insertion point.

> **note**
>
> If you are new to using the mouse, it may take you a few days to get used to clicking the I-beam where you want the insertion point.

Exercise 1-3

1. To move the insertion point to the end of the document, hold (**Ctrl**) and press (**End**).

2. To move the insertion point into the final text paragraph, press (**↑**) once.

3. To move the insertion point to the beginning of the current paragraph, hold (**Ctrl**) and press (**↑**).

4. To move the insertion point up one screen, press (**Page Up**).

5. To move the insertion point down one screen, press (**Page Down**).

6. To return the insertion point to the beginning of the document, hold (**Ctrl**) and press (**Home**).

7. Take a few minutes to practice using the keys to move through the document.

Press	To Move
←	One character to the left
→	One character to the right
↑	One line up
↓	One line down
Ctrl + ←	One word to the left
Ctrl + →	One word to the right
End	To the end of a line
Home	To the beginning of a line
Ctrl + ↑	To the beginning of the current paragraph
Ctrl + ↓	To the beginning of the next paragraph
Ctrl + ↑ twice	To the beginning of the previous paragraph
Page Up	Up one screen
Page Down	Down one screen
Ctrl + Page Down	To the bottom of the screen
Ctrl + Page Up	To the top of the screen
Alt + Ctrl + Page Up	To the top of the previous page
Alt + Ctrl + Page Down	To the top of the next page
Ctrl + End	To the end of the document
Ctrl + Home	To the beginning of the document
Shift + F5 (GoBackKey)	To previous editing location (Word remembers last three)

Table 1-2

MOVING WITH COMMANDS

You can use the Go To command on the Edit menu to move to various locations in your document. You can also display the Go To dialog box (see Figure 1-3) by double-clicking the page number on the status bar.

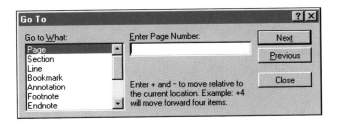

Figure 1-3
The Go To command on the Edit menu lets you move to a specific location in your document.

When the Go To dialog box appears, the insertion point is in the Enter Page Number box. You can use the Go To command to move to a page, section, line, bookmark, annotation, footnote, endnote, field, table, graphic, equation, or object. (You will learn about many of those items in later lessons.) You can use plus and minus signs to move relative to the current location.

You can also use the Find command on the Edit menu to move to a position in your document. For example, if you know you want to do some editing near the words *relational database* somewhere in your document, you can use the Find command to get there quickly and easily without scrolling and watching the display.

As you can see in the Find dialog box shown in Figure 1-4, you enter the word or words you want to find. Then you tell Word to search forward, backward, or all through the document. You can also match case, find whole words only, use pattern matching, or look for phonetic matches, formatting, or special characters. You will learn about those features in a later lesson.

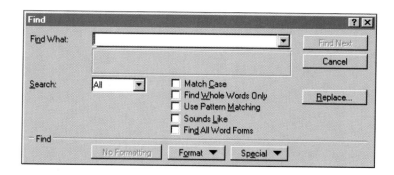

Figure 1-4
The Find command on the Edit menu can help you move to a position in the document.

You can also use the Bookmark command on the Edit menu to move around a document efficiently. Place a bookmark at a position in your document that you often return to for editing. Whenever you have to reach that position, simply use the Bookmark or the Go To command.

You must first create the bookmark by using the Bookmark command (see Figure 1-5).

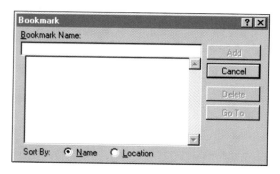

Figure 1-5
The Bookmark command on the Edit menu lets you mark a position in your document so you can move to it quickly.

You can use the Bookmark dialog box to sort the list of bookmarks by name or by location in the document, to add bookmarks, to delete bookmarks, or to go to a bookmark.

Exercise 1-4

1. To open the menu, click **Edit** on the menu bar.

2. To open the Go To dialog box, click **Go To.**

3. To move the insertion point to the top of page 3, type **3** in the Enter Page Number box, and click the **Go To** command button.

4. To close the Go To dialog box, click the **Close** command button.

5. To display the Go To dialog box again, double-click the page number on the status bar.

6. To go back two pages, type **-2** and click **Go To.**

7. To close the Go To dialog box, click the **Close** button.

8. To display the Find dialog box, click **Edit** and then **Find.**

9. To find the words *relational database,* type **relational database** and click **Find Next.** You now see the first occurrence of the text you entered, and the text is selected. It is much easier to find text this way than to scroll through a page to find the proper place for editing.

10. To cancel the selection, click in the document to activate it and press ⊖. You will learn more about selecting and canceling selections later in this lesson. Notice Word still displays the dialog box, but its title bar has no color.

11. To activate the Find dialog box, click in the dialog box.

12. To find the next occurrence of the words *relational database*, click the **Find Next** command button.

13. To close the dialog box, click **Cancel.**

14. To display the Bookmark dialog box to place a bookmark at this occurrence of *relational database,* click the **Edit** menu and then **Bookmark.**

15. To add a bookmark, type **relational** to name the Bookmark, and click the **Add** command button to add the bookmark to the list box.

16. To return the insertion point to the beginning of the document, hold (Ctrl) and press (Home).

17. To display the Bookmark dialog box, click the **Edit** menu and then **Bookmark.**

18. To move to the bookmark, click **Go To** because relational is already selected.

19. To close the dialog box, click **Close.**

20. To save the document, click the **Save** tool.

21. To close the document, click the document **Close** button on the menu bar. If you click the application Close button on the title bar, you will close the Word application.

Remember, the Go To, Find, and Bookmark commands can make it much easier to edit your documents.

❖ ENTERING TEXT

When you enter text, you press (**Enter**) only at the end of a paragraph. Word will automatically wrap text to the next line within a paragraph. When you finish a paragraph, press (**Enter**) to signal you want to move to a new line.

❖ SELECTING TEXT

In Windows applications, you select and then do. That means before you can format, move, or delete text or graphics, you must select the area you want to change. In older programs, selecting is sometimes called highlighting or blocking.

Remember also that (unless you change the setting in the Options comand), whenever there is something selected in your document, the first character you type replaces the entire selection. This feature can sometimes cause problems when you first work in Windows 95. Because it is really much faster to work that way, however, you should not change the option unless you find it impossible to adjust to it.

You can cancel a selection by:

❖ Pressing an arrow key.

or

❖ Clicking outside the selection.

SELECTING WITH THE MOUSE

You will probably do most of your selecting with the mouse once you are comfortable with it. Table 1-3 describes how to select with the mouse.

When you click in the middle of a word and drag into a second word, Word automatically selects both words and the spaces after them. To turn off this feature, you can click the Tools menu and then Options and use the Edit tab in the Options dialog box to turn off automatic word selection.

note

When clicking outside a selection to cancel it, be sure you do not click a part of the window that will change your display. Click on white space on the right side of the document.

To Select	Do This
Any item or amount of text	Drag over the text you want to select
Word	Double-click the word
Graphic	Click the graphic
Line of text	Click in the selection bar to the left of the line (your mouse pointer will take the upward-right pointing shape)
Multiple lines of text	Drag in the selection bar to the left of the lines
Sentence	Hold **Ctrl** and click anywhere in sentence
Paragraph	Double-click in selection bar by paragraph, or triple-click in paragraph
Entire document	Triple-click in selection bar
Vertical block of text	Hold **Alt** and drag over vertical block

> **note**
>
> You can use the Vertical Block feature to select the first letter in each line of a list. This feature is not available within a table.

Table 1-3

Exercise 1-5

1. To open the **Exercise 01-05 Modifying a Document** file, click the **Open** tool and double-click **Exercise 01-05 Modifying a Document.**

2. To move the insertion point to the end of the document, hold **Ctrl** and press **End**.

3. To enter a paragraph, type the following text. You need not correct errors you make while keyboarding (you will learn text-editing features later). If Word displays a wavy red line under a word, it means the word is not in Word's dictionary. You will learn to use the Spelling feature in Lesson 4. Do not press **Enter** at the end of each line. Word will wrap the text to the next line for you.

```
This is my first opportunity to type a paragraph using
the Word program. Before too long I will know many
of the Word features for creating documents. I will
also save this file.
```

4. To return the insertion point to the beginning of the document, hold **Ctrl** and press **Home**.

5. To select *Microsoft Office*, drag across **Microsoft Office.**

6. To cancel the selection, click on white space on the right side of the document window.

7. To select the whole line with *Microsoft Office*, click in the **selection bar** to the left of the line.

8. To cancel the selection, click on white space on the right side of the document (not in the selection bar).

9. To select the first four-line paragraph, click and drag down in the **selection bar** to the left of the paragraph.

10. To select the paragraph beginning *In the Windows*, triple-click the insertion point anywhere in the paragraph. You may have to try that a few times before you are successful.

11. To select the word *Microsoft* in the heading line, double-click the word **Microsoft**.

12. Practice using the mouse to select text until you feel very comfortable about selecting. Don't worry if you feel clumsy at first.

SELECTING WITH THE KEYBOARD

Table 1-4 describes the keystrokes you use to select text and graphics with the keyboard.

Exercise 1-6

1. To move to the beginning of the document, hold **Ctrl** and press **Home**.

2. To select one character to the right of the insertion point, hold **Shift** and press **→**.

3. To select the word to the right of the insertion point, hold **Ctrl** and **Shift** and press **→**.

4. To select to the end of the line, hold **Shift** and press **End**.

5. To cancel the selection, press an **arrow key.**

6. To return to the beginning of the document, hold **Ctrl** and press **Home**.

7. To get comfortable using keystrokes to select, practice using any of the keystrokes shown in Table 1-4 that you think you might use to select text.

To Select	Press
One character to the right	(Shift)+(→)
One character to the left	(Shift)+(←)
To the end of a word	(Ctrl)+(Shift)+(→)
To the beginning of a word	(Ctrl)+(Shift)+(←)
To the end of a line	(Shift)+(End)
To the beginning of a line	(Shift)+(Home)
To same location on next line	(Shift)+(↓)
To same location on preceding line	(Shift)+(↑)
To the end of a paragraph	(Ctrl)+(Shift)+(↓)
To the beginning of a paragraph	(Ctrl)+(Shift)+(↑)
To same location on next screen	(Shift)+(Page Down)
To same location on previous screen	(Shift)+(Page Up)
To the end of a document	(Ctrl)+(Shift)+(End)
To the beginning of a document	(Ctrl)+(Shift)+(Home)
To include the entire document	(Ctrl)+(A)

note

You also can select the entire document by using the Select All command on the Edit menu.

Table 1-4

8. To save the document, click the **Save** tool.

9. To close the document, click the **Close** button on the menu bar.

❖ INSERTING TEXT

Word's default setting for entering text is called insert mode. That means text you type is entered at the insertion point to the left of anything that may be there already.

In Overtype mode, text overwrites text that already exists in the document. Even if you are accustomed to using Overtype mode, you should leave Word's setting as is because it is faster and easier to work in insert mode. You can press (Insert) to toggle Overtype mode on or off. OVR is displayed on the right side of the status bar when Overtype mode is turned on.

To insert text:

- ❖ Move the insertion point with the mouse or keyboard to the position where you want to insert text.

- ❖ Type the text.

Exercise 1-7

1. To open the **Exercise 01-07 Inserting Text** file, click the **Open** tool and double-click **Exercise 01-07 Inserting Text.**

2. To reach the end of the document, drag the **scroll box** to the bottom of the scroll bar.

3. To position the insertion point at the end of the document, click the I-beam at the end-of-document line.

4. To enter some text, type the following paragraph and press (Enter) at the end of the paragraph.

   ```
   Before too long I will be able to use many of
   Microsoft Word's features to create professional
   documents. I may still feel a bit clumsy with all
   I have learned, but I know with a little practice
   that clumsy feeling will disappear.
   ```

5. To move the insertion point to the beginning of the document, hold (Ctrl) and press (Home).

6. To move to the end of the line, press (End).

7. To insert the word *Suite*, press (SpaceBar) and type **Suite.**

8. To switch to Overtype mode, press (Insert). Notice that OVR is showing on the right side of the status bar.

9. To display the Find dialog box, click the **Edit** menu and then click **Find.**

10. To enter the text for Word to find, type **An added benefit.**

11. To move to the paragraph beginning with *An added benefit*, click the **Find Next** command button.

12. To close the Find dialog box, click **Cancel.**

13. Type **Any Windows application can share data with any other Windows application with the greatest of ease.** Notice that the first character you enter replaces the selection. Then each character overstrikes a character. Notice you still have extra text that must be deleted.

14. To delete *the remaining text*, press the (Delete) key 23 times.

15. To turn off Overtype mode, press (Insert).

16. To save the document, click the **Save** tool.

17. To close the document, click the document **Close** button on the right side of the menu bar.

❖ DELETING TEXT

There are several ways of deleting text in Word. You can:

- ❖ Press **Delete** to delete a character after the insertion point.
- ❖ Press **Backspace** to delete a character just before the insertion point.
- ❖ Hold **Ctrl** and press **Delete** to delete a word after the insertion point.
- ❖ Hold **Ctrl** and press **Backspace** to delete a word before the insertion point.
- ❖ Select text and then click the Cut tool, click Cut on the Edit menu, or press **Backspace** or **Delete**.

❖ USING UNDO AND REDO

You can undo many but not all of the actions you take in Word with the Undo command on the Edit menu or with the Undo tool. The Undo command on the Edit menu lets you undo your most recent action.

The Undo tool undoes the last action if you click the left side. If you click the drop-down button to the right of it, you see a list of many actions you can undo. It is important to undo a mistake immediately, because the drop-down list can be confusing. If you undo the third item on the list, the first two are undone as well. You may not remember what those actions were or see what happens when they are undone.

You can use the Redo tool when you have used Undo and would like to redo the last canceled action.

Exercise 1-8

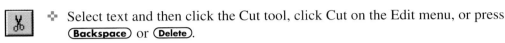

1. To open a clean version of the document you have been using, click the **Open** tool and double-click **Exercise 01-08 Using Undo.**

2. To select the first sentence in the paragraph beginning *One of the major benefits*, drag the I-beam over the sentence until the whole sentence and the two blank spaces after it are selected.

3. To delete the sentence, press **Delete**. Notice the selected sentence is gone.

4. To undo the delete, click the left side of the **Undo** tool.

5. To cancel the selection, press ⏎.

6. To delete the blank line after *Microsoft Office,* press **Backspace**.

7. To see the list of actions you can undo, click the **drop-down button** on the **Undo** tool and notice it lists typing as the most recent action.

8. To undo the deletion, click **typing.**

9. To redo the undo, click the **left side** of the **Redo** tool.

10. To restore the deletion again, click the **left side** of the **Undo** tool.

11. To delete the character to the right of the insertion point, press (**Delete**).

12. To restore the character you just deleted, click the left side of the **Undo** tool again.

❖ USING SHOW/HIDE

¶ You can use the Show/Hide tool, which looks like a paragraph mark, to show or hide paragraph marks, spaces, tabs, and other nonprinting symbols. It is often wise to have the paragraph marks displayed when editing text.

Word defines a paragraph as any amount of text or graphics with a paragraph mark after it. The preceding *Using Show/Hide* heading is considered a paragraph because the typist pressed (**Enter**) after those words.

Exercise 1-9

1. To hide paragraph marks and other nonprinting characters, click the **Show/Hide** tool.

2. To move the insertion point to the beginning of the document, hold (**Ctrl**) and press (**Home**).

3. To move the insertion point to the end of the line before the paragraph mark, press (**End**).

4. To delete the paragraph mark, press (**Delete**). Notice the blank line after the heading is gone.

5. To return the paragraph mark to its position, click the left side of the **Undo** tool.

❖ USING CUT, COPY, AND PASTE

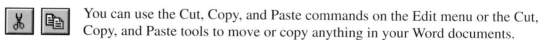 You can use the Cut, Copy, and Paste commands on the Edit menu or the Cut, Copy, and Paste tools to move or copy anything in your Word documents.

When you cut or copy a selection with the Cut or Copy command, Windows stores a copy of the selection in an area of memory called the Clipboard. The Clipboard stores the cut or copied selection until you cut or copy another selection or until you quit the program.

You use the Paste command or tool to position the contents of the Clipboard at a new location. Because the selection remains in the Clipboard until you cut or copy another selection, you can paste the selection as often as you want.

You can also use the drag-and-drop feature to move or copy text. When you move or copy a selection using the drag-and-drop method, the selection is not stored in the Clipboard.

To move a selection using the drag-and-drop feature:

❖ Point to the selected text or graphics.

❖ Hold down the mouse button until you see the drag-and-drop pointer.

❖ Drag the dotted insertion point to the new location and release.

To copy a selection using the drag-and-drop feature:

❖ Hold **Ctrl** and point to the selected text or graphics.

❖ Drag the dotted insertion point to the new location and release.

❖ Release **Ctrl** after you release the mouse button.

You can use the Paste Special command when you are pasting material from another Word document or from another application (such as Excel) into your document. Paste Special links the item pasted in a Word document to the original item in its source file so it can be updated automatically when changes are made in the source file.

When you paste text between Word documents without including either a section break or the final paragraph mark, the text takes on the section formatting of the document into which you paste it.

note

When copying or moving paragraphs, include the paragraph marks at the end of a paragraph in your selection so you do not have to go back to adjust line spacing.

Exercise 1-10

1. To open the file, click the **Open** tool and double-click **Exercise 01-10 Moving Text.**

2. To select the paragraph beginning *In the Windows environment*, double-click in the **selection bar.**

3. To move the selection, point to it and hold down the mouse button until you see the drag-and-drop pointer. Drag the dotted insertion point up to the beginning of the paragraph before it and release when the dotted insertion point is just before the *O* in *One*.

4. To cancel the selection, press ➡. Notice that the line spacing between paragraphs needs to be adjusted.

5. To insert a blank line between the two paragraphs, press **Enter**.

6. To remove the extra line space left behind, press ⬇ five times and press **Delete**.

7. To select the paragraph beginning *One of the major benefits*, including the blank line after the paragraph, drag in the **selection bar** until the four lines and the blank line are selected.

8. To remove the paragraph from its current position and put it in the Clipboard, click the **Cut** tool. Notice the paragraph disappears from the document.

9. To paste the paragraph, position the insertion point before the first letter of the preceding paragraph, which begins *In the Windows,* and click the **Paste** tool. Notice that this time there is no need to correct line spacing. Remember, you still have the paragraph in the Clipboard and can paste it again until you do another Cut or Copy with the menu commands or tools.

10. To create a new document to practice some pasting between documents, click the **New** tool.

11. To display the three documents that are currently open, click the **Window** menu and then **Arrange All.** Notice the insertion point is in the document you just created.

12. To enter the Clipboard contents in the new document, click the **Paste** tool.

13. Click the **Maximize** button on the new document's title bar so that it fills the screen.

14. To display the Close All command, hold **Shift** and click the **File** menu.

15. To use the Close All command, click **Close All.** Respond **No** when asked to save changes.

❖ S U M M A R Y

You have learned a good many Word basics including how to move around within documents; select text or graphics; insert and delete text; use undo and redo; work with the Cut, Copy, and Paste commands and tools; and move and copy using the drag-and-drop feature.

Try the exercises on the following pages to test how well you remember what you learned. Don't be afraid to go back and look up procedures—you won't be able to remember everything you did. Using Help or looking back through this book will reinforce what you learned.

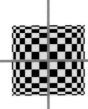

activities

❖ T R U E / F A L S E

*On the blank line before each sentence, place a **T** if the statement is true or an **F** if it is false.*

_____ 1. You should try to work from files on the A drive when using Word.

_____ 2. The easiest way to move through a long document to find an area that needs editing is to scroll line by line.

_____ 3. If you click the mouse in the left margin, you select the line.

_____ 4. "Typing Replaces Selection" means each character you type replaces one character in the document.

_____ 5. You will probably do most of your selecting with the mouse once you are familiar with using it.

_____ 6. Hold (Ctrl) and press (↑) to go to the beginning of the next paragraph.

_____ 7. An easy way to find every occurrence of the word *mountain* in a document is to use a bookmark.

_____ 8. The opposite of Overtype mode is insert mode.

_____ 9. Word's drag-and-drop feature lets you quickly move selected text to a new location.

_____ 10. When you copy text, it is stored in the Clipboard.

❖ COMPLETION

Fill in the blanks in the following statements.

1. You cancel a selection by pressing a(n) _____ key.

2. When you click to close a menu, you should be careful to click in _____ space.

3. You can hold _____ and press _____ to move to the beginning of a document.

4. You can click _____ on a word to select it.

5. You can click _____ times on a paragraph to select it.

6. When you delete something by mistake, click the _____ tool immediately.

7. The _____ command lets you mark specific locations in a document so that you can move quickly to them.

8. When you use the Cut tool or the Copy command on the Edit menu, a copy of the cut or copied text is placed in the _____.

9. When you cut or copy a whole paragraph, select all of the text and the _____.

10. It is wise to use the _____ tool to display paragraph marks while you are editing text.

review

Review Exercise 1-1

1. Open document **Review 01-01 Revise Document** and make the following revisions:

   a. In the first paragraph:

      ✦ Insert the word **Microsoft** before the first occurrence of the word *Windows*.

      ✦ Delete *and Windows.*

      ✦ Delete the words *that* and *easily* in the first sentence.

      ✦ Change the words *any other* to **another.**

      ✦ Move the second sentence to the beginning of the paragraph.

   b. In the second paragraph:

      ✦ Delete the words *For instance* in the second sentence and capitalize *the*.

      ✦ Delete the *comma* after the word *cut*.

   c. In the third paragraph:

      ✦ Delete *of applications* in the first sentence.

      ✦ Change the words *integrated into* to **used in**.

   d. In the fourth paragraph:

      ✦ Move the first sentence to the end of the paragraph.

      ✦ Change *The toolbar* to **The Shorcut Bar.**

      ✦ Delete the word *very* before *easy* in what is now the first sentence.

2. Save the document as **Review 01-01.** Be sure that you save it in your personal folder.

3. Select the entire document and use the Copy command to put it on the Clipboard.

4. Print and close the document.

Review Exercise 1-2

Find, read, and print the Help screens for the drag-and-drop feature.

On Your Own

1. Create a new document.

2. Paste the contents of the Clipboard (from Review Exercise 1-1) in the new document.

3. Save the document as **On Your Own 01**. Be sure you save it in your personal folder.

4. Print and close the document.

notes

File: New

Memo Wizard

lesson 2

Creating, Printing, and Sending a Document

❖ OBJECTIVES

When you complete this lesson, you will be able to:

1. Use templates and wizards.
2. Use the Print Preview Feature.
3. Print a document.
4. Create and print an envelope.
5. Route and send documents.

Estimated Time: $1\frac{1}{2}$ hours

❖ INTRODUCTION

Now that you are familiar with Word basics, you are ready to create your own documents. In this lesson you will learn about using Word wizards and Word templates to create memos. You will preview a document before you print it and then create and print an envelope. In addition, you will learn about routing and sending documents electronically.

❖ USING TEMPLATES AND WIZARDS TO CREATE NEW DOCUMENTS

You can work more efficiently by basing many of your new documents (such as memos, letters, fax cover sheets, and reports) on templates that Word provides. A template is a master copy for a certain type of document.

Templates contain the settings for margins, the page size and orientation, and any text or graphics that are standard for the type of document. Instead of having to create a layout each time you want to create a memo, for instance, you can use one of the memo templates.

Wizards take you step-by-step through creating the type of document you choose and let you make more decisions than a template would about the format of the document.

In an earlier lesson you used the New tool to create a new document. When you use the New tool, the new document automatically uses Word's normal or blank template. The normal template is a general-purpose template for any document. Unless you choose another template in the New dialog box, Word uses the blank document when you create a new document. Even the blank document, however, contains default settings for various aspects of a document.

In the next exercise you will create a document using a memo template. To choose a template other than the blank one, you *must* use the New command on the File menu. The New dialog box contains tabs for the various kinds of templates you can use. You can see the templates and Wizards on the Memo tab in Figure 2-1.

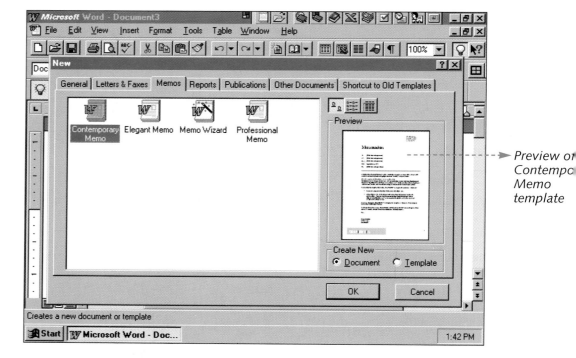

Preview or Contempo Memo template

Figure 2-1
Word displays a preview of a template when you select it.

The New dialog box lets you preview what each of the templates (except the blank document) looks like when you select a template. Create New Document is automatically selected at the bottom right of the dialog box. You can select Template if you want to create a template for a document format you need. You might want, for instance, to create templates based on those Microsoft has already provided.

If you choose the Memo Wizard in the New dialog box, Word displays the first of the dialog boxes that will walk you through creation of the memo (see Figure 2-2). You can use the Next and Back buttons to move forward or backward through the steps. When you are finished answering the wizard's questions, the Next button will be dimmed. Click the Finish button to display the memo with your entries.

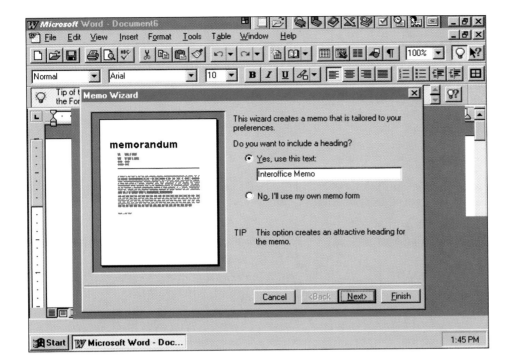

When you create a new document using the Contemporary Memo template, Word displays the screen shown in Figure 2-3. The template provides all of the formatting for an easily recognizable memo. Word inserts the current date and among other changes displays page layout view and 69% magnification. To complete the memo, you must click within each set of square brackets and type your information.

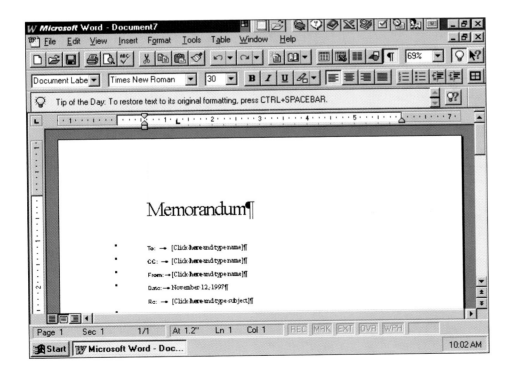

❖ AUTOMATIC SPELL CHECKING

As you enter text, Word checks for typos and spelling errors and enters a wavy red line under any word it does not recognize. If you see the wavy red line under a word, you can point to the word and click the right mouse button to display a shortcut menu. Use the shortcut menu to correct the word if it is incorrect or to ignore the word if it is okay as is.

❖ USING WATERMARKS

You can use watermarks in your documents to add a professional touch (see Figure 2-4). You will be able to experiment with adding watermarks in the Header and Footer view

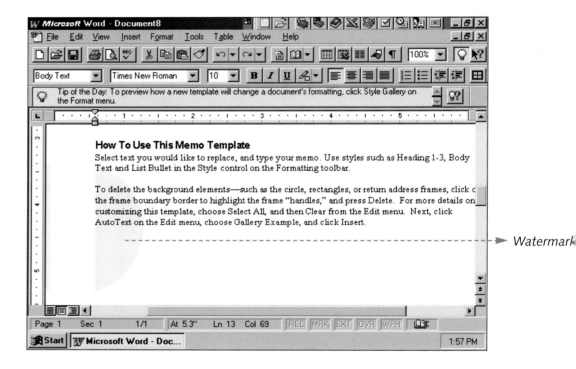

Figure 2- 4
You can see
an example of
a watermark
in this memo.

after you learn about adding headers and footers and using the Drawing toolbar.

❖ USING AN ELECTRONIC ADDRESS BOOK

If you use an electronic personal address book, the Memo Wizard lets you access it to insert names on the To: and Cc: lines of memos. Key in the names yourself if you don't have an address book.

You also can use the Insert Address button on the Standard toolbar to enter an address in any document.

❖ USING THE HIGHLIGHT BUTTON

You can use the Highlight button on the Formatting toolbar to emphasize text with color shading. (You will learn more about sending documents electronically later in this lesson.) This feature is really useful for highlighting text in documents to be reviewed or read on a computer monitor.

Exercise 2-1

1. To open the New dialog box, click the **File** menu and click **New.**

2. To display the Memos tab if it is not already displayed, click the **Memos** tab.

3. To create a memo using the Contemporary Memo template, click the **Contemporary Memo** icon and click **OK.**

4. To enter a name on the To: line, click anywhere **within the brackets** on that line and enter *a friend's name.* Do not press (Enter) after keying the name.

5. To enter a name on the Cc: line, click anywhere **within the brackets** on that line and enter *another friend's name.* Do not press (Enter) after keying the name.

6. To enter your name on the From: line, click anywhere **within the brackets** on that line and enter *your name.* Do not press (Enter) after keying the name.

7. To enter a subject on the Re: line, click anywhere **within the brackets** on that line and type **Using a Template.** Do not press (Enter) after keying the subject.

8. To enter the text shown below, select all the text in the message section of the memo and type the following paragraphs.

   A Word template is a blueprint for the text, graphics, and formatting of a document. Templates also store the styles, macros, AutoText entries, and customized command settings you need to work faster on particular types of documents.

   Word provides templates for commonly used types of documents. You can create your own templates from scratch, or you can tailor an existing template to suit your needs.

9. Look over the text you entered. If you find any wavy red lines and the words are actually incorrect, point to the word, click the **right mouse button,** and choose one of the options displayed.

10. To highlight the first sentence in your memo, select the sentence, click the **drop-down button** on the **Highlight** tool, and click a color you like.

❖ USING PRINT PREVIEW

With the Print Preview tool or the Print Preview command on the File menu, you can preview entire pages of your document before printing. You save time and paper when you use Print Preview because you reduce the number of times you print a document before getting exactly the look you want. You can zoom in and out to see different magnifications of your document and even edit the document in this view.

Word displays the current page of your document when you click Print Preview. If you or another user has not changed the default setting, you should see a one-page display similar to the one in Figure 2-5.

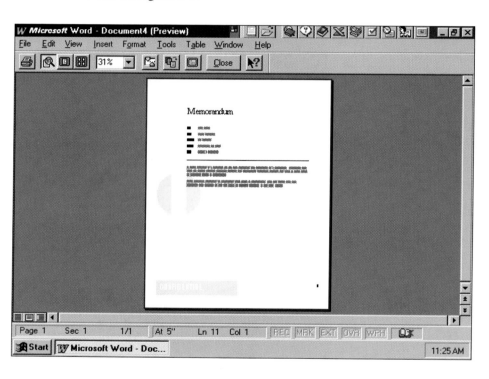

Figure 2-5
Click the Print Preview button to see your document before printing.

USING THE PRINT PREVIEW TOOLBAR

The Print Preview toolbar has many useful tools you can use to work with your document while preparing it for printing.

 Use the Print tool to print the document. You will not see the Print dialog box, so you will not be able to change any of the default settings.

 Use the Magnifier tool to zoom in on an area of your document. Notice the Magnifier tool is automatically selected (its button looks pushed in).

 Use the One Page tool if more than one page is displayed and you would prefer to see just one page at a time.

 Use the Multiple Pages tool when you want to see more than one page at a time. Drag over the grid to select the number of pages.

Use the Zoom Control box to select a greater or lesser magnification. You can enter a figure or choose one in the drop-down box.

 Use the View Ruler tool to display the ruler for making changes to the margin settings by dragging boundaries.

 Use the Shrink to Fit tool to make a document with a short paragraph on a new page fit without the short page.

 Use the Full Screen tool to display just the page and the toolbar. Click Full Screen again to return to the original display.

When you move the mouse pointer onto the document page, the pointer changes to a magnifying glass. The Magnifier tool is turned on when you access Print Preview.

You can zoom in on an area of your document by moving the magnifier to the area you want to see and clicking. To return to the original magnification, click the Magnifier tool. Then click the magnifying glass pointer within the document page again.

note

If you want to edit your document, click the Magnifier tool to turn it off. When you see the I-beam, you can use it to edit your document.

Exercise 2-2

1. To preview your document, click the **Print Preview** tool.

2. To display just one page if you see more than one, click the **One Page** tool.

3. To zoom in on the area at the bottom left of the page that appears to have some text, point to the location and click. Notice the memo template contains the Confidential notation.

4. To turn off the magnifying glass and see the I-beam on the screen, click the **Magnifier** tool.

5. To enter a middle name for the addressee, scroll up to the addressee line, position the I-beam just before the addressee's last name, click the **I-beam,** type a *middle name,* and press (SpaceBar).

6. To leave edit mode, click the **Magnifier** tool.

7. To zoom back to the original display, click the **magnifying glass pointer.**

8. To set up for a two-page display, click the **Multiple Pages** tool and drag over the first two pages on the top row. Notice the original page has moved to the left side of the screen to make room for a second page if there is one.

9. To return to the one-page display, click the **One Page** tool.

10. To hide all but the Print Preview toolbar, click the **Full Screen** tool.

11. To return to the original display, click the **Full Screen** tool again.

CHANGING MARGINS

 You can use the View Ruler tool to display the rulers across the top of the page and down the left side of the screen (see Figure 2-6).

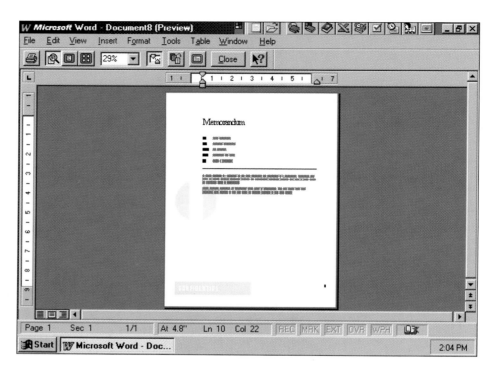

Figure 2-6
Drag markers
on the rulers to
change margins.

PRINTING AND SAVING DOCUMENTS

 You can use the Print tool on the Print Preview toolbar to print your document. However, if you want to make any changes in the Print dialog box shown in Figure 2-7, you must use the Print command on the File menu.

You can use the Save command on the File menu to save your document while in Print Preview. When your document has not been saved before, the Save As dialog box appears.

USING THE PRINT COMMAND

You can use the Print command on the File menu to access the Print dialog box to:

❖ Choose the printer you want to use.

❖ Print to a file.

❖ Print either all or specified parts of the document. To enter specific pages, type **1-10** to print pages 1 through 10. Type **1,10** to print pages 1 and 10.

❖ Specify the number of copies to print.

❖ Collate copies of documents.

❖ Print the document, Summary Info, annotations, or other information you will learn about in later lessons.

❖ Print all pages in a range, or print only odd or even pages in the range.

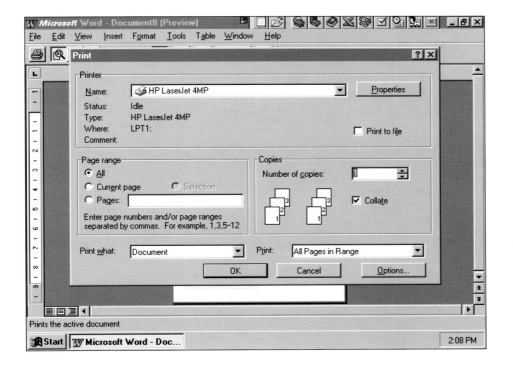

Figure 2-7
The Print dialog box provides various printing options.

CANCELING A PRINT JOB

When Word is printing your document, you will see a printer icon at the right side of the task bar. (Double-click the icon to display the dialog box in which you can cancel the print job.) To cancel the print job, select the document you want to cancel, click the Document menu, click Cancel Printing, and click the Microsoft Word button on the task bar to return to Word.

Exercise 2-3

1. To display rulers across the top of the page and down the left side of the screen, click the **View Ruler** tool.

2. To make the top margin larger, point to the **Ruler** on the left side of the window (see Figure 2-6). When the double-pointing arrow appears, drag the arrow down about one-half inch. Notice the text in your memorandum move down on the page.

3. To undo the formatting change, click the **Undo** tool on the Standard toolbar.

4. To print your memo, click the **File** menu and click **Print**. Notice the options you have available in the Print dialog box. Click **OK.**

5. To save your memo, click **File** and **Save**. When the Save As dialog box appears, type **Exercise 02-03 Create Memo.** Click **Save.**

6. To exit from Print Preview, click **Close** on the Print Preview toolbar.

CREATING AN ENVELOPE

Word makes creating and printing envelopes easy. You use the Envelopes and Labels command on the Tools menu to create the envelope (see Figure 2-8). If your document happens to be a letter, Word picks up the inside address and adds it to the Delivery Address without your having to key it in. If you have more than one address in the letter, select the address before using the Envelopes and Labels command.

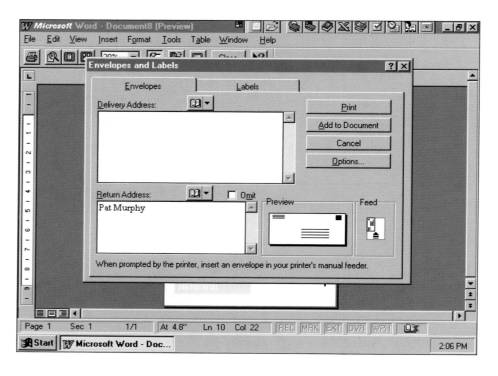

Figure 2-8
The Envelopes and Labels command on the Tools menu lets you create envelopes easily.

The Add to Document button lets you add the envelope to the beginning of the document so you can print the two together.

Use the Options button to change the envelope size, add bar codes for the Postal Service, and change the position and fonts for the addresses. You will learn more about fonts in a later lesson.

In the envelopes exercise, you will have to enter an address because the memo does not have an address Word can recognize.

Exercise 2-4

1. To display the Envelopes and Labels dialog box, click the **Tools** menu and click **Envelopes and Labels.**

2. Click the **Envelopes** tab.

3. To enter an address in the Delivery Address box, type the ***name and address*** of the person to whom you addressed the memo.

4. If it is necessary to enter your name and address in the Return Address box, select the text that is displayed and type ***your name and address.*** Notice the preview of the envelope and also how to feed the envelope for your printer.

5. To see that you can change the envelope size, add bar codes for the Postal Service, and change fonts and positions for the delivery and return addresses, click the **Options** button.

6. To return to the Envelopes and Labels dialog box, click **Cancel.**

7. To see whether you have to insert an envelope in your printer before you click Print or whether you click Print and wait for a prompt to insert the envelope, read and follow the directions on the **bottom line** of the dialog box.

8. To print the envelope, click **Print.** If you changed the return address, you will be prompted to save the new address. Respond **No.**

9. To close the document, click the **Close** button on the menu bar. Because you already saved the document, click **No** when asked to save changes.

❖ SENDING DOCUMENTS ELECTRONICALLY

Word provides three options for sharing documents electronically:

1. Sending a document

2. Routing a document

3. Posting a document

USING THE SEND COMMAND

Use the Send command on the File menu to send a copy of the current document. When you choose Send, Word starts your electronic mail application (see Figure 2-9) using Microsoft Exchange. When you use the Send command, the current document is included as an icon in the message. The recipient can double-click the icon to open the document.

You can enter the recipients, the subject, additional documents, and a message. Microsoft recommends you use this option when you want to distribute a document quickly to a specific list of reviewers.

> **note**
>
> To send electronic mail, you must have Microsoft Mail, cc:Mail, Microsoft Exchange, or another compatible mail system installed on your computer.

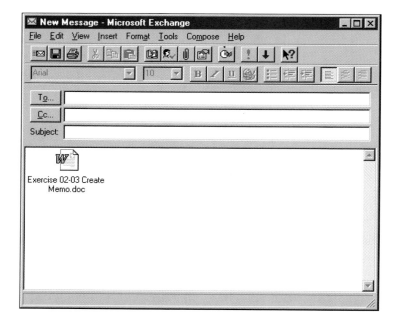

Figure 2-9
Your document
appears as an icon
in the message.

> **note**
>
> You can protect
> your document
> so reviewers
> can add only
> revision marks
> or annotations.
> You will learn
> more about
> those options
> in later lessons.

USING THE ADD ROUTING SLIP COMMAND

Use the Add Routing Slip command when you want to send a single copy of a document to reviewers in an order you specify. When you choose Add Routing Slip, Word starts your electronic mail application (see Figure 2-10). When a reviewer finishes reviewing the document and clicks the Send command on the File menu, the document is automatically routed to the next reviewer. When the last reviewer finishes with the document, Word returns it to you.

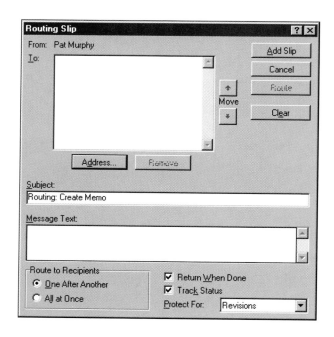

Figure 2- 10
You can make
reviewing decisions
in the Routing Slip
dialog box.

USING THE POST TO EXCHANGE FOLDER

Use the Post to Exchange Folder command on the File menu when you want to send a copy of a document to a Microsoft Exchange public folder so others can access the document over the network. You can use this command when you have a document, such as a company manual, that needs to be available to many network users.

note

To post a document, you must be connected to a network with Microsoft Exchange Server.

❖ SUMMARY

You have now learned how to use a Word template to create a document, how to enter text, how to use the Print Preview feature, how to print documents and envelopes, and how to use electronic document sharing.

Try the exercises on the following pages to test how well you remember what you have learned. Once again, remember that going back through parts of the first three lessons and using Help will reinforce learning. Good luck!

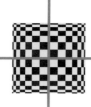

activities

On the blank line before each sentence, place a **T** *if the statement is true or an* **F** *if it is false.*

_____ 1. You can use the New tool to create a document using a template.

_____ 2. The normal or blank template is the only template you can access with the New tool.

_____ 3. You can tailor a Word template to suit your needs.

_____ 4. You cannot edit your document in Print Preview.

_____ 5. You can change margins in Print Preview.

_____ 6. You cannot use any menu commands while in Print Preview.

_____ 7. You have more options available when you use a wizard rather than a template.

_____ 8. You can click the left mouse button on a word with a wavy red line under it to see the shortcut menu to correct it.

_____ 9. You must have Microsoft Network, Microsoft Mail, cc:Mail, or another compatible system to send documents electronically.

_____ 10. You can use the Add Routing Slip command on the File menu to put a document in a public folder for general distribution in an organization.

COMPLETION

Fill in the blanks in the following statements.

1. The Envelopes and Labels command on the _____ menu makes creating envelopes and labels easy.

2. You can use the _____ tool in Print Preview to squeeze a little extra text onto a page.

3. You can use the _____ tool when you want to see more than one page in Print Preview.

4. You must use the _____ command on the File menu to create a document with a wizard or template.

5. The _____ template is a general-purpose template for any document.

6. When you are in Print Preview, you can use the _____ tool to enlarge a particular area of the document.

7. To view only a single page when you are in Print Preview, click the _____ tool.

8. A(n) _____ gives you step-by-step instructions for creating a particular type of document.

9. When Word comes across a word it does not recognize, it places a(n) _____ under the word.

10. You can use the _____ command to specify that a document should be electronically routed to a list of people.

review

Review Exercise 2-1

1. Use the Memo Wizard to send a memo to yourself, from you, with the subject Learning Word, and with a copy to your instructor.

2. Write a short paragraph about how you feel about learning Word.

3. Save, print, and close the document.

4. Give your instructor a copy.

Review Exercise 2-2

1. Search online Help for information on Print Preview.

2. Print a copy of the information you find.

On Your Own

Edit the Contemporary Letter template to make a template with stationery for your personal use.

Replace the company name at the top of the template with your initials. After you have inserted your personal information, choose the Save As command from the File menu. Under Save as type, select Document Template. Now you can use this template whenever you want to write a letter.

lesson 3

Working with Basic Writing Tools

❖ OBJECTIVES

When you complete this lesson, you will be able to:

1. Use the AutoText and AutoCorrect features.
2. Check spelling.
3. Use the Thesaurus.
4. Use the Grammar command.
5. Use the Hyphenation, Language, and Word Count commands.
6. Insert symbols.
7. Enter and remove a password.

Estimated Time: 1 hour

❖ INTRODUCTION

You have learned to create and print documents and to do some basic text editing. Now you will work with some of the Word features that make proofreading and protecting documents easier. You will check spelling, correct grammatical errors, and look up synonyms. You will also use the AutoCorrect and AutoText features, and insert symbols. In addition, you will learn to put a password on a document to ensure that others cannot open confidential files.

❖ USING AUTOTEXT

You can use the AutoText tool or the AutoText command on the Edit menu to store or access text and graphics you use often. The closing of a standard business letter is a good example of a likely AutoText entry.

To store an AutoText entry:

+ Type the entry.
+ Select the entire entry.

❖ Click Edit and then click AutoText to display the AutoText dialog box (shown in Figure 3-1).

❖ To add the entry to the AutoText list, click Add.

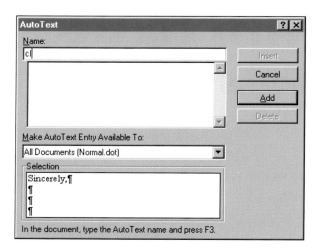

To edit an AutoText entry:

❖ Enter the AutoText entry in a document.

❖ Make any changes you want.

❖ Select the entry.

❖ Click Edit and then click AutoText.

❖ Select the original entry name.

❖ Click Add.

❖ When you are asked if you want to redefine the entry, click Yes.

Word stores AutoText entries with the template you are using when you create the entry. If you want to use the entry with all templates, be sure to use the Blank Document template at the time you create the AutoText entry.

Exercise 3-1

1. To open a document, click the **Open** tool and double-click **Exercise 03-01 Using AutoText.**

2. To select the entire closing for the letter beginning with the word *Sincerely,* drag across all of it (see Figure 3-2).

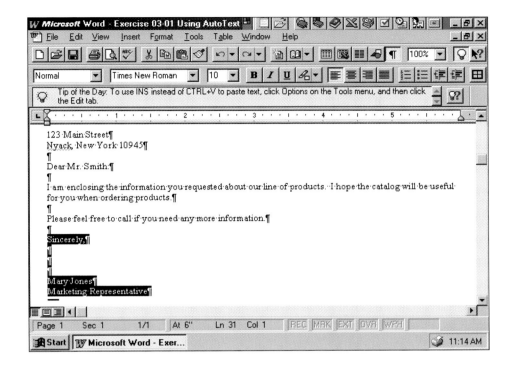

123·Main·Street¶
Nyack,·New·York·10945¶
¶
Dear·Mr.·Smith:¶
¶
I·am·enclosing·the·information·you·requested·about·our·line·of·products.··I·hope·the·catalog·will·be·useful·
for·you·when·ordering·products.¶
¶
Please·feel·free·to·call·if·you·need·any·more·information.¶
¶
Sincerely,¶
¶
¶
Mary·Jones¶
Marketing·Representative¶

Figure 3-2
This closing is selected before being stored in AutoText.

3. To display the AutoText dialog box shown in Figure 3-1, click the the the **Edit** menu and then click **AutoText.** Notice the beginning of the AutoText selection is displayed for the AutoText name and you can see the first line of the closing in the Selection box.

4. To give the closing a shorter name that will be easier to use, type **cl**. Notice that instructions for inserting an AutoText entry are at the bottom of the dialog box. Notice also you can add, insert, or delete AutoText entries.

5. To add the entry to the AutoText list, click **Add.**

6. To create a new document, click the **New** tool.

7. To enter the AutoText entry in the new document, click the **Edit** menu, click **AutoText,** select **cl,** and click **Insert.**

8. To move the insertion point down a few lines, press **Enter** a few times.

9. To enter the AutoText entry with **F3**, type **cl,** and then press **F3**.

10. To close the new document without saving changes, click the **File** menu and then click **Close.** Respond **No** when asked to save changes.

11. To save and close **Exercise 03-01 Using AutoText,** click the **Save** tool. Then click the **File** menu and click **Close.**

❖ USING AUTOCORRECT

You can also use the AutoCorrect command on the Tools menu for items you want to insert in your documents frequently. As you can see in Figure 3-3, AutoCorrect can easily replace typed characters with symbols and automatically correct common typing errors such as typing *teh* for *the*. Because the feature is so much faster to use than AutoText, you might want to consider using it for text you often type.

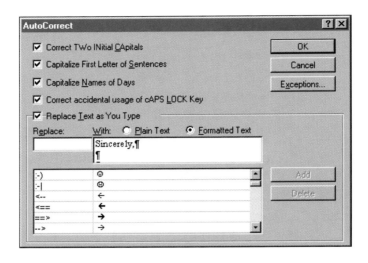

Figure 3-3 AutoCorrect automatically corrects frequently misspelled words and offers other spelling and capitalization options.

note

If your initials are also a common word or abbreviation, don't use this shortcut.

You could, for instance, enter in AutoCorrect your initials to be replaced by your name. Every time you type the initials followed by a space, Word will automatically enter your full name. If you type your initials followed by '*s*, Word will form the possessive of your name.

Word keeps track of words you don't want AutoCorrect to change. If you undo a change Word makes, Word will not make the same automatic change in the future. You can turn AutoCorrect off by turning off the Replace Text as You Type option in the AutoCorrect dialog box.

Word can automatically correct two initial caps, capitalize names of days, correct accidental usage of Caps Lock, and replace text as you type.

The list at the bottom of the dialog box contains the characters and words that Word changes automatically.

You can opt to replace with plain or formatted text. Most times you will probably want to replace with plain, so the insertion follows the formatting of the text around it.

Exercise 3-2

1. To create a new document based on the Normal template, click the **New** tool.

2. To display the AutoCorrect dialog box, click the **Tools** menu and then click **AutoCorrect.**

3. To set your options to match those shown in Figure 3-3, click any of the options that do not match.

4. To see the entire list of words that Word changes, scroll through the list.

5. To set up Word to replace your initials with your complete name, type *your initials* in the Replace box, click the insertion point in the **With** box, and type *your full name.*

6. To enter the AutoCorrect entry, click the **Add** button and then click **Close.**

7. To have AutoCorrect enter your full name, type the initials you entered followed by a space. Notice Word entered your name.

8. To save the document, click the **Save** tool. Type **Exercise 03-02 AutoCorrect** for the document's name. Click **Save.**

9. To close the document, click the **File** menu and click the **Close** button on the right side of the menu bar.

❖ CHECKING SPELLING

Word can check spelling while you type and enter a wavy red line under any words not in its dictionary. To display suggested spellings for an underlined word, point to the word with the wavy line and click the right mouse button. Then click the correct spelling or one of the other options. Alternatively, you can ignore the wavy red lines and check spelling for the entire document when you finish entering text. You can use either the Spelling tool or the Spelling command on the Tools menu to check your document for spelling errors. You can check a selection or the entire document.

Word's main dictionary contains most common words. If Word finds a word in your document that does not appear in its main dictionary, it gives you options for correcting the possible misspelling.

The Spelling dialog box shown in Figure 3-4 shows the options available to you when checking spelling.

You probably use some words that are not in Word's main dictionary. You can add those words to a custom dictionary. You also can ignore a word or ignore all occurrences of a word. You can change a word or change all occurrences of a word.

note

If you find you often type the same word incorrectly, add the word to the AutoCorrect list.

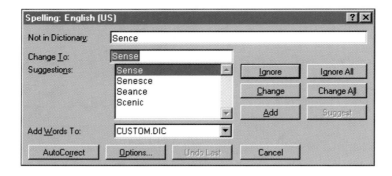

Figure 3-4
The Spelling
tool checks
your document
for spelling errors.

note

If you are using
Microsoft
Office, any word
you add to the
custom diction-
ary in any of
the Office pro-
grams is avail-
able for all
programs.

note

If you are work-
ing on a net-
work, you can
share with other
users a diction-
ary with words
commonly
used in your
organization.

When you use the Spelling feature, Word checks the entire document from the insertion point forward, and then works from the beginning of the document to the insertion
point. If you would like to check only a word or an area of your document, select the
word or the area before starting Spelling.

It is important to remember that the Spelling tool does not do away with the need to
proofread a document. If your misspelling results in another English word, the Spelling
feature will not notice it. The Spelling tool does not distinguish between homonyms
such as *there* and *their*. You must always proofread carefully.

If the following exercise (see Figure 3-5) does not work exactly as shown, it may be
that it was done on your computer already. If words do show a correct suggestion in the
list, just select them and click change.

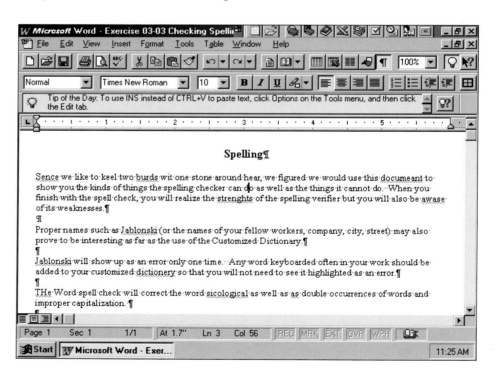

Figure 3-5
The Exercise 03-03
Checking Spelling
file to be used in
Exercise 3-3.

Exercise 3-3

1. To open a document, click the **Open** tool and double-click **Exercise 03-03 Checking Spelling.** Notice the many spelling errors.

2. To begin checking spelling, click the **Spelling** tool.

3. To correct the word *Sence*, which is not in the main dictionary and does not produce a correct suggestion, type **Since** and click the **Change** button.

4. To correct the word *burds*, type **birds** and click the **Change** button. Notice Word did not select the words *keel, wit,* or *hear* as being misspelled. Those words are in the dictionary.

5. To add *document* to the AutoCorrect list because you often type it incorrectly, click the **AutoCorrect** button.

6. To undo adding the word to the AutoCorrect list, click **Undo Last** in the dialog box.

7. To enter the correct spelling for *documeant*, click **Change.**

8. To enter the correct spelling for *strenghts*, click **Change.**

9. To enter the correct spelling for *awase*, click **aware** and the **Change** button.

10. To have Word ignore all occurrences of the proper name Jablonski in this document, click **Ignore All.**

11. To add *dictionary* to the AutoCorrect list because you often misspell it, click **AutoCorrect.**

12. To undo adding the word to the AutoCorrect list, click **Undo Last.**

13. To change the word in the document without adding *dictionary* to the AutoCorrect list, click **Change.**

14. To change the incorrect initial caps for the word *THe*, click **Change.**

15. To enter the correct spelling for *sicological*, click **psychological** and click **Change.** Notice Word can find a correct spelling for a word entered phonetically.

16. To delete the repetition of the word *as,* click the **Delete** button in the Spelling dialog box.

17. To respond to the prompt that the spell check is complete, click **OK.**

18. To move to the beginning of the document hold (Ctrl) and press (Home).

19. To enter some text that Word will underline, type your entire name and press (Enter) twice. Notice the wavy red line under names not in the Word dictionary.

20. To display suggested spellings for a word with a wavy red line, click the right mouse button on it.

21. To ignore the suggestion, click **Ignore All.**

22. To print the document, click the **Print** tool.

23. To save the file, click the **Save** tool.

24. To close the file, click the **Close** button on the right side of the menu bar.

If you choose Add for any word, Word adds it to your custom dictionary. The word you add will not appear as a misspelling again. We did not use Add or AutoCorrect in this lesson because we do not want to permanently change either the custom dictionary or the AutoCorrect list.

❖ USING THE THESAURUS

You can use the Thesaurus to improve your choice of words when writing. You can find synonyms and sometimes antonyms for words you enter. Select the word for which you want to find a synonym or antonym, and click the Thesaurus command on the Tools menu to display the Thesaurus dialog box shown in Figure 3-6.

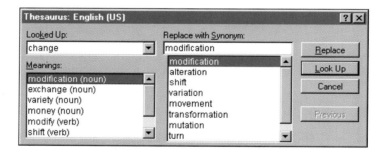

Figure 3-6
The Thesaurus dialog box displays synonyms and antonyms for words you wish to replace.

You can use the Replace button to replace the selected word with the selection in the Replace with Synonym box. You can use the Look Up button to look up a selected word in the Replace with Synonym box. You can select Antonym in the Meanings box when you want to see antonyms for the selected word.

Exercise 3-4

1. To open the document, click the **Open** tool and double-click **Exercise 03-04 Using Thesaurus.**

2. To select the word *change* in the last line of the paragraph, double-click **change.**

3. To display the Thesaurus dialog box, click **Tools** and then **Thesaurus.** Notice the different meanings for the word *change*.

4.   To select the *modify (verb)* meaning, click **modify (verb).** The words in the Replace with Synonym box change to reflect synonyms for the selected meaning.

5.   To replace the word *change* with *modify*, click the **Replace** button.

6.   To print the document, click the **Print** tool.

7.   To save the file, click the **Save** tool.

8.   To close the document, click the **Close** button at the right side of the menu bar.

❖ USING THE GRAMMAR TOOL

You can use the Grammar tool to identify sentences that contain possible grammatical or stylistic errors. Word offers suggestions about how to improve the sentences. The Grammar tool is particularly useful for finding sentences containing the passive voice. You can see the Grammar dialog box in Figure 3-7.

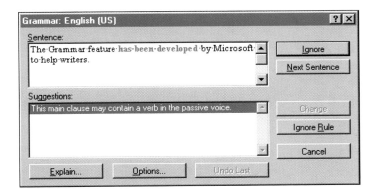

**Figure 3-7
The Grammar dialog box helps you find grammatical errors in your document.**

When you use the Grammar command, Word automatically checks spelling at the same time. When the grammar check is finished, Word displays the Readability Statistics dialog box.

Just as the Spelling tool does not do away with the need to proofread documents for spelling errors, the Grammar tool is not foolproof. You must still proofread your documents for grammatical errors.

Exercise 3-5

1.   To open the document for this exercise, click **Open** and then double-click **Exercise 03-05 Checking Grammar.**

2.   To begin the grammar check, click **Tools** and then **Grammar.** Word selects the first sentence and displays the passive verb in red. The suggestion box tells you the verb is in the passive voice.

3. To see an explanation of the problem with using passive voice, click **Explain.**

4. To close the Grammar Explanation box after you read the explanation, click its **Close** button in the upper-right corner.

5. To correct the sentence, select it in the dialog box and then type **Microsoft developed the Grammar tool to help writers.** Then click **Change.**

6. When Word selects the next sentence and suggests you use *was* instead of *were*, click **Change** to correct the agreement error.

7. To correct the spelling of *checls* (Word checks spelling during the grammar check), click **Change.**

8. To correct the word *speling*, click **Change.**

Readability Statistics, as shown in Figure 3-8, appear when you finish checking grammar. You can use these statistics to determine how easily a reader can understand your document. The last four Readability Statistics are scores calculated using different readability formats.

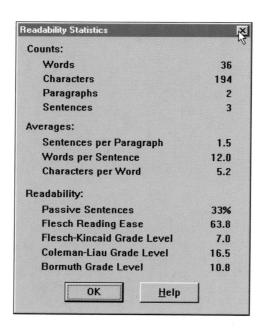

Figure 3-8
Readability
Statistics calculate
the ease with
which a reader
can understand
your text.

Exercise 3-6

1. To see information about the various readability statistics, click **Help** in the Readability Statistics window.

2. To close Help after you have read the information, click the **Close** button in the Help window.

3. To close the Readability Statistics window, click **OK.**

4. To see a list of the errors the Grammar tool searches for, click **Tools,** click **Options,** click the **Grammar** tab, click **Customize Settings** (see Figure 3-9). Scroll through the list, and click **Cancel** without making any changes.

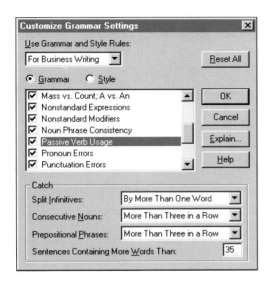

Figure 3-9
You can click on Customize Settings to see the errors for which the Grammar tool searches.

5. To close the Options dialog box, click **Cancel.**

6. To practice using the Grammar tool, write a few sentences after the paragraph you just corrected, and use the Grammar tool to check the sentences.

7. To save the document, click the **Save** tool.

8. To close the document, click the **Close** button at the right side of the menu bar.

❖ USING HYPHENATION

Hyphenation reduces the ragged appearance of text at the right margin. Hyphenation is not usually necessary unless you are using narrow text columns. Use the Hyphenation command on the Tools menu when you want to use hyphenation in your documents.

A *nonbreaking* hyphen is one that joins two words together that should not be separated at the end of a line by word wrap.

To insert a nonbreaking hyphen in your text:

❖ Hold (Ctrl) and (Shift) and press ⊙ (hyphen).

   or

❖ Click the Symbol command on the Insert menu, click the Special Characters tab, select Nonbreaking Hyphen, and click OK.

note

A narrow hyphenation zone reduces the raggedness of the right margin. A wide zone reduces the number of hyphens.

Word displays the Hyphenation dialog box shown in Figure 3-10 when you use the Hyphenation command. It is considered incorrect style to hyphenate a capitalized proper noun. You might want to toggle that option off. You also might want to limit the number of consecutive hyphens because more than about three on a page is distracting to the reader.

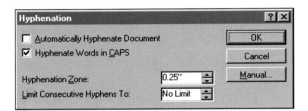

Figure 3-10
Use the Hyphenation dialog box to insert hyphens in a document.

Exercise 3-7

1. To open the document for this exercise, click **Open** and double-click **Exercise 03-07 Hyphenating.**

2. To display the Hyphenation dialog box, click **Tools** and then **Hyphenation.**

3. To **Automatically Hyphenate Document,** click that option and click **OK.** Notice Word entered one hyphen in the first paragraph and one in the title of the second paragraph.

4. To move to the end of the document to enter some text, hold **Ctrl** and press **End**. Type **My friend's married surname is Mary Jones-Smith.** Notice when you use a regular hyphen, the last name separates.

5. To insert a nonbreaking hyphen, select the original hyphen and hold **Ctrl** and **Shift** and press ⊙ (hyphen). Notice Word now treats the name as one word and keeps it together.

❖ WORKING IN OTHER LANGUAGES

You can use the editing and proofing tools to check text in other languages. First you must install the language dictionary for each language you want to check; then you can use the Language command on the Tools menu to mark the text and identify the language.

Figure 3-11 displays the Language dialog box you would use to check text in another language. You can also select an area of your document and mark it for no proofing. This feature is useful when you enter text that is purposely misspelled. You might have to use the scroll bar to move up the list to see the no-proofing selection.

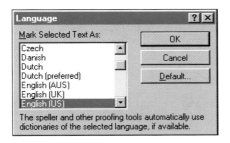

Figure 3-11
The Language command lets you check text in another language.

❖ USING WORD COUNT

You can use the Word Count command on the Tools menu to count the number of pages, words, characters, paragraphs, and lines in a document or in a selection (see Figure 3-12).

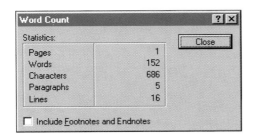

Figure 3-12
Use the Word Count command to count the number of pages, words, characters, paragraphs, or lines in a document.

Word Count does not count headers or footers. You can include footnotes and endnotes. Character Count includes letters, numbers, and punctuation marks. Blank lines are counted in the line count but not in the paragraph count.

Exercise 3-8

1. To see the count for the pages, words, characters, paragraphs, and lines in the hyphen document, click **Tools** and then **Word Count.**

2. To close the Word Count dialog box, click **Close.**

❖ INSERTING SYMBOLS

You can use the Symbol command on the Insert menu to insert symbols such as those shown on the Symbols tab in Figure 3-13 or on the Special Characters tab in Figure 3-14.

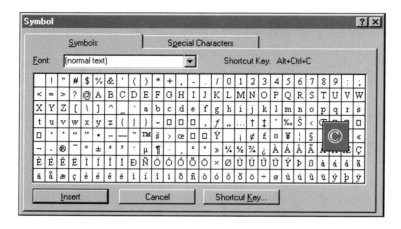

Figure 3-13
Various symbols are available on the Symbols tab.

Figure 3-14
The Special Characters tab contains the special characters you might need.

If you do not see the symbol you need on the Symbols tab, you can select a different font in the Font box and check the symbols in that font. When you click a symbol, Word enlarges that symbol. Click Insert when you find the symbol you need, and Word inserts it at the insertion point.

The nonbreaking space is a special character on the Special Characters tab. You should get accustomed to using the nonbreaking space.

Word's wraparound feature will wrap text to the next line whenever it finds a normal space, but there are certain pairs that should never be separated. For example, you will not see the title *Ms.* on one line and a first or last name on the next. Also, you will not see the month on one line and the day on the next. You should use the nonbreaking space as you enter such pairs.

note

You can type a nonbreaking space by holding **Ctrl** and **Shift** and pressing **SpaceBar**.

Exercise 3-9

1. To move the insertion point to the end of the document and begin a new paragraph, hold (Ctrl) and press (End) and then press (Enter) twice.

2. To display the Symbol dialog box, click the **Insert** menu and then **Symbol.**

3. To make sure the Symbols tab is displayed, click the **Symbols** tab.

4. To display the symbols on the Symbol font, select **Symbol** in the drop-down font box.

5. To enter the copyright symbol, click the symbol (see Figure 3-13), click **Insert**, and then click **Close**. Notice the copyright symbol in your document.

6. To use the Special Characters tab in the Symbols dialog box to enter the copyright symbol, click the **Insert** menu, click **Symbol,** click the **Special Characters** tab, scroll through the list to see the various special characters, click **Copyright** to select it, click **Insert,** and click **Close.** Notice the copyright symbol is a little different from the one on the Symbols tab.

7. To enter a nonbreaking space, type **September,** hold (Ctrl) and (Shift) and press (SpaceBar), and type **19, 1997.** To display nonprinting marks if they are not already displayed, click the Show/Hide tool. Notice the mark that signals the nonbreaking space and will not allow *September* and *19* to be split at the end of a line.

8. To browse through all of the symbols to become familiar with the symbols you can insert in your documents, click the **Insert** menu and click **Symbol** again.

9. To close the Symbol dialog box when you have seen all of the fonts and their symbols, click **Cancel.**

❖ PROTECTING A DOCUMENT WITH A PASSWORD

You can use the Save Options dialog box shown in Figure 3-15 to enter a password to prevent others from opening a document. You can open the Options dialog box from the Save As dialog box when you first save your document. If you decide later to add a password, choose the Save As command on the File menu to access the Options dialog box.

A document can be opened only by those who know the password.

You must be very careful when putting a password on a document. *If you forget your password, you cannot open your document.* Be sure to choose a password that you will remember weeks or months from now.

You can remove a password, but you must be able to open the document with the password before you can remove it.

note

Write down your password and keep it in a safe place so you can always check on it.

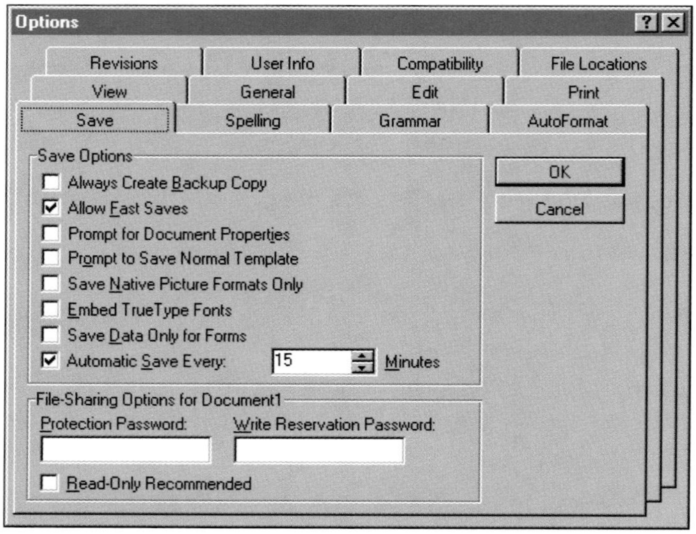

Figure 3-15
In the Options dialog box you can enter a password, which keeps those who don't know the password from opening your document.

Always check your fingers on the keyboard when entering passwords to make sure your fingers are not on the wrong keys. Word always displays a Confirm Password dialog box (see Figure 3-16) so you can enter your password a second time. Even when entering the password a second time, you have no way of knowing from the screen if you are actually typing what you think you are typing unless you check the position of your fingers on the keyboard.

Figure 3-16
The Confirm Password dialog box.

A password can contain up to 15 characters and can include letters, numbers, symbols, and spaces. Remember also that passwords are case sensitive. *PASSWORD*, *password*, and *PaSsWoRd* are three different passwords.

Exercise 3-10

1. To display the Save Options dialog box, click **File,** click **Save As,** and click **Options.**

2. To enter a password, click the insertion point in the **Protection Password** box, type **password,** and notice Word inserts asterisks for each character you enter. Click **OK.**

3. To confirm the password, type **password** again and click **OK.**

4. Before saving **Excercise 03-07 Hyphenating,** make certain that it will be saved in your personal folder. To save the document with its original name and the added password, click **Save** in the Save As dialog box.

5. To close the document, click the **File** menu and click **Close.**

6. To open the document with the password, click the **File** menu and click **Exercise 03-07 Hyphenating** on the bottom of the File menu (make certain that you click the version of the file stored in your personal folder). Type **password** in the dialog box, and click **OK.**

7. To remove the password, click **File,** click **Save As,** click **Options,** select the **asterisks** in the Protection Password dialog box, and press (Delete). Click **OK** in the Options dialog box, and click **Save** again in the Save As dialog box.

8. To close the document, click the **Close** button on the right side of the menu bar.

9. To be sure you removed the password, try opening and closing the document again.

❖ S U M M A R Y

You have now learned to use the AutoText and AutoCorrect features; check spelling; use the Thesaurus; use the Grammar, Hyphenation, and Word Count commands; insert symbols; and enter and remove a password.

Try the exercises on the following pages to test how well you remember what you learned. Don't be afraid to go back and look up answers or procedures, because that will help to reinforce what you learned.

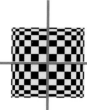

activities

❖ T R U E / F A L S E

On the blank line before each sentence, place a **T** *if the statement is true or an* **F** *if it is false.*

_____ 1. AutoText stores the entry with the template you are using.

_____ 2. The spelling feature checks for double occurrences of a word.

_____ 3. There is no need to proofread a document when you use the Grammar and Spelling commands.

_____ 4. Hyphenation is generally used for all documents.

_____ 5. The Grammar command checks for sentences using passive voice.

_____ 6. Word Count displays Readability Statistics.

_____ 7. You can check text in more than one language with the dictionary that comes with Word.

_____ 8. You can use the nonbreaking space to ensure that pairs of words are not separated at the end of a line.

_____ 9. A nonbreaking hyphen ensures the hyphenated word is not separated at the end of a line.

_____ 10. If you forget your password, Microsoft will help you access your document.

❖ COMPLETION

Fill in the blanks in the following statements.

1. The _____ tool automatically changes *teh* to *the*.

2. The Thesaurus lets you to find _____ and _____ for a selected word.

3. The _____ command is rarely used unless you are working with very narrow columns.

4. You can use the _____ command to mark text that you do not want Spelling to check.

5. The _____ command counts the number of pages, words, characters, paragraphs, and lines in a document.

6. _____ are case sensitive.

7. The Symbol command is on the _____ menu.

8. The _____ command checks for double occurrences of a word.

9. The _____ command checks for agreement errors.

10. _____ help you determine how easily others can read your document.

review

Review Exercise 3-1

1. Use the Answer Wizard command on the Help menu to find information about how Word arrives at Readability Statistics.

2. Read the information and then print it.

Review Exercise 3-2

1. Open the **Review 03-02 Check Document** document.

2. Use the Grammar command on the file. Spelling is automatically checked when you use the Grammar command.

3. Use the Word Count command.

4. Print, save, and close the document.

On Your Own

You have been asked to provide monthly calendars to hang by participants' desks.

1. Use the Calendar Wizard to create calendars for the next two months. To open the Calendar Wizard, click the File menu and then click New. Click the Other Documents tab. Click Calendar Wizard.

2. Print two copies of the calendars.

3. There is no need to keep a file copy.

4. Close the file.

lesson 4

Using Basic Formatting Techniques

❖ OBJECTIVES

When you complete this lesson, you will be able to:

1. Use the Page Setup command.

2. Use the Ruler to set margins.

3. Control pagination.

4. Apply character formatting.

5. Apply paragraph formatting.

Estimated Time: $1\frac{1}{2}$ hours

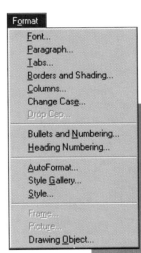

❖ INTRODUCTION

In this lesson you will learn to use Word's formatting features to change the appearance of text on a page. You will learn how to change page size and orientation, change margins, use the Pagination feature, and apply character and paragraph formatting.

❖ SETTING UP THE PAGE

One of the first things you might want to do when you begin working with a new document is format the page.

You can use the Page Setup command on the File menu to set margins, choose paper size and paper source, and set the page layout.

SECTIONS

You can divide a Word document into sections and format each of the sections differently. A section can be as small as a single paragraph or as long as an entire document. As you look at the Page Setup options, you will see how using sections helps you to more easily format a document.

PAPER SIZE

You can use the Paper Size tab in the Page Setup dialog box (see Figure 4-1) to set the size of the paper or envelope you want to use. You can change paper size and orientation for the whole document or for part of the document.

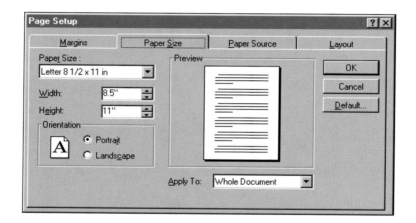

In the Paper Size drop-down box, you can choose one of the given sizes or you can choose Custom Size. If you choose Custom Size, use the Width and Height boxes to specify the custom size.

You can also choose Portrait (vertical) or Landscape (horizontal) orientation.

You can apply changes in paper size or orientation to the whole document, from just the insertion point forward, or to selected text. If you change the paper size or orientation from the insertion point forward, Word inserts a section break before the insertion point. If you change the paper size or orientation for selected text, Word inserts a section break before and after the selected text.

Exercise 4-1

1. To open a file, click the **Open** tool and double-click **Exercise 04-01 Page Setup.**

2. To display the Page Setup dialog box, click the **File** menu and then **Page Setup.**

3. To display the Paper Size dialog box, click the **Paper Size** tab.

4. To see the paper sizes available, click the **drop-down button** in the **Paper Size** box. Notice the Custom Size item; you might want at some time to use a paper size not shown on the list. Be sure **Letter 8 1/2 x 11 in** is selected.

5. To change to a horizontal orientation, click **Landscape.** Notice the Preview box changed the orientation of the paper.

6. To return to the vertical orientation, click **Portrait.**

7. To see the list in the Apply To box, click the **drop-down button.**

8. To apply the changes to the whole document, be sure **Whole Document** is selected.

MARGINS

As you can see in Figure 4-2, the default margins for the Blank template are 1 inch at the top and bottom of the page and 1.25 inches at the right and left of the page. You can change the margins with the Page Setup command or with the Ruler.

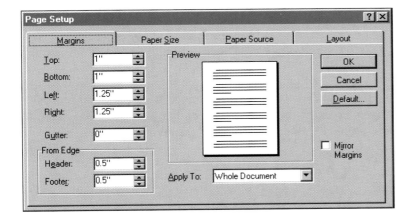

Figure 4-2
Use the Page
Setup command to
change margins.

> **note**
>
> Most printers cannot print all the way to the edge of the paper. You can check your printer's documentation to see what your minimum margin settings and header and footer settings must be.

You can change margins for the whole document, from the insertion point forward, or for a selection. As you learned with paper size, Word inserts section breaks if you choose from the insertion point forward or for a selection.

You can also use the Page Setup command to determine how far from the edge of the page Word prints headers and footers. Word prints headers and footers in the top and bottom margins, respectively.

You can choose Mirror Margins when you intend to print on both sides of the paper. Facing pages will mirror each other's margins. If you choose Mirror Margins, the Preview box changes to show you facing pages.

If you choose Mirror Margins, you can change the gutter measurement to allow extra space between the pages for binding.

PAPER SOURCE

If you have more than one paper tray available for your printer, you can use the Paper Source tab in the Page Setup dialog box (see Figure 4-3) to set options for the type of printer paper you want to feed. You must know your printer's capabilities and the number of trays available. You can set the paper feed for the whole document, for sections, or for selections.

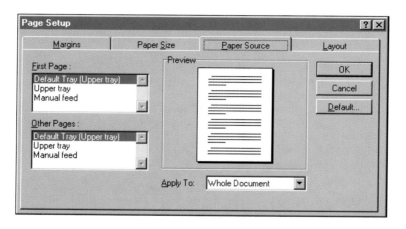

Figure 4-3
Use the Paper Source tab in the Page Setup dialog box to choose the type of printer paper you want to use.

LAYOUT

You can use the Layout tab in the Page Setup dialog box (see Figure 4-4) to designate how new sections are formatted. You can also tell Word whether headers should be on the first page and whether they should be positioned differently on odd and even pages, how text should be vertically aligned on the page, and whether Word should display line numbers or endnotes.

You can use the Section Start box to designate whether a new section begins on a new page, an odd-numbered page, an even-numbered page, a new column, or on the same page as the preceding section.

> **note**
>
> You must also use the Headers and Footers command on the View menu or the Page Numbers command on the Insert menu to actually insert your headers and footers in the document.

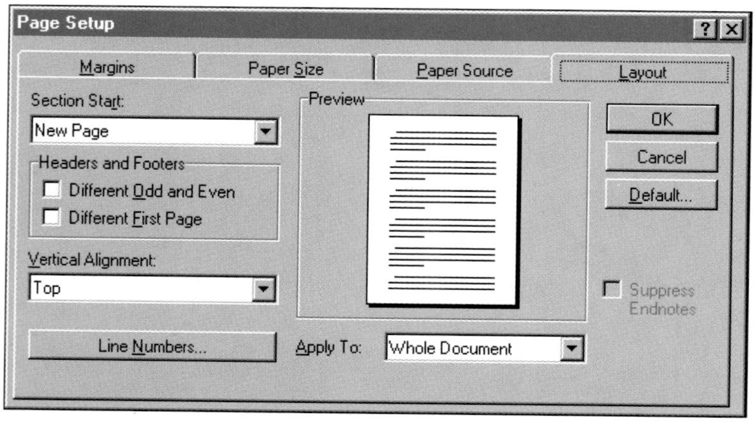

Figure 4-4
Use the Layout tab in the Page Setup dialog box to choose different formatting options.

You can use the Headers and Footers options to decide whether you want different headers and footers on odd and even pages if you are using facing pages. You can also decide whether you want a header or footer to print on the first page of a document or a section.

You can use the Vertical Alignment box to designate whether Word aligns the section or document at the top margin, aligns it between the top and bottom margins, or expands space between paragraphs to align the top line with the top margin and the bottom line with the bottom margin.

You can use the Line Numbers button to display line numbers for a section or for the whole document and to designate how the numbers are determined.

Exercise 4-2

1. To display the margins choices, click the **Margins** tab.

2. To change the left margin to 1 inch, click the **down button** on that box until you see **1".**

3. To change the right margin to 1 inch, drag over the **1.25"** to select it. Then type **1.**

4. To set up for facing pages, click **Mirror Margins.** Notice the Preview.

5. To see the binding area increase, enlarge the gutter by clicking the Gutter box **up arrow** until it reaches **.5".** Notice the Preview.

6. To remove mirror margins, click **Mirror Margins** again.

7. To reset the gutter, click the **down arrow** in the Gutter box until it returns to **0.**

8. To execute the changes you made, click **OK.**

❖ SETTING MARGINS WITH THE RULER

You can also use the Ruler to set margins for your document. Before you can use the Ruler to set margins, however, you must be sure you are in Print Preview or page layout view. You changed margins in Print Preview in an earlier lesson. You will work in page layout view to change margins in this lesson.

 You can use the Page Layout command on the View menu or the Page Layout button on the horizontal scroll bar to display page layout view.

 You can use the Normal command on the View menu or the Normal button on the horizontal scroll bar to display normal view.

The normal view shown in Figure 4-5 displays a simplified version of a document. It does not show, for example, how graphics will be displayed on the printed page or display top and bottom margins.

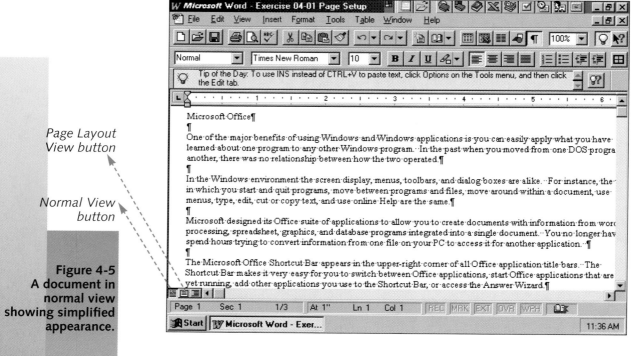

Page Layout View button

Normal View button

Figure 4-5
A document in normal view showing simplified appearance.

Page layout view, displayed in Figure 4-6, is called WYSIWYG (what you see is what you get). In page layout view, you can see the margin areas at the top and at the bottom of the page. Page layout view can slow editing and scrolling, but it is useful for checking the final appearance of a document.

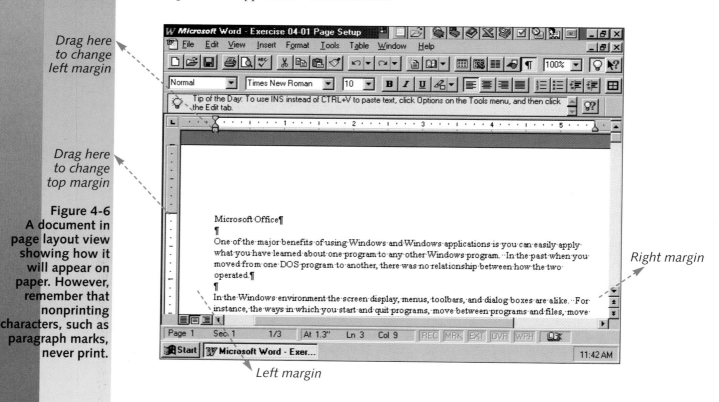

Drag here to change left margin

Drag here to change top margin

Figure 4-6
A document in page layout view showing how it will appear on paper. However, remember that nonprinting characters, such as paragraph marks, never print.

Right margin

Left margin

When you change margins, the margins change for the entire document if your document has only one section. If it has more than one section, the margins change for the section containing the insertion point.

You can display the measurements of the text area and the margins while you change the margins by holding (Alt). The mouse pointer becomes a double-headed arrow when it is on a margin boundary.

As you can see in Figure 4-6, the gray areas on the rulers indicate the margins.

Exercise 4-3

1. If the Ruler is not displayed, click the **View** menu and click **Ruler.**

2. To switch to page layout view, click the **View** menu and then click **Page Layout.**

3. To increase the top margin to 1.5 inches, hold (Alt) while you drag the margin boundary on the Vertical Ruler until you see the **1.5-inch mark** on the top section and release.

4. To return to the original 1-inch margin, click **Undo.**

5. To set a 1.5-inch left margin, hold (Alt) and point to the left edge of the Hortizontal Ruler until the pointer changes to a two-sided arrow (←→). Drag right to the **1.5-inch mark** and release.

6. To reverse the action, click **Undo.**

❖ CONTROLLING PAGINATION

Word automatically starts a new page when the current page is full. Page breaks entered by Word are called *soft page breaks*. As you reformat or edit, Word continually adjusts soft page breaks. You cannot delete a soft page break. As you can see in Figure 4-7, in normal view a soft page break appears as a dotted line across the page.

You can use the Break command on the Insert menu or hold (Ctrl) and press (Enter) to insert a hard page break. When you insert a hard page break, Word always breaks the page at that point. Word will not move a hard page break when rearranging after editing. You must go back and select and delete the hard page break if you want to change it. In normal view, a hard page break appears as a dotted line with the words *Page Break*.

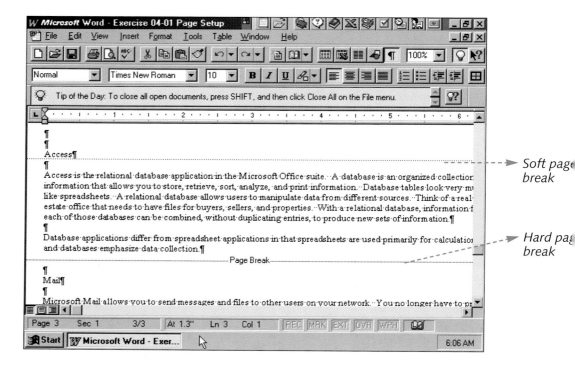

Soft page break

Hard page break

Figure 4-7
In normal view a soft page break appears as a dotted line; a hard page break appears as a dotted line with the words *Page Break*.

Exercise 4-4

1. To return to normal view, click the **Normal View** button on the horizontal scroll bar.

2. To go to page 2, click the **Edit** menu and the **Go To** command. Type **2,** click **Go To,** and click **Close.**

3. To see the soft page break as well as the hard page break, press ⬆ once.

4. To delete the hard page break (lower one), scroll down to see it, click the I-beam on the **hard page break,** and press (Delete).

5. Try clicking the I-beam on the **soft page break.** You cannot select the page break because you cannot delete it.

❖ APPLYING CHARACTER FORMATS

Characters are letters, numbers, symbols, punctuation marks, and spaces. You can select text and apply one or more character formats.

The character formats you can apply are font, font size, font style (regular, italic, bold), underline, color, strikethrough, superscript, subscript, hidden, small caps, and all caps.

To apply character formats to selected text:

❖ Click a button on the Formatting toolbar, shown in Figure 4-8.

   or

❖ Choose the Font command on the Format menu to access the Font dialog box displayed in Figure 4-9.

   or

❖ Press shortcut keys (use the Search command on the Help menu to search for shortcut keys).

Word displays formatted text as it will look when you print it.

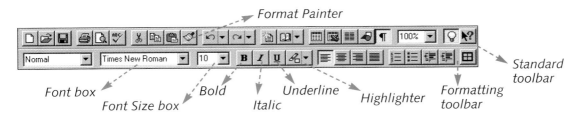

Format Painter

Font box   *Font Size box*   *Bold*   *Italic*   *Underline*   *Highlighter*   *Formatting toolbar*   *Standard toolbar*

Figure 4-8
The Formatting toolbar lets you apply character formats to your document.

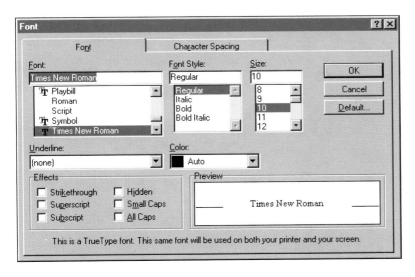

Figure 4-9
The Font command gives you another way to choose character formats.

FORMATTING CHARACTERS USING THE FORMATTING TOOLBAR

You can use the Formatting toolbar to apply most of the commonly used character formatting. You can change the font and font size. You can highlight a section with a color to make it stand out when you send a document electronically. You can also choose bold, italic, or underline. You can use the Format Painter on the Standard toolbar to apply character formats as well.

You can see the name of the font and the font size currently in use on the Formatting toolbar. If either or both of those boxes are blank, you have selected text containing more than one font or font size.

CHOOSING FONTS

Word displays your text in the font and point size in which it will print your text. The font is the design of the letters and numbers. Here are some examples:

Times New Roman

Arial

Arial Narrow

Arial Rounded Bold

You can see a list of your available fonts in the drop-down list on the Formatting toolbar or in the same list in the Font dialog box. Fonts used in the current document are displayed at the beginning of the list as well as in alphabetical order below the list of current fonts.

TrueType fonts are provided with Microsoft Windows 3.1 and later. They are *scalable fonts,* which means they can be displayed and printed in any size. You can print them on any printer capable of printing graphics.

Font sizes are measured in points. Point size measures the height of characters. A point is approximately equal to $\frac{1}{72}$ inch. A 10-point font is approximately $\frac{10}{72}$ inch high. These examples show what different point sizes look like:

8 Point

12 Point

24 Point

36 Point

Font styles fall into four categories:

Regular

Italic

Bold

Bold Italic

Here are examples of other formats you can apply to characters:

~~Strikethrough~~

Super^{script}

Sub_{script}

SMALL CAPS

ALL CAPS

Use Hidden for notes (such as to yourself) that do not display or print. You can see hidden text if you use the Show/Hide tool to display nonprinting characters. All Caps and Small Caps affect only lowercase letters.

In addition to the Superscript and Subscript formats, you can select the Character Spacing tab in the Font dialog box and use the Position option to adjust the vertical position of any character or graphic.

Word can underline text with a _single_, _dotted_, or _double line_. You _can_ _also_ _choose_ _to_ _underline_ _just_ _the_ _words_ _and_ _not_ _the_ _spaces_ _between_ _them_.

You can add color to text and condense or e x p a n d character spacing with the Font command.

All text has some format even if you do not apply any. Word automatically applies the Normal style when you enter text. Normal style when you install Word is the Times New Roman font and 10-point size.

note

There are not many times when you need to underline words. Instead use bold or italic styles to set text apart.

Exercise 4-5

1. To change the font size from 10 to 12 points for the whole document, click the **Edit** menu and then **Select All.** Then click the **Format** menu and click **Font.** Click **12** in the **Size** box and click **OK.**

2. To be sure your insertion point is at the beginning of the document, hold `Ctrl` and press `Home`.

3. Select the title, **Microsoft Office.**

4. To display the toolbar Font list, click the drop-down **Font** button on the toolbar.

5. To change the heading to a different font, click **Arial** in the Font list.

6. To apply the Bold style, click the **Bold** button on the toolbar. Notice when you apply the Bold style, the toolbar button appears pushed in.

7. To change the font size, click the drop-down **Size** button and click **18.**

8. To select _you can easily apply what you have learned about one program to any other Windows program_ in the first sentence, drag across it.

9. To change the style to italic, click the **Italic** tool.

10. To change the same text to bold italic, click the **Bold** tool.

11. To remove the italic from the selected text, click the **Italic** tool.

12. To select _In the past_ in the next sentence, drag the mouse across it.

13. To add strikethrough, click the **Format** menu, click **Font,** click the **Font** tab, click **Strikethrough,** and click **OK.**

14. To select the word _no_ near the end of the paragraph, double-click it.

15. To underline the word, click the **Underline** tool.

16. To select the word _relationship_ near the end of the paragraph, double-click it.

17. To underline with a double line and add color, click the **Format** menu, click **Font,** click the **Underline** drop-down button, click **double,** click the **Color** drop-down button, click **Red,** and click **OK.**

18. To select the word *two* near the end of the paragraph, double-click it.

19. To underline with a dotted line, click the **Format** menu, click **Font,** click the **Underline** drop-down button, click **dotted,** click **OK.**

20. To select *In the Windows environment* on the first line of the next paragraph, drag the mouse across it.

21. To underline the words but not the spaces between them, click the **Format** menu, click **Font,** click the **Underline** drop-down button, click **Words Only,** and click **OK.**

22. To select the third paragraph, double-click in the **selection bar** to the left of the paragraph.

23. To highlight the selected paragraph, click the **Highlight** tool.

24. Scroll down through the document until you see the heading *Word* at the left margin and select **Word.**

25. To change to caps, click the **Format** menu, click **Font,** click **All Caps,** and check the Preview box. Click **Small Caps,** click **Arial** in the Font list, click **Bold Italic** in the Font Style list, click **14** in the Size box, and click **OK.**

You can format text when you enter it or at any time thereafter. If you are formatting text as you enter it, all the text you enter immediately after takes on the same formatting. You will usually have to turn the formatting off before typing text you do not want to format.

REMOVING CHARACTER FORMATTING

You can remove any character formats applied with the Font dialog box, keystroke combinations, or the Formatting toolbar by selecting the text and holding **Ctrl** and pressing **SpaceBar**.

USING FORMAT PAINTER

Once you have applied formatting to text, you can select the formatted text to use the Format Painter tool on the Standard toolbar to add the same formatting to other parts of your document.

❖ Click the Format Painter once when you want to copy the format to one location.

or

❖ Double-click the Format Painter to copy a format to more than one location.

❖ When the mouse pointer changes to a paintbrush with an I-beam, select the text you want to format.

❖ If you double-clicked the Format Painter, continue formatting by selecting other text.

❖ Click the Format Painter tool again to toggle it off.

Exercise 4-6

1. Make sure the word *Word* with the attributes you gave it is still selected.

2. To use the same formatting on the words *Excel, PowerPoint, Access*, and *Mail*, double-click the **Format Painter** tool.

3. To add the formatting to the word *Excel*, scroll down through the document until you come to the word *Excel* at the left margin. Click the paintbrush on **Excel.**

4. To add the same formatting to the words *PowerPoint, Access*, and *Mail*, click the paintbrush on each of them.

5. To toggle off Format Painter, click the **Format Painter** tool.

6. To return to the beginning of the document, hold ⟨Ctrl⟩ and press ⟨Home⟩.

7. To remove the formatting from *Microsoft Office*, select the two words and then hold ⟨Ctrl⟩ and press ⟨SpaceBar⟩.

8. To print the document, click the **Print** tool.

9. To save the document, click the **Save** tool.

10. To close the document, click the **Close** button at the right side of the menu bar.

USING THE CHANGE CASE COMMAND

You can use the Change Case command on the Format menu to quickly change the case of text. The Change Case command affects character capitalization you type, but it does *not* affect characters you formatted with All Caps or Small Caps.

You must first select the text you want to change. Then select one of the options in the Change Case dialog box (see Figure 4-10):

❖ *Sentence case* capitalizes the first word in each sentence.

❖ *lowercase* changes all characters to lowercase.

❖ *UPPERCASE* changes all characters to caps.

❖ *Title Case* capitalizes the first character of each word.

❖ *tOGGLE cASE* changes each character to the opposite of what it is.

Toggle case can help you fix things quickly if you have accidentally typed text with ⟨Caps Lock⟩ on.

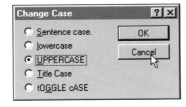

Figure 4-10
The Change Case command gives you several options for changing the case of text.

Exercise 4-7

1. To open a file, click the **Open** tool and double-click **Exercise 04-07 Change Case.**

2. To select all of the text, click the **Edit** menu and **Select All.**

3. To change to lowercase, click **Format,** click **Change Case,** and click **lowercase.** Then click **OK.**

4. To change to uppercase, click **Format,** click **Change Case,** and click **UPPERCASE.** Then click **OK.**

5. To change to title case, click **Format,** click **Change Case,** and click **Title Case.** Then click **OK.**

6. To use toggle case, click **Format,** click **Change Case,** and click **tOGGLE cASE.** Then click **OK.**

7. To return to the original, click **Undo** four times.

8. To save the file, click the **Save** tool.

9. To close the document, click the **Close** button at the right side of the menu bar.

❖ FORMATTING PARAGRAPHS

The appearance of your document depends on the formatting you apply to blocks of text. Word refers to any amount of text or other items followed by a paragraph mark as a *paragraph.*

To apply paragraph formatting to a paragraph, position your insertion point anywhere in that paragraph. Word will apply any paragraph formats you select to the entire paragraph. You cannot apply paragraph formatting to just a selection within the paragraph.

To apply paragraph formatting, you can use the Formatting toolbar (see Figure 4-11), the Paragraph command on the Format menu, or keystrokes.

Figure 4-11
You can choose paragraph formatting with the Formatting toolbar.

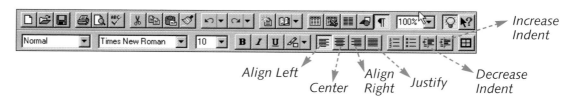

Increase Indent

Align Left Center Align Right Justify Decrease Indent

As you can see in Figure 4-12, the options on the Indents and Spacing tab in the Paragraph dialog box let you control indentation from the left and right margins, spacing before and after paragraphs, line spacing within paragraphs, special indents such as first line indents and hanging indents, and alignment with margins. Figure 4-13 displays a first line indent, margin alignment, and a hanging indent.

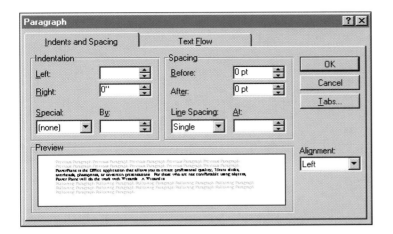

Figure 4-12
The Indents and Spacing tab provides options for indentation and spacing.

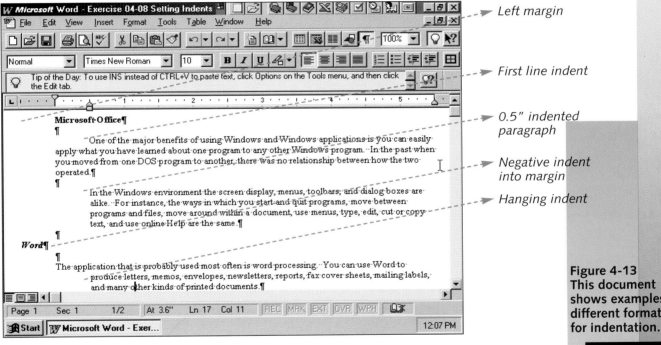

Left margin

First line indent

0.5" indented paragraph

Negative indent into margin

Hanging indent

Figure 4-13
This document shows examples of different formats for indentation.

You can also use the Tabs button on the Indents and Spacing tab to set tabs for the paragraph. Tabs are automatically set every half inch.

As you see in Figure 4-14, the Text Flow tab lets you to control how pagination is determined for each paragraph and to control line numbering and hyphenation.

For example, if you turn on line numbers in the Layout tab of the Page Setup dialog box, you can suppress (prevent Word from printing) line numbers for selected paragraphs. You can also select paragraphs that you do not want hyphenated by the Hyphenation command.

note

You will rarely use the Tab feature in Word. The Indent feature and the Tables feature (which is covered in a later lesson) make tabs almost unnecessary.

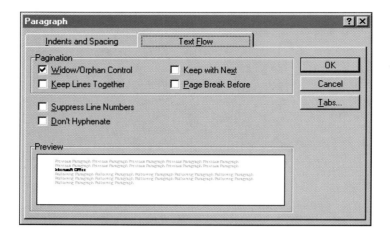

Figure 4-14
The Text Flow tab options control pagination, line numbering, and hyphenation.

When Widow/Orphan Control is toggled on, Word does not allow single lines to appear at the top or bottom of a page. You can use the Keep Lines Together option to specify that selected lines in a paragraph be kept together on a page. You can use the Keep with Next option to specify that selected paragraphs be kept together on a page. You can use the Page Break Before option to specify that the paragraph containing the insertion point always be on the top of a page.

SETTING INDENTS

You can see in Figure 4-13 that there are several ways you can use indenting to set paragraphs off from other text in your documents.

You should not press **Tab** or **SpaceBar** numerous times to indent lines of text. Nor should you try to control indentation by pressing **Enter** at the end of each line. Each of these methods worked with the typewriter or with early word processing programs. However, they make editing a document or converting a document to another file format very difficult in Word.

You can set precise measurements for paragraph indents with the Paragraph command on the Format menu. Left and right indents are measured from the left and right margins. Negative indents run the text into the margins. You can also use first line indents and hanging indents.

Exercise 4-8

1. To open **Exercise 04-08 Setting Indents,** click the **Open** tool and then double-click **Exercise 04-08 Setting Indents.**

2. To enter the first line indent in the paragraph beginning *One of the major*, click the I-beam before the word *One* and press **Tab**.

3. To indent the paragraph beginning *In the Windows environment*, click the I-beam anywhere in the paragraph, and then click the **Increase Indent** tool. Notice Word indented the paragraph 0.5 inch to the first tab stop.

4. To indent the paragraph 1 inch, click the **Increase Indent** tool again.

5. To move back to the 0.5-inch indent, click the **Decrease Indent** tool.

6. To indent the heading into the margin, click anywhere in the *Word* heading, click the **Format** menu, click the **Paragraph** command, click the **down arrow** on the **Left Indentation** box until it reaches **-0.5",** and click **OK.**

7. To paint the format on the *Excel* heading, select **Word** and the **Paragraph mark** after it, click the **Format Painter** tool, and drag the paintbrush I-beam over the **Excel** heading.

8. To set the hanging indent, click the I-beam anywhere in the paragraph beginning *The application that is probably used*, click the **Format** menu, click **Paragraph,** click **Hanging** in the Special box, make certain that the By box reads **0.5",** and click **OK.**

9. To remove the hanging indent, click the **Format** menu, click **Paragraph,** click **(none)** in the Special box, and click **OK.**

10. To print the document, click the **Print** tool.

11. To save the file, click the **Save** tool.

12. To close the document, click the **Close** button at the right side of the menu bar.

CENTERING AND ALIGNING TEXT

You can left justify, justify, right justify, or center paragraphs in Word. Each of the alignments is shown in Figure 4-15.

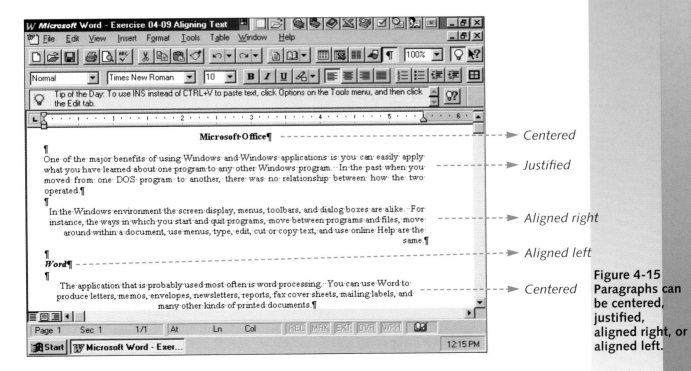

Figure 4-15
Paragraphs can be centered, justified, aligned right, or aligned left.

Word defaults to *left justified*, which aligns text flush with the left margin and leaves a ragged right edge.

Justified aligns text flush with the left margin and flush with the right margin. Word adds extra space between words to even out the lines.

Right justified aligns text with the right margin and leaves a ragged left edge.

Center centers the text between the margins.

Exercise 4-9

1. To open **Exercise 04-09 Aligning Text**, click the **Open** tool and then double-click **Exercise 04-09 Aligning Text.** The insertion point should be before the words *Microsoft Office.*

2. To center the title between the margins, click the **Center** tool. Notice the Center tool appears pushed in when it is turned on.

3. Move the insertion point into the *One of the major benefits* paragraph.

4. To justify the paragraph, click the **Justify** tool.

5. Move the insertion point into the *In the Windows* paragraph.

6. To align the paragraph with the right margin, click the **Align Right** tool.

7. Move the insertion point into the *The application that is* paragraph.

8. To center the lines of the paragraph between the margins, click the **Center** tool.

9. To print the document, click the **Print** tool.

10. To save the file, click the **Save** tool.

11. To close the document, click the **Close** button at the right side of the menu bar.

SETTING LINE SPACING

Line spacing determines the height of each line of text in a paragraph. Word defaults to single line spacing.

The height of each line for single line spacing depends on the size of the font characters. The line will be just a little taller than the number of points you are using. When you choose double-spacing, the line will be approximately twice the number of points you are using. If a line contains a large character or a graphic or a formula, Word increases the spacing for that line.

You can use either the Paragraph command on the Format menu or shortcut keys to designate Single, 1.5 lines, Double, At Least, Exactly, or Multiple line spacing.

Exercise 4-10

1. To open **Exercise 04-10 Line Spacing**, click the **Open** tool and then double-click **Exercise 04-10 Line Spacing.**

2. To see 1.5 line spacing, position the insertion point in the paragraph beginning *One of the major benefits.* Click the **Format** menu, click **Paragraph,** click the drop-down button in the **Line Spacing** box, click **1.5 Lines,** and click **OK.**

3. To see double-spacing, click the **Format** menu, click **Paragraph,** click the drop-down button in the **Line Spacing** box, click **Double,** and click **OK.**

4. To see at least a 15-point line space, click the **Format** menu, click **Paragraph,** click the drop-down button in the **Line Spacing** box, click **At Least,** change *12* points to **15** points, and click **OK.**

5. To see exactly 14 points, click the **Format** menu, click **Paragraph**, click the drop-down button in the **Line Spacing** box, click **Exactly**, change *12* points to **14** points, and click **OK**.

6. To see multiple line spacing, click the **Format** menu, click **Paragraph,** click the drop-down arrow in the **Line Spacing** box, click **Multiple,** change *3* to **4,** and click **OK.**

7. To return to single-spacing, click the **Format** menu, click **Paragraph,** click the drop-down button in the **Line Spacing** box, click **Single,** and click **OK.**

8. To save the file, click the **Save** tool.

9. To close the document, click the **Close** button at the right side of the menu bar.

ADDING AND REMOVING SPACE BETWEEN PARAGRAPHS

You can add space before or after a paragraph without pressing (Enter) by entering measurements in the Spacing Before and After boxes on the Indents and Spacing tab. You can, for instance, specify how much space should appear before and after a heading.

SETTING AND CLEARING TABS

Tab stops are set at 0.5-inch intervals from the left margin. You can use either the Ruler (see Figure 4-16) or the Tabs command on the Format menu (see Figure 4-17) to change tab positions or the way text lines up at a tab stop.

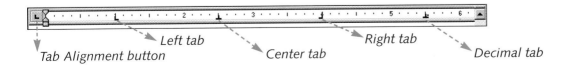

Tab Alignment button   Left tab   Center tab   Right tab   Decimal tab

> **note**
>
> The Spacing Before and After feature can be useful when working with lengthy documents or when using styles. You will learn more about styles in a later lesson. When you only needed to press (Enter) once in the Memo template, the Spacing Before and After feature was used.

Figure 4-16 Tabs may be set using the Ruler.

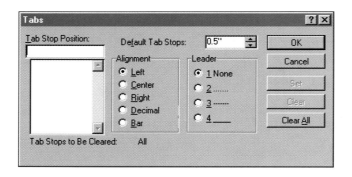

Figure 4-17
Another way to set tabs is to use the Tabs command on the Format menu.

note

Be sure to use Word's Table feature, which is covered in a later lesson, whenever you are setting up columns of text and/or numbers. Do not use tabs for those items.

You can change the default tab spacing in a document. Custom tab stops you have set for existing paragraphs in the document are not affected.

Word offers four types of tab stops:

❖ *Left* aligns text flush left at the tab stop.

❖ *Right* aligns text flush right at the tab stop.

❖ *Center* centers text at the tab stop.

❖ *Decimal* aligns characters at the decimal point.

You can use the Bar tab option in the Tabs dialog box to run a vertical line between columns.

To set tab stops in existing text, select the paragraph or paragraphs in which you want to set or change tab stops. Tabs you set are displayed on the Ruler only when the insertion point is in the area selected for tabs. If you are at the beginning of a document and set tab stops, they will be stored in the paragraph mark.

To set or change the type of tab alignment:

❖ Click the Tab Alignment button at the far left of the Horizontal Ruler until you see the tab you want—left, right, center, or decimal.

❖ Click the spot on the Ruler where you want to position the tab stop.

❖ To remove a tab stop, drag it off the Ruler; to move a tab stop, drag it to another location on the Ruler.

Exercise 4-11

1. To create a new document, click the **New** tool. Notice the left tab is displayed at the far left of the Horizontal Ruler. (If it isn't, click the tab until the left tab is displayed.)

2. To insert a left tab, click the approximate spot on the Ruler where the left tab is set in Figure 4-16.

3. To display the center tab, click the **left tab** at the left of the Ruler. Notice Word now displays the center tab.

4. To insert a center tab, click the approximate spot where the center tab is set in Figure 4-16.

5. To display the right tab, click the **center tab** at the left of the Ruler.

6. To set a right tab, click the approximate spot where the right tab is set in Figure 4-16.

7. To display the decimal tab, click the **right tab** at the left of the Ruler.

8. To set a decimal tab, click the approximate spot where the decimal tab is set in Figure 4-16.

9. Tab to the first tab position and begin typing the following data. For each entry, press (Tab) and then just type the entry. Press (Enter) at the end of each line.

   ```
   Left            Center          Right       342.16

   Justify       Center Align    Right Tab      2.43
   ```

   Notice column 1 is aligned at the left, column 2 is centered around the tab stop, column 3 is aligned at the right, and column 4 is aligned at the decimal points.

10. To print the document, click the **Print** tool.

11. To save the document, click the **Save** tool, type **Exercise 04-11 Using Tabs,** and click **Save.**

12. To close the document, click the **Close** button at the right side of the menu bar.

To fill the empty space before a tab stop with leaders—dotted, dashed, or solid lines:

❖ Select the paragraphs where you want the leaders.

❖ Use the Tabs command on the Format menu to choose the leader character.

Figure 4-18 shows an example of dotted leaders.

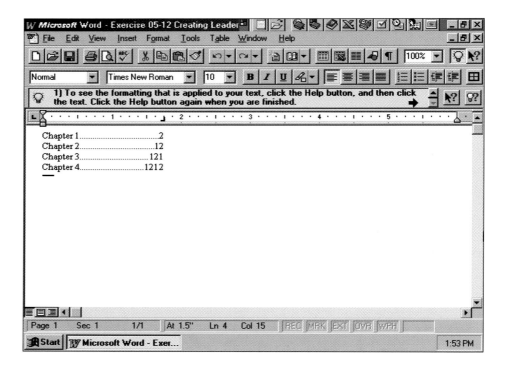

Figure 4-18
Use the Tabs
Command on the
Format menu
to create dotted
leaders.

Exercise 4-12

1. To open a file, click the **Open** tool and then double-click **Exercise 04-12 Creating Leaders.**

2. To select the entire file, click the **Edit** menu and **Select All.**

3. To enter leaders, click the **Format** menu and click **Tabs.** Notice the tab position is already selected. Click the **2** option for dotted leaders and click **OK.**

4. To print the document, click the **Print** tool.

5. To save the document, click the **Save** tool.

6. To close the document, click the **Close** button at the right side of the menu bar.

You have learned a good many of Word's formatting features, including how to use the Page Setup command, how to use the Ruler to set margins, how to control pagination, and how to apply character and paragraph formatting.

Try the activities on the following pages to test how well you remember what you learned. Don't be afraid to go back and look up procedures; you won't be able to remember everything you did. Using Help or looking back through this book will reinforce what you learned.

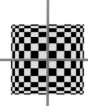

activities

On the blank line before each sentence, place a **T** *if the statement is true or an* **F** *if it is false.*

_____ 1. Sections let you to use different margins or paper orientation within the same document.

_____ 2. You can set custom sizes for paper with the Paragraph command on the Format menu.

_____ 3. You must be in the page layout view to set margins with the Ruler.

_____ 4. You can delete a soft page break that Word enters in the document.

_____ 5. You must select existing text before you can apply character formatting.

_____ 6. Font names describe the design of characters, and point sizes measure the height of characters.

_____ 7. You should use underlining as frequently as possible to set words off from the rest of the text.

_____ 8. You can remove character formats you apply by selecting the text and holding (Ctrl) and pressing (SpaceBar).

_____ 9. Any amount of text or other items followed by a paragraph mark is considered a paragraph.

_____ 10. The best way to indent whole paragraphs is with (Tab).

❖ COMPLETION

Fill in the blanks in the following statements.

1. You can use the _____ command on the _____ menu to change paper orientation from portrait to landscape mode.

2. You must be in _____ view to use the Ruler to change margins.

3. You can use the _____ command on the _____ menu to add tabs and leaders.

4. You can use the _____ command on the _____ menu when you have accidentally typed text with (Caps Lock) turned on.

5. You can use the _____ command on the _____ menu to change the line spacing from single to double.

6. You can set a(n) _____ tab when you want to align columns at the decimal points.

7. You can use the _____ tool to align text at both the left and right margins.

8. You can insert a(n) _____ break when you want to change a page in your document to landscape mode.

9. You can use the _____ tool to center a paragraph.

10. You can use the Page Layout View button on the _____ to switch to page layout view.

review

Review Exercise 4-1

1. Open **Review 04-01 Printing Document**.

2. Print the document.

3. Open **Review 04-01 Formatting Document** and follow the formatting directions you find on the printed document.

4. Print, save, and close the document you formatted.

Review Exercise 4-2

1. Use online Help to find information about line numbers.

2. Read the information you find.

3. Print a copy of each of the Help screens.

On Your Own

1. Find the symbols for the mouse, disk, and computer in the Symbol dialog box. You will have to search through the different fonts to find the symbols.

2. Insert each of the symbols in a document. Press (Enter) a couple of times after each symbol you enter.

3. Select each of the symbols and change the font size to 72 points.

4. Print the document.

5. Save and close the file.

Enhancing Documents

❖ O B J E C T I V E S

When you complete this lesson, you will be able to:

1. Add bullets and numbering to lists.

2. Add borders and shading to paragraphs.

3. Use the AutoFormat feature.

4. Work with styles.

5. Use the Heading Numbering command.

6. Use the Drop Cap command.

7. Format text in newspaper columns.

Estimated Time: $1\frac{1}{2}$ hours

❖ I N T R O D U C T I O N

In this lesson you will learn to use features that can really enhance the look of your documents. You will work with bullets and numbering, add borders and shading, explore Word's AutoFormat and Style features, use heading numbering and drop caps, and format in newspaper columns.

❖ A D D I N G   B U L L E T S   A N D   N U M B E R I N G   T O   L I S T S

You can easily create bulleted or numbered lists with the Bullets and Numbering tools. You can use the Bullets and Numbering command on the Format menu to modify the bullets or the numbering, or to create a multilevel list.

When you use the numbering feature, Word automatically renumbers your list when you insert, move, copy, or delete items.

You can use the Bullets tool when you want to add bullets to your list. You can use the Numbering tool when you want to add numbers to your list.

✦ You can select an existing list and then click the Bullets or Numbering tool to add bullets or numbers.

or

✦ You can click the tools before you type a list to have Word add the bullets or numbers as you type. When you finish typing the list, press **Enter** and click the same tool again to turn it off.

You can use the Bullets and Numbering shortcut menu if you want Word to skip numbering. If you want blank lines between items in your bulleted or numbered list (see Figure 5-1), it is easier to enter the list first and then add the bullets or numbering. Word will not add bullets or numbers to the blank lines, and you will not have to stop to choose Skip Numbering each time you use a blank line.

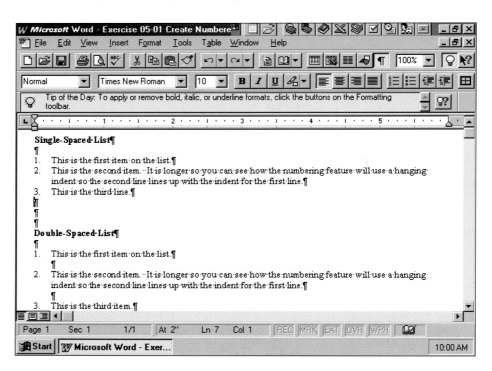

Figure 5-1
Numbers can easily be added to a list using the Numbering tool.

Exercise 5-1

1. To open a file for this exercise, click **Open** and double-click **Exercise 05-01 Create Numbered List.**

2. To add bullets to the first list, drag down the **selection bar** in the left margin to select the four lines, and click the **Bullets** tool.

3. To change the bullets to numbers, click the **Numbering** tool.

4. To remove the numbering, click the **Numbering** tool again.

5. To return to numbering, click the **Numbering** tool again.

6. To insert a numbered item before item 2 so you can see how Word renumbers when you edit, position the insertion point before the word *This* in item 2, type **This is an inserted item,** and press (**Enter**).

7. To delete the item you just entered so you can see how Word renumbers after a deletion, click in the **selection bar** at the left margin to select the item, and press (**Delete**).

8. To display nonprinting marks if they are not displayed, click the **Show/Hide** tool.

9. To add an item to the list, position the insertion point just before the Paragraph mark at the end of the third item, press (**Enter**), type **This is item 4,** and press (**Enter**).

10. To remove the extra number and turn off numbering, click the **Numbering** tool.

11. To number the second list, select the three items on the list and click the **Numbering** tool. Notice the blank lines do not have numbers.

12. To enter a list with numbering turned on before you begin, hold (**Ctrl**) and press (**End**) to move to the end of the document, and click the **Numbering** tool. Type the following items and let Word enter the numbers each time as you press (**Enter**).

    This is the first item for the list.

    This is the second item for the list, and it is longer. You will be able to see how Word uses a hanging indent to line up the second line with the first.

    This is the third item for the list.

13. To stop the numbering, press (**Enter**), notice the number *4,* click the **right mouse button** on the number **4** to display the shortcut menu, and then click **Stop Numbering.** Notice the number *4* is deleted.

14. To print the list, click the **Print** tool.

15. To save and close the document, click the **Save** tool and click the **Close** button at the right side of the menu bar.

USING THE BULLETS AND NUMBERING COMMAND

You can use the Bullets and Numbering command on the Format menu to modify the appearance of bulleted or numbered lists. You can change the bullet symbol or number format, the alignment of the bullets or the numbers, or the amount of space between a bullet or a number and an item in a list. You can see the formats available for bullets in Figure 5-2 and for numbered lists in Figure 5-3.

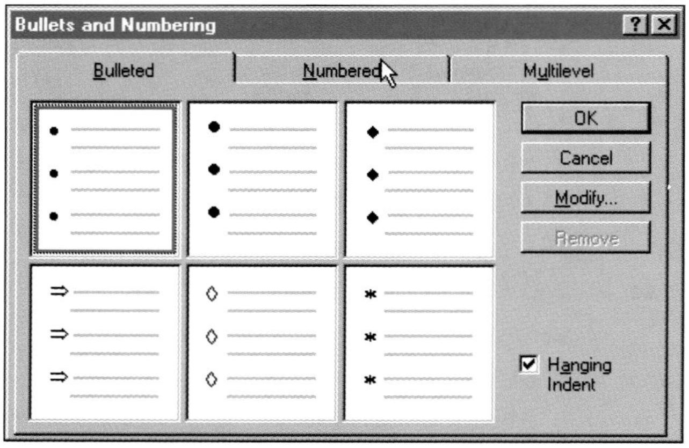

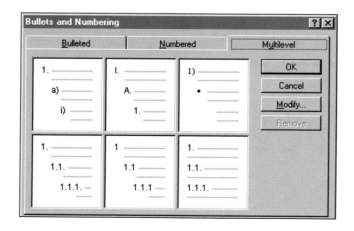

Figure 5-2
Available formats for creating bullets.

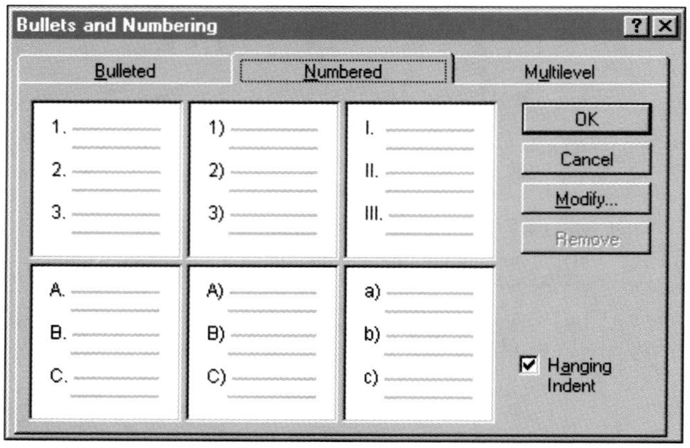

Figure 5-3
Available formats for creating numbered lists.

You can use the Modify button to create a number format that includes parentheses or a format that starts list items with a word or phrase such as *Action Required*.

You can also use the Bullets and Numbering command on the Format menu to create multilevel lists for outlines and legal and technical documents. You can have a list of up to nine levels in your document.

Word comes with six multilevel formats, as shown in Figure 5-4. You can define new formats by using the Modify button.

Figure 5-4
The Bullets and Numbering command can also be used to create multilevel lists.

You can use as many multilevel formats in a document as you want, as long as you separate the document into sections. Each section can have a different multilevel format.

 You can use the Increase Indent tool up to eight times to create up to nine levels in your list.

 You can use the Decrease Indent tool when you want to move back either to a previous indent position or to the left margin. To return to the left margin, click the Decrease Indent tool as often as you clicked the Increase Indent tool.

Exercise 5-2

1. To open a document, click the **Open** tool and double-click **Exercise 05-02 Multilevel List.**

2. To select the entire document, click the **Edit** menu and **Select All.**

3. To add numbering to the list, click the **Format** menu and then **Bullets and Numbering,** click the **Multilevel** tab, click the **middle** format on the **top** row, and click **OK.**

4. To deselect the list and move the insertion point to the last paragraph mark, press ⬇.

5. To return the insertion point to the left margin, click the **Decrease Indent** tool once.

6. To start a new Level 1 heading, press (**Enter**), click the **Numbering** tool, type **Starting a New Level,** and press (**Enter**).

7. To skip numbering on the blank line, click the **right** mouse button on the blank line, and click **Skip Numbering** with the **right** mouse button.

8. To move to the next line, press (**Enter**).

9. To move to a new level and begin numbering again, click **Decrease Indent** and the **Numbering** tool.

10. To enter an item at this level, type **This is an example of how to enter text when multilevel numbering is turned on.** Then press (**Enter**).

11. To turn the numbering off, click the **Numbering** tool.

12. To print the document, click the **Print** tool.

13. To save and close the document, click the **Save** tool and click the **Close** button at the right side of the menu bar.

❖ ADDING BORDERS TO PARAGRAPHS

You can add borders or lines to any side of a paragraph, and you can add background shading.

You can use the Borders tool to display or hide the Borders toolbar shown in Figure 5-5.

> **note**
>
> Your Borders toolbar may appear on one line instead of three somewhere else on your screen if a previous user has moved it.

You can also use the Toolbars command on the View menu to display or hide the Borders toolbar.

You can use the Borders and Shading command on the Format menu for even more choices of border styles, shading, and positioning (see Figure 5-6).

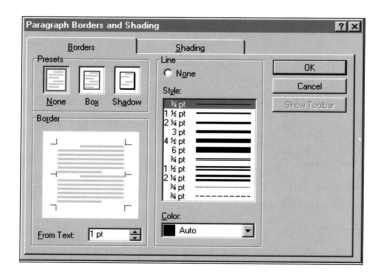

Figure 5-6
The Borders and
Shading command
gives you many
options for
creating borders.

Borders and shading extend from the left indent of the selected paragraph to the right indent of the paragraph. If you want to change the width of the bordered or shaded area in a short paragraph, you can adjust the indent markers shown in Figure 5-7.

Figure 5-7
Adjust the left
or right indent
markers to change
the width of
a bordered
or shaded area.

Left indent marker

Right indent marker

Exercise 5-3

1. To open a file, click the **Open** tool and double-click **Exercise 05-03 Creating a Border.**

2. To put a border and shading around the title, position your insertion point in the title paragraph. Click the **Borders** tool to display the Borders toolbar. Click the **Outside Border** button. Click the **drop-down Shading button** and click **25%.**

3. To increase the distance between the top and bottom of the text and the border, and increase the thickness of the line, click the **Format** menu, click the **Borders and Shading** command, increase the **From Text** measurement to **5 pt**, click **3 pt** in the Line Style box, and click **OK.**

4. To decrease the width of the border, drag the **right indent marker** to the **4.5**-inch mark and the **left indent marker** to the **1.5**-inch mark. Markers are shown in Figure 5-7.

5. Experiment with adding and removing borders and shading for a few minutes.

6. To hide the Borders toolbar, click the **Borders** tool on the Formatting toolbar.

7. To print the document, click the **Print** tool.

8. To save and close the document, click the **Save** tool and then click the **Close** button at the right side of the menu bar.

❖ USING THE AUTOFORMAT COMMAND

You can have Word automatically format text you have typed. To do so, you use the AutoFormat tool or the AutoFormat command on the Format menu. AutoFormat can quickly improve a document's appearance.

Word provides ready-to-use styles for all documents. The styles are for formatting common document elements such as headings, body text, bulleted lists, quotations, inside addresses, and so on.

If you use the AutoFormat tool, Word automatically formats either the selected area or the entire document if no area is selected.

If you use the AutoFormat *command* on the Format menu, the dialog box shown in Figure 5-8 appears. When you use the menu command, you can review, accept, or reject changes. You can click the Options button to see the AutoFormat options in effect (see Figure 5-9).

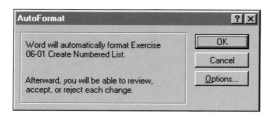

Figure 5-8
Use the AutoFormat
command to
format text you
have typed.

note

Use the Undo
command
immediately if
you do not like
the results of
the AutoFormat.

Figure 5-9
The Options
button displays
available
AutoFormat
options.

note

When you type
three or more
hyphens or
equal signs and
press **Enter**,
Word enters
either a single
or double-line
border.

When the Styles option under Preserve is turned on, styles you applied to text yourself are not changed. Word applies styles only to paragraphs formatted with the Normal or Body Text style.

When Headings is turned on, Word will apply heading styles for you.

When Lists is turned on, and you begin a list with the number 1, Word will insert a consecutive number each time you press **Enter**. When Automatic Bulleted Lists is turned on, you can type an asterisk at the beginning of the bulleted list and Word will enter a bullet each time you press **Enter**. When Other Paragraphs is turned on, Word applies paragraph styles to paragraphs that are not headings or lists.

AutoFormat will replace straight quotes with smart quotes (curly ones) and symbol characters such as (C), (R), and (TM) with the symbols ©, ®, and ™.

After the AutoFormat command has formatted your document, you see the dialog box shown in Figure 5-10.

Figure 5-10
When the
AutoFormat
command has
finished formatting
your document, this
dialog box appears.

This dialog box lets you access the Style Gallery (see Figure 5-11), which lets you use any of Word's templates for the document. You can also use the Style Gallery command on the Format menu to display the Style Gallery and format from it.

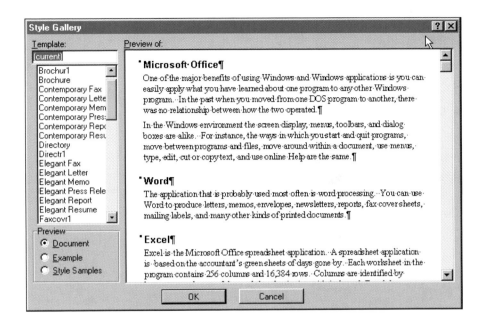

Figure 5-11
Style Gallery lets you apply templates to your document.

Exercise 5-4

1. To open a document, click the **Open** tool and double-click **Exercise 05-04 Using AutoFormat.**

2. To print the document, click the **Print** tool.

3. To format the document automatically, click the **AutoFormat** tool.

4. To print the document with the new formatting, click the **Print** tool.

5. To return to the original document, click the drop-down button on the **Undo** tool and click **AutoFormat.**

6. To use the AutoFormat menu command, click the **Format** menu and click **AutoFormat.**

7. To see the options in effect for AutoFormat, click **Options.**

8. To return to the AutoFormat dialog box, click **Cancel.**

9. To start the AutoFormat, click **OK.** The AutoFormat dialog box displayed in Figure 5-10 gives you the option to accept all formatting, reject all formatting, review and reject individual changes, or choose a custom look with Style Gallery.

10. To look at the other styles available, click **Style Gallery.**

11. To preview how your document looks with various templates, click on the various templates in the list of templates.

12. To choose the Contemporary template, click **Contemporary Report,** click **OK,** and click **Accept.**

13. To print the document again, click the **Print** tool.

14. To save and close the document, click the **Save** tool and then click the **Close** button at the right side of the menu bar.

❖ USING STYLES

You can use the Styles feature to record paragraph and character formats and to easily apply that same formatting to paragraphs. You can also easily edit a style to change all paragraphs throughout the document with the same style name.

All Word documents contain built-in styles. You use paragraph styles to format whole paragraphs; you use character styles to format such items as page numbers or text you want to emphasize. You can easily distinguish between paragraph and character styles in the Style drop-down box because paragraph styles have a paragraph icon before the name, and character styles have an underscored, lowercase *a* before the name.

The Style box displays the name of the style in effect at the insertion point. When you want to format headings or other common items, apply a style from the Style drop-down box on the Formatting toolbar displayed in Figure 5-12.

When you begin working with Word, not all of the built-in styles are displayed in the Style box. You can hold (Shift) while you click the drop-down button to display the entire list of built-in styles.

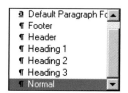

You can display the style names applied to text (see Figure 5-13) by using the Options command on the Tools menu.

In the AutoFormat exercise, you used Style Gallery to format your document with the Contemporary Report template, as displayed in Figure 5-13.

There are some general guidelines you can follow to make it easier to maintain consistent formatting for your documents. You should base new documents on a template, format all text with a style, and change formatting when necessary by updating styles.

note

When you begin typing a document, Word automatically applies the Normal style. Normal style when you install Word is 10-point Times New Roman font, single line spacing, and left paragraph alignment.

Figure 5-12
Choose a style from the Style drop-down box.

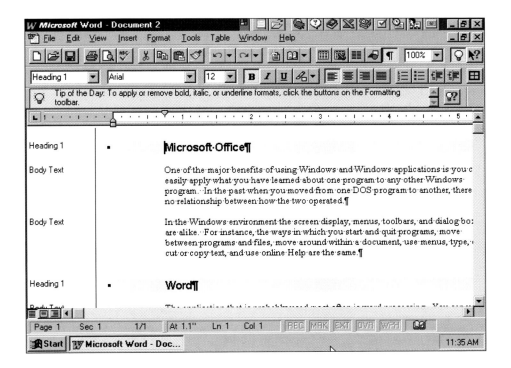

Figure 5-13
Style names can be displayed in the margin when you choose the Options command.

It is particularly important that you use the Heading 1 through Heading 9 styles in documents where you want to be able to use a Master Document, Heading Numbering, or the Table of Contents feature. You will learn about those features later.

APPLYING STYLES TO TEXT

You can use the Style box on the Formatting toolbar to apply styles to existing text. When you apply a paragraph style, Word applies all the formats defined for the style to all text in the selected paragraphs.

To apply a *paragraph* style to a paragraph, you do not have to select the entire paragraph; just position the insertion point anywhere in the paragraph.

To apply a *character* style, you must select all the text you want to format. You can also apply a character style for text you will enter. Choose the style you want to use for text you will enter at the insertion point, and then type the text.

REMOVING CHARACTER STYLES

You can remove a character style by selecting the text formatted with the character style and holding **Ctrl** and pressing **SpaceBar**.

DETERMINING HOW FORMATTING WAS APPLIED

You can click the Help tool on the Standard toolbar and then click on text to find out whether formats are from a style or direct formatting. You can see an example in Figure 5-14.

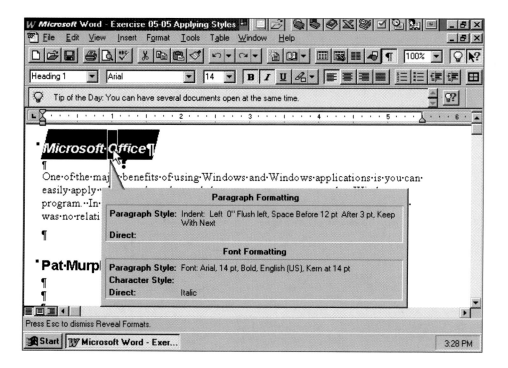

Figure 5-14
Help dialog box
showing the style
used in this
document.

Exercise 5-5

1. To open a file, click the **Open** tool and double-click **Exercise 05-05 Applying Styles.**

2. To change the paragraph beginning *One of the major benefits* to Body Text style, click anywhere in the paragraph, click the **Style** box drop-down button, and click the **Body Text** style.

3. To move to the end of the document, hold (**Ctrl**) and press (**End**).

4. To start a new paragraph, press (**Enter**) twice.

5. To change the style before you begin to type, click the **Style** box drop-down button, and click **Heading 1.**

6. To see the style, type ***your name*** and press (**Enter**) twice. Notice the style has returned to Normal because the Heading 1 style is set to return to Normal for the next paragraph. Notice also if nonprinting marks are displayed; a black mark appears before any paragraph with a heading style.

7. To return to the beginning of the document, hold (**Ctrl**) and press (**Home**).

8. To apply Heading 1 style to *Microsoft Office,* click the **Style** box drop-down button, and click **Heading 1**.

9. To change the heading to italic using direct formatting, select ***the heading*** and click the **Italic** tool.

10. To see what formatting is applied to the heading (see Figure 5-14), click the **Help** tool on the Standard toolbar and click *the heading*.

11. To turn off the Help tool, click the **Help** tool again.

12. To remove the character formatting, be sure the heading is still selected and hold ⟨Ctrl⟩ and press ⟨SpaceBar⟩. Notice the character formatting applied with the Italic tool is removed and the paragraph formatting remains in effect.

13. Experiment for a few minutes applying various styles to the heading and body text paragraphs in the document.

14. To print the document, click the **Print** tool.

15. To save and close the document, click the **Save** tool and then click the **Close** button at the right side of the menu bar.

MODIFYING AN EXISTING STYLE

The easiest way to change the appearance of text is to modify its style. When you modify a style, all text formatted with the style is automatically formatted with the modified style. If you change the font and font size for a built-in style, Word will update all text in the active document formatted with that style.

You can use the toolbar to modify a style. You can see in this exercise how easy it is to change the format of all text in a document that is formatted with the same style.

Exercise 5-6

1. To open a document, click the **Open** tool and double-click **Exercise 05-06 Modifying a Style.**

2. To display the style names to the left of the text in your document, click the **Tools** menu, click **Options,** click the **View** tab if it is not on top, increase the number in the Style Area Width box to **1"** (not 0.1"), and click **OK.**

3. To see that *Heading 1* and *Body Text* are the two styles used in the document, scroll down through the document.

4. To return to the beginning of the document, hold ⟨Ctrl⟩ and press ⟨Home⟩.

5. To see how easily you can change the Body Text style from Arial font to Times New Roman, select the first paragraph of Body Text, click the **Font** drop-down button, click **Times New Roman**, click the insertion point in the **Style** box, press ⟨Enter⟩, and respond **OK** when asked if you want to redefine the style using the selection as an example (see Figure 5-15). Notice all the paragraphs formatted with Body Text style are reformatted.

Figure 5-15
A style can be
changed using the
Reapply Style
dialog box.

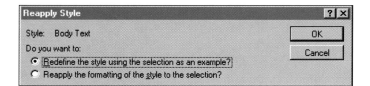

6. To return to the original style format, click the **Undo** tool twice.

You can also use the Style command on the Format menu (see Figure 5-16) to modify a style (see Figure 5-17). You will see in this exercise how one style is often based on another and the many changes you can make.

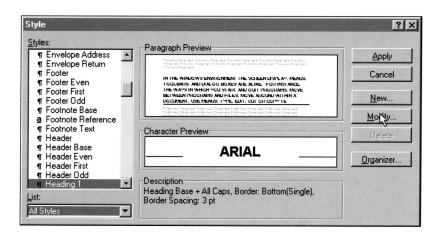

Figure 5-16
The Style command
on the Format
menu also lets you
change a style.

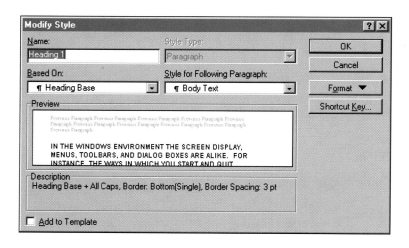

Figure 5-17
The Modify Style
dialog box.

Exercise 5-7

1. To move the insertion point to the beginning of the document, in the paragraph with the Heading 1 style, hold **Ctrl** and press **Home**.

2. To see the Style dialog box, click the **Format** menu and click **Style.** Notice the Heading 1 style is selected. Notice the paragraph and character previews. Notice also the description of all the settings in the style.

3. To move to the Normal style, scroll down the list until you see **Normal** and click it. Once again, notice the character and paragraph previews and the description of the style.

4. To see the description of the Normal Indent style, click it. Notice in the description that it is the Normal style plus a left indent.

5. To select Heading 1 again, scroll up until you see it and click it.

6. To see the Modify dialog box shown in Figure 5-17, click the **Modify** button. Notice the name of the style, the style type, the style it is based on, the style for the following paragraph, the preview, and the description. Notice you can assign a shortcut key and access all of the paragraph and character formats. Notice also the Add to Template option that you can turn on to use the updated style in new documents using the current template.

7. To change the font size of the Heading 1 style, click the **Format** command button, click **Font,** click **16,** click **OK** to return to the Modify Style dialog box, click **OK** again to return to the Style dialog box, and click **Close.** Notice the heading format changed.

8. To undo the style modification, click **Undo.**

9. To remove the style names from the document, click the **Tools** menu, click **Options,** return the Style Area Width to **0",** and click **OK.**

10. Close the file without saving it.

CREATING A NEW PARAGRAPH STYLE BY EXAMPLE

You can format a paragraph with the font, font size, alignment, and other formats you want, and then create a new style using that paragraph as an example. To create a paragraph style, you must use the Style command on the Format menu.

Exercise 5-8

1. To open a document, click the **Open** tool and double-click **Exercise 05-08 Creating Style By Example.**

2. To format a paragraph for use as an example for a new style, select the **first paragraph** beginning *One of the major benefits*, click the **Font Size** drop-down button, click **12**, and click the **Bold** tool.

3. To create a new style by example, click the insertion point in the **Style** box, type the name **Bold,** and press (**Enter**).

4. To apply the new style to the next paragraph, click anywhere in the paragraph, click the Style drop-down button, and click the **Bold** style.

5. To undo the changes, click the **Undo** tool four times.

6. To save and close the document, click the **Save** tool and then click the **Close** button at the right side of the menu bar.

❖ NUMBERING HEADINGS

You can use the Heading Numbering command on the Format menu to have Word number headings that are formatted with built-in heading styles (see Figure 5-18). Word will number only those paragraphs where you have used a heading style. Word starts the numbering at the beginning of the document. You must create a new section if you want to restart numbering within the document.

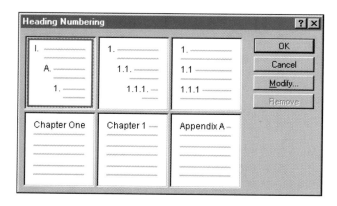

Figure 5-18
The Heading Numbering command lets you number headings in selected styles.

Exercise 5-9

1. To open a file, click the **Open** tool and double-click **Exercise 05-09 Numbering Headings.**

2. To see the Heading 1, Heading 2, and Heading 3 formatting, use ⊕ to move through the document. Notice the changes in the Style list box as you scroll.

3. To number the headings with the default format, click the **Format** menu, click **Heading Numbering,** and click **OK.**

4. To see that Word has numbered the headings, scroll through the document.

5. To save and close the document, click the **Save** tool and then click the **Close** button at the right side of the menu bar.

❖ USING DROP CAPS

You can use the Drop Cap command on the Format menu to have a large or dropped initial capital letter (see Figure 5-19) or a large first word.

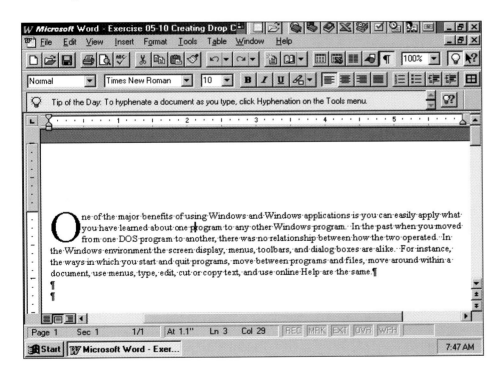

Figure 5-19
You can create a dramatic-looking initial capital letter using the Drop Cap command.

When you want to drop the first letter of the paragraph, you simply put the insertion point anywhere in the paragraph and choose the Drop Cap command to access the Drop Cap dialog box shown in Figure 5-20. When you want to drop the first word, select the entire word before you choose the Drop Cap command.

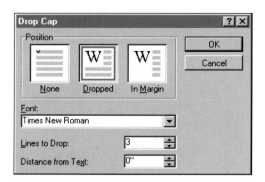

Figure 5-20
The Drop Cap
dialog box offers
several options.

note

You must be in
page layout
view or Print
Preview to see
the dropped
cap.

Word places the first letter of the paragraph or the selected word in a frame (see Lesson 9 for more about frames). The text can wrap around the frame, or you can position the dropped text in the margin.

You can remove a dropped cap from a paragraph by placing the insertion point in the paragraph, choosing Drop Cap from the Format menu, selecting None in the Drop Cap dialog box, and clicking OK.

Exercise 5-10

1. To open a document, click the **Open** tool and double-click **Exercise 05-10 Creating Drop Caps.**

2. To drop the first character in the paragraph, *be sure the insertion point is in the paragraph,* click the **Format** menu, click the **Drop Cap** command, click the **Dropped** box, and click **OK.** Click **Yes** to switch to page layout view.

3. To remove the dropped cap, *be sure the insertion point is in the paragraph,* click the **Format** menu, click the **Drop Cap** command, click the **None** box, and click **OK.**

4. To save and close the document, click the **Save** tool and then click the **Close** button at the right side of the menu bar.

❖ WORKING WITH NEWSPAPER-STYLE COLUMNS

You can use the Columns command on the Format menu to format all or part of your document with newspaper-style columns. The Columns command also lets you create columns of unequal width.

note

You must be in
page layout
view or Print
Preview to see
multiple columns
on your screen.

You can also use the Columns tool on the Standard toolbar to create multiple columns of equal width.

Text flows from the bottom of one column to the top of the next (see Figure 5-21) when you use the column format. You can vary the number of columns and the width of individual columns.

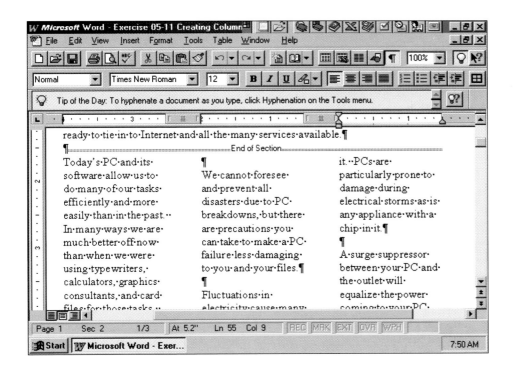

Figure 5-21
Newspaper-style columns can be created with the Columns command or the Columns tool.

Do not use the column format when you want to display text in side-by-side paragraphs such as you would see in a resume. Use the Tables feature (Lesson 7) for side-by-side paragraphs.

In the Columns dialog box displayed in Figure 5-22, you can see the various selections available for formatting columns.

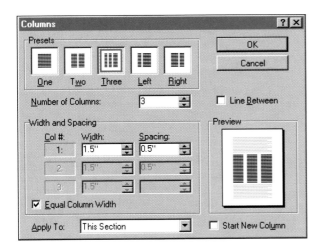

Figure 5-22
The Columns dialog box shows options for formatting columns.

Word will automatically add section breaks at the beginning and at the end of the text formatted for newspaper columns.

Exercise 5-11

1. To open a document, click the **Open** tool and double-click **Exercise 05-11 Creating Columns.**

2. To switch to page layout view, click the **Page Layout** button on the horizontal scroll bar.

3. To put the four paragraphs beginning with *Today's PC* in three-column format, select the four paragraphs, click the **Columns** tool, drag across **three columns,** and release.

4. To see the section breaks and the three-column layout, scroll up through the document.

5. To undo the column layout, be sure everything in the column section is selected, click the **Format** menu, click **Columns,** click **One,** and click **OK.**

6. To delete the section breaks, click the insertion point on each of them and press (Delete).

7. Experiment with the Columns command and tool for a few minutes.

8. To save and close the document, click the **Save** tool and then click the **Close** button at the right side of the menu bar.

❖ SUMMARY

You have now learned how to use the bullets and numbering features, add borders and shading to paragraphs, use the AutoFormat feature, work with styles, use the Heading Numbering and Drop Cap commands, and create newspaper-style columns.

Try the exercises on the following pages to test how well you remember what you learned. Don't be afraid to go back and look up the answers, because that will help to reinforce what you learned.

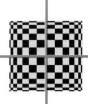

activities

*On the blank line before each sentence, place a **T** if the statement is true or an **F** if it is false.*

_____ 1. You cannot leave a blank line between items in a numbered list.

_____ 2. You can use the Increase Indent and Decrease Indent tools to set up a multilevel list.

_____ 3. You can select an existing list and use the Bullets tool to add bullets to the list.

_____ 4. You can have only one multilevel list in a document.

_____ 5. You can use the Borders tool to hide the Borders toolbar.

_____ 6. The AutoFormat tool formats the document and lets you reject individual changes.

_____ 7. You can display the style names used in your document in the left margin.

_____ 8. You should use the columns feature for a resume with side-by-side paragraphs.

_____ 9. You can hold (Ctrl) and press (Enter) to remove character styles from a selection.

_____ 10. The Style box displays the style in effect at the insertion point.

❖ COMPLETION

Fill in the blanks in the following statements.

1. You can use the _____ command to create a multilevel list.

2. You can use the _____ command to number headings.

3. A(n) _____ is a group of formats identified by a name.

4. You can create heading numbers if you use the _____ styles in your document.

5. Word _____ your list as needed when you delete a numbered item from the list.

6. The _____ displays the name of the style in effect at the insertion point.

7. Word automatically applies the _____ style when you start entering text in a document.

8. You can use the _____ command or tool to create newspaper-style columns in which text flows from the bottom of one column to the top of the next.

9. You can assign _____ keys to a style.

10. You can use the _____ menu when you want Word to skip numbering a line.

review

Review Exercise 5-1

1. Open the **Review 05-01 Create List** file.
2. Add bullets shaped like diamonds to the first list.
3. Use the Numbering tool to add numbers to the second list.
4. Use the Print tool to print your finished document.
5. Save and close the document.

Review Exercise 5-2

1. Open the **Review 05-02 AutoFormat** file.
2. Use the AutoFormat command to enhance its appearance.
3. After the initial AutoFormat, use the Style Gallery to preview how various Word templates will affect the document.
4. Print the finished document using the Print command on the File menu.
5. Save and close the document.

Review Exercise 5-3

1. Use online Help to find out how to use shortcut keys with styles.
2. Read and print the information you find.

On Your Own

1. Use the Fax Wizard to create a template for a fax cover sheet.
2. Print a copy of the fax cover sheet.
3. Save and close the document.

lesson 6

Using Timesaving Features

❖ OBJECTIVES

When you complete this lesson, you will be able to:

1. Use the Replace command.

2. Record and run a macro.

3. Enter page, section, and column breaks.

4. Use the Annotation feature.

5. Work with fields.

6. Use the Headers and Footers and Page Numbers commands.

Estimated Time: $1\frac{1}{2}$ hours

❖ INTRODUCTION

In this lesson you will use many of Word's timesaving features. You will use the Replace command to quickly replace text or formatting throughout a document. You will record a series of actions and then run the macro to repeat the actions. You will also learn to enter page, section, and column breaks.

You will use the Annotation feature, which allows others to comment on your document without altering it. You will use Revision Marking, which can also be used when you route documents to others. You will use *fields* to enter information contained in the system (dates, file names, and so on) in your documents. You will also use the Headers and Footers and Page Numbers commands to enter information that will repeat on each page.

❖ USING THE REPLACE COMMAND

Use the Replace command on the Edit menu to find and replace text, formats, and styles. This is a very useful feature if you have documents in which you must change names or other often used text or formatting.

You can also use the Special button in the Replace dialog box shown in Figure 6-1 to find and replace special characters, such as paragraph marks, tab characters, and manual page breaks.

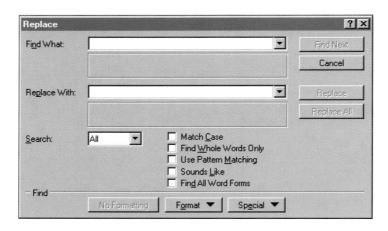

Word searches the entire document, including headers, footers, footnotes, endnotes, and annotations. You can limit the search by selecting part of a document or by selecting Up or Down in the Search list box. If you use the Up or Down options for the search, you limit the search to the main document and exclude headers and footers, footnotes, and so on.

You specify text and formatting in the Replace dialog box the same way you did in the Find dialog box. In addition to replacing text or formatting with the contents of the Replace With box, you can make changes directly in the document without closing the dialog box. You click the document to make it active, make your changes, and then click the dialog box to reactivate it.

You can turn on the Match Case option to find text with the same capitalization as the text in the Find What box. You can turn on Find Whole Words Only so Word will not find words like *his* in *history*. You can turn on Sounds Like when you want to find words that sound the same but are spelled differently, such as *there* and *their*.

You can turn on Use Pattern Matching to find text using multiple search criteria. For instance, if you search for *t?e*, Word will find all words containing a character string beginning with *t*, having any character in the second position, and ending with *e*.

Word can even find and replace inflected forms of a word. For example, you could use the Find All Word Forms option and instruct Word to replace all occurrences of *tell* and *telling* with *narrate* and *narrating*.

You can also refine searches using operators and expressions. An *operator* is a symbol that controls the search. An *expression* is any combination of characters and operators that specifies a pattern. A simple expression is *t?e*.

To specify formats, you can use formatting dialog boxes, tools on the toolbar, or key combinations.

Both the Find and Replace boxes limit the number of characters you can enter. If you want to replace an item with a large block of text or graphics, copy the text or graphics to the Clipboard. Then use the Special button and select Clipboard Contents from the list.

note

If you need more information about using operators or expressions, you can use online Help for advanced search criteria.

You can use the Replace All command button to replace all occurrences at once without confirming each. Be very sure when you use Replace All that you really want to replace all occurrences. For instance, you can run into trouble using Replace All when changing a person's name, such as Jackson to Johnson. If a company name or city name in the document contains the name Jackson, Replace All changes it to Johnson also.

You can use the Replace button to replace the text or formatting of the selected text and find the next occurrence. The Find Next button leaves the text or formatting unchanged and searches for the next occurrence.

In the document shown in Figure 6-2, you will search for and replace occurrences of the company name, which has changed. You will search for and replace the addressee's last name. You will also search for and replace formatted text.

note

You can use the Undo tool if you are not happy with the results of a find-and-replace operation.

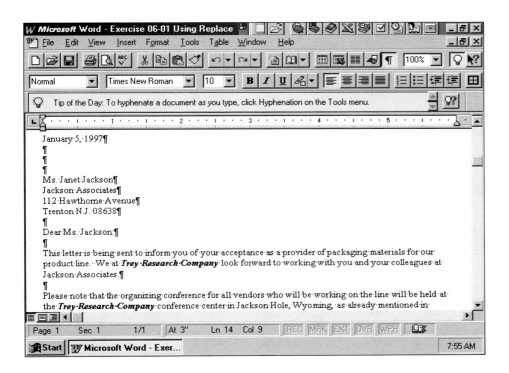

Figure 6-2
The document you will use in the find-and-replace exercise.

Exercise 6-1

1. To open the document, click the **Open** tool and double-click **Exercise 06-01 Using Replace.**

2. To open the Replace dialog box, click the **Edit** menu and then **Replace.**

3. To enter the Find What text, type **Trey Research Company.**

4. To enter the Replace With text, press ⌧Tab and type **Trey-Davis Research Corporation.**

5. To replace the several words where an unexpected result is not likely all at once, click the **Replace All** button.

6. To close the dialog box shown in Figure 6-3 telling you three replacements were made, click **OK.**

Figure 6-3
Word reports
the number of
replacements
made.

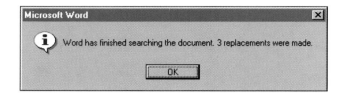

Microsoft Word

ⓘ Word has finished searching the document. 3 replacements were made.

OK

7. To close the Replace dialog box, click the **Close** button.

Because you did not specify formatting in the dialog box, the formatting in place for each of the original instances of *Trey Research Company* remained as it was.

If your replace operation did not produce the expected results,

❖ Be sure you entered the text in the Find What box exactly as specified. Otherwise, Word may search for something that is not in the document.

❖ Be sure there are no extra spaces in the text. Otherwise, Word will be searching for two spaces instead of a space and a character.

If the insertion point is not at the beginning of your document when you begin a find and replace, Word will prompt that it has reached the end of the document and ask if you want to continue searching at the beginning of the document.

If you have text selected when you begin a find and replace, Word will search through the selection, report that it has searched the selection, and ask if you would like to search the rest of the document.

note

If you cannot
see the selected
items during a
find-and-replace
operation be-
cause the dialog
box covers
them, you can
move the dialog
box by dragging
its title bar. Try
positioning it
at the bottom
center of your
screen.

Exercise 6-2

1. To begin another replace, be sure nothing is selected in your document, click the **Edit** menu, and click **Replace.** Type **Jackson** in the Find What box, press Ⓣⓐⓑ to move to the Replace With box, type **Johnson,** and click the **Find Next** button.

2. To replace the first occurrence of Janet Jackson's last name, which is selected, with *Johnson*, click the **Replace** button.

3. To leave the selected name of Janet Jackson's company unchanged, click the **Find Next** button.

4. To replace Janet Jackson's last name, which is selected, click the **Replace** button.

5. To skip the company name again, click **Find Next.**

6. To leave *Jackson Hole* unchanged, click **Find Next.**

7. To leave the letter writer's name unchanged, click **Find Next.**

8. To remove the dialog box telling you the search is finished (shown in Figure 6-4), click **OK.**

Figure 6-4
When Word reports that the search is finished, you click OK.

9. To close the Replace dialog box, click the **Close** button.

You know from the first replace exercise that there are three instances of *Trey-Davis Research Corporation*. Scroll through the document to find them. The first one is at the top of the page, and the other two are in the body of the letter. The two in the body of the letter have additional formatting. You will now search for *Trey-Davis Research Corporation* with bold and italic formatting and replace it with italic formatting only.

Exercise 6-3

1. To see the formatting applied to *Trey-Davis Research Corporation*, click the **Help** tool on the Standard toolbar and click on **Trey-Davis Research Corporation** in the body of the letter. Notice Bold and Italic formatting were applied directly.

2. To remove the Help screen and the Help pointer, click the **Help** tool again.

3. To begin the replace operation, be sure nothing is selected, click the **Edit** menu, click **Replace**, and type **Trey-Davis Research Corporation** in the **Find What** box.

4. To add bold and italic to the search criteria, click the **Bold** and the **Italic** tools on the Formatting toolbar. Notice the format is entered directly under the Find What box.

5. To move to the Replace With box, press ⟨Tab⟩.

6. To enter the replacement text, type **Trey-Davis Research Corporation.**

7. To format the replacement text with italic but not bold, click the **Format** command button in the dialog box, click **Font,** in the Style box click **Not Bold,** and click **OK.**

8. To replace the text with the differently formatted text, click **Replace All.**

9. To close the dialog box telling you Word replaced two selections, click **OK.**

10. To remove the Format criteria from the **Find What** box, click the Find What box and click the **No Formatting** command button. Word would now search for all occurrences of the text.

11. To close the Replace dialog box, click **Close.**

12. To print the document, click the **Print** tool.

13. To save and close the document, click the **Save** tool and then click the **Close** button at the right side of the menu bar.

❖ RECORDING AND RUNNING A MACRO

A *macro* is a recording of a series of Word commands. Macros can simplify repetitive tasks. You can make a macro as easy to use as any Word command by assigning it to a menu, a toolbar, or shortcut keys.

If you owned or worked for Trey Research Company when its name changed to Trey-Davis Research Corporation, you might have to use the Replace command on hundreds or even thousands of documents. A macro would certainly speed your task. You would need only to click a menu command or tool or type a few keystrokes to run the macro for each document.

To create a macro,

❖ Use the Macro command on the Tools menu and click the Record button.

or

❖ Double-click REC on the status bar to display the Record Macro dialog box (see Figure 6-5).

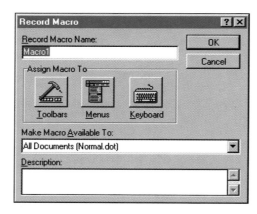

Figure 6-5
Use the Record Macro dialog box to create a macro.

You then enter a name for your macro and assign the macro to a toolbar, menu, or shortcut keys. When you click OK, the recording begins and Word displays the Macro Record toolbar shown in Figure 6-6.

 You can use the Pause tool to turn the recorder off when you don't want to record certain actions. Clicking the Pause tool again returns you to recording mode.

 You can use the Stop tool to signal you are finished recording.

To remind you that the recorder is on, Word attaches a re-corder graphic to your mouse pointer.

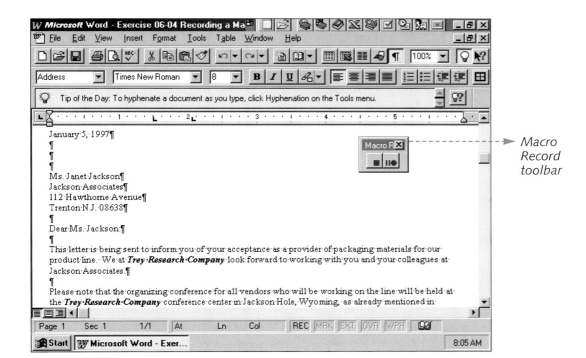

Figure 6-6
The Macro Record
toolbar appears
after the recording
of a new macro
begins.

When recording a macro, try to think of any prompts or dialog boxes that might interfere with your macro. For example, if your macro will use the Replace command, you must type the correct text in the Find What and Replace With boxes while you are recording the macro.

It doesn't matter whether the correct text is already in the Find What and Replace With boxes when you display them. The boxes are empty when you turn on your computer each day, so you must retype the text to be sure entering it becomes part of the macro.

By default a macro you create is available in all your documents. If a template is attached to your document, you can store the macro in the attached template so that it is available only to documents that are based on that template.

The macro is not saved until you save the template in which it is stored. You can save the template by choosing the Save All command on the File menu or by responding *yes* when asked whether you want to save changes to the template.

You can use the Macro command on the Tools menu to run a macro, or you can run the macro by using the menu command, toolbar button, or shortcut keys you assign to the macro.

In the following exercise you will create a macro for the find-and-replace operation you just completed so you can run it for each document that needs the company name changed.

Exercise 6-4

1. To open a document, click the **Open** tool and double-click **Exercise 06-04 Recording a Macro.**

2. To start the macro process, double-click **REC** on the status bar.

3. To name your macro, type *your initials.*

4. To assign shortcut keys to the macro, click the **Keyboard** button and hold (Alt) and press (R).

5. To assign the keys, click the **Assign** button and click the **Close** button. Notice the Macro Record toolbar and the recorder attached to your mouse pointer. The recorder is now on.

6. To be sure the insertion point is always at the beginning of the document and nothing is currently selected, hold (Ctrl) and press (Home).

7. To begin recording the find-and-replace operations, click the **Edit** menu, click **Replace,** type **Trey Research Company,** and click the **No Formatting** button if there are formats displayed under the Find What box.

8. To finish recording the find-and-replace operations, press (Tab), type **Trey-Davis Research Corporation,** click the **No Formatting** command button if there are formats displayed under the Replace With box, click **Replace All,** click **OK** to respond to the number of replacements, and click **Close.**

9. To stop recording, click the **Stop** button on the Macro Record toolbar.

10. To test the macro on another document, click the **Open** tool, double-click **Exercise 06-04 Test Macro,** and hold (Alt) and press (R). Notice how quickly Word replaced the original text.

11. To close both documents without saving the documents or the macro, hold (Shift) while you click the **File** menu and click **Close All.** Respond **No** when asked whether to save the documents.

❖ ENTERING PAGE, SECTION, AND COLUMN BREAKS

You can use the Break command on the Insert menu to insert hard page breaks and to insert section and column breaks (see Figure 6-7).

Figure 6-7
The Break command lets you insert hard page breaks and section and column breaks.

You have already learned that Word adjusts pagination and how to insert a hard page break with **Ctrl**+**Enter**. The end of a chapter is an example of a place where you will always want the page to break.

You have already learned that section breaks are required when you want to change the size or orientation of the page, the margins, or the vertical alignment of text on a page. You have also seen that Word will sometimes enter the required section breaks for you (for example, when you use the column feature for a selection within a document). You might also want to insert a section break to change the contents and position of headers and footers for just a portion of your document.

As you can see in the Break dialog box in Figure 6-7, you can control whether section breaks you insert start on the next page, an even page, or an odd page, or are continuous.

In this exercise you will work with the different options available for section breaks.

Exercise 6-5

1. To open a document, click the **Open** tool and double-click **Exercise 06-05 Section Breaks.**

2. To make a separate section of the title, position the insertion point just before the heading below it, *Windows*. Click the **Insert** menu and then click **Break.** Click **Next Page** to leave the title on a page by itself and click **OK.**

3. To see what the document looks like, click the **Print Preview** tool, click the **Multiple Pages** tool, drag over **three pages** on the top line, and release. Notice the title is positioned at the top of the page. Click **Close.**

4. To use the Page Setup command to center the title vertically on the page, move the insertion point onto the title, click the **File** menu, click **Page Setup,** click the **Layout** tab, click the **Vertical Alignment** drop-down button, click **Center,** and click **OK.**

5. To see how the title section looks now, click the **Print Preview** tool. Notice the title is centered vertically on the page.

6. To print the document, click the **Print** tool.

7. To close Print Preview, click the **Close** button on the toolbar.

8. To save and close the document, click the **Save** tool and then click the **Close** button at the right side of the menu bar.

❖ USING THE ANNOTATION FEATURE

You can use annotations when you want reviewers to comment on your document rather than make changes to it. *Annotations* are numbered comments in a special separate pane (see Figure 6-8). If you have the necessary hardware, you can include voice and pen annotations.

When several reviewers comment on a document, Word enters each reviewer's initials so you can easily tell who made a comment.

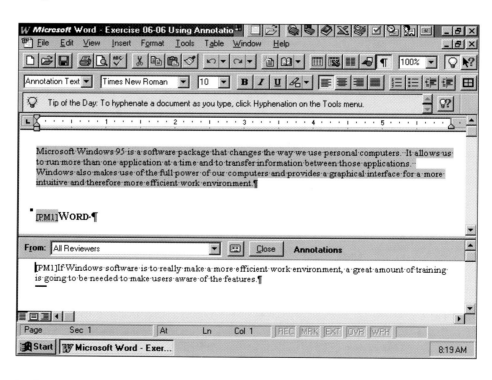

Figure 6-8
Annotations
(comments) can be
added to your
document.

Before you insert an annotation, you should select the text about which you will comment. When you choose the Annotations command from the Insert menu, Word opens the annotation pane where you type your comments. Word takes the user's initials from the User Info tab in the Options dialog box and adds them with the number of the annotation as hidden text in the document. You can move from pane to pane by clicking in the pane in which you want to work to make it active.

Each annotation has an annotation mark in the document, which you can see when you use the Show/Hide tool to display nonprinting marks. You can use the Annotations command on the View menu to view the annotation pane in a document. When the annotation pane is open, it displays the annotations corresponding to the part of the document displayed. Word will highlight the text to which the annotation refers. If nonprinting marks are displayed, you can also double-click an annotation mark to view the annotation.

To put a copy of an annotation into your document:

❖ Select the annotation.

❖ Choose Copy from the Edit menu.

❖ Position the insertion point where you want the annotation.

❖ Choose Paste from the Edit menu.

To delete an annotation:

❖ Select the annotation mark in the document window.

❖ Press (**Backspace**) or (**Delete**).

You can use the Print command to print annotations only or a combination of the document and the annotations. Word prints the annotation number and the text if you print only annotations. If you print the document and the annotations, Word prints the annotation number and the text at the end of the document.

note

When you copy, move, or delete an annotation, Word automatically renumbers the annotations.

❖ USING REVISION MARKS

Annotations are comments that do not make changes in the document. Revision marks show changes, such as insertions and deletions, that have been made in the document.

Use the Revisions command on the Tools menu to turn on revision marks. The Revisions dialog box shown in Figure 6-9 appears.

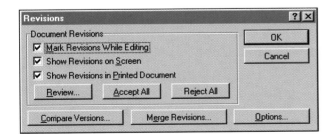

**Figure 6-9
The Revisions
Dialog Box.**

The following options are available in the Revisions dialog box:

❖ Mark Revisions While Editing

❖ Show Revisions on Screen

❖ Show Revisions in Printed Document

You can also choose:

❖ Compare Versions to compare the current document with another document.

❖ Merge Revisions to make the changes marked in the revised document in the original document.

❖ Options for color and style of inserted text; eight reviewers can revise a document before colors repeat, so you can easily route documents electronically for revisions.

Exercise 6-6

1. To open a document that contains an annotation, click the **Open** tool and double-click **Exercise 06-06 Using Annotations.**

2. To display nonprinting marks if they are not already displayed, click the **Show/Hide** tool. Notice the annotation mark just before the *Word* heading.

3. To view the annotation pane, click the **View** menu and click **Annotations.**

4. To save and close the document, click the **Save** tool and then click the **Close** button at the right side of the menu bar.

5. To open another document, click the **Open** tool and double-click **Exercise 06-06 Adding an Annotation.**

6. To select text you will comment on, drag down the **selection bar** in the left margin until the whole paragraph beginning *Microsoft Windows 95* is selected.

7. To insert an annotation, click the **Insert** menu, click **Annotation,** and notice the Reviewer's initials taken from the User Info tab. Type **Annotations are a really great way of getting students working on a project or employees in workgroups to comment on a document.**

8. To close the annotations pane, click **Close** on the Annotations toolbar.

9. If nonprinting marks are not displayed, click the **Show/Hide** tool. Notice the annotation mark is inserted at the end of your selection.

10. To print the document and the annotations, click the **File** menu and click **Print.** Then click **Options,** click **Annotations** in the Include with Document list, and click **OK** twice.

11. Experiment with annotations on your own for a few minutes.

12. To save and close the document, click the **Save** tool and then click the **Close** button at the right side of the menu bar.

13. To open a document with revision marking, click the **Open** tool and double-click **Exercise 06-06 Revision Marks.**

14. To be sure revision marking is still turned on, click the **Tools** menu and click **Revisions.** Be sure there is a check mark in the Mark Revisions While Editing, the Show Revisions on Screen, and the Show Revisions in the Printed Document boxes.

15. To see revision marks entered as you enter text, type **perfect** before the word *example* on the first line.

16. To see revision marks as you delete text, delete the word *turned* on the first line.

17. To save and close the document, click the **Save** tool and then click the **Close** button at the right side of the menu bar.

❖ WORKING WITH FIELDS

Fields are codes that tell Word to insert information in a document. Word contains more than 60 fields you can use to manage documents.

Probably the most often used field is the Date and Time field. You can use the Date and Time command on the Insert menu to insert the date and time (see Figure 6-10). As you can see in Figure 6-10, you can choose the format for the date or time.

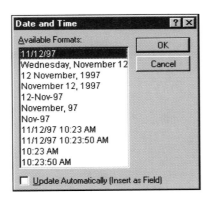

Figure 6-10
The Date and Time command lets you select the format for the date and time.

If you turn on the Insert as Field option, Word automatically updates the date or time when you print the document. If you do not want Word to change the date, be sure to turn off that option.

Field results are visible as text, graphics, or a combination of the two. *Field codes* are instructions enclosed within field characters, which look like braces {}. You can use the shortcut menu to view the field codes for a single field. You can view all of the field codes in your document (see Figure 6-11) by holding **Alt** and pressing **F9**.

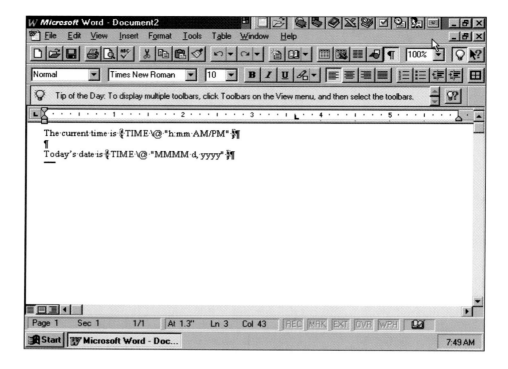

Figure 6-11
This document shows time and date field codes.

You can update the date or time at any time when it is inserted as a field. To do so:

❖ Position the I-beam on the date.

❖ Click the right mouse button.

❖ Click Update Field.

You can also update fields by selecting one or more fields, or the whole document and pressing **F9**.

To update fields when you are printing:

❖ Choose Options from the Tools menu.

❖ Select the Print tab.

❖ Turn on the Update Fields option.

You can also use the Field command on the Insert menu to insert one of Word's fields in your document (see Figure 6-12). You can use the Date and Time category to insert the current date, the current time, the date a document was created, the date it was last printed, the date it was last saved, or the total time it was edited. You then use the Options button to select a format for a field.

note

Many users enter the FileName field as a footer in the document. That way the name of the file is displayed on all pages.

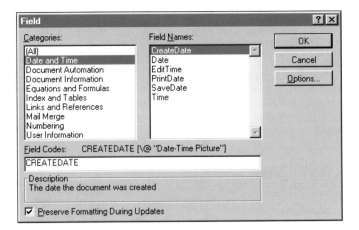

Exercise 6-7

1. To create a new document, click the **New** tool.

2. Type **The current time is** and type a *space.*

3. To enter a time field, click the **Insert** menu, click the **Date and Time** command, and click the **first** time format. Be sure **Update Automatically (Insert as Field)** is turned on and click **OK.**

4. To enter the date, press **(Enter)** twice, type **Today's date is** and a *space,* click the **Insert** menu, click **Date and Time,** click the **fourth** format on the list, and click **OK.**

5. To display the field codes instead of the actual date and time, hold **(Alt)** and press **(F9)**.

6. To return to the original display, hold **(Alt)** and press **(F9)** again.

7. To enter the document's creation date, hold **(Ctrl)** and press **(End)**, press **(Enter)** twice, type **This document was created on** and a *space,* click the **Insert** menu, click **Field,** click the **Date and Time** category, and click the **Create Date** field.

8. To select the format for the date, click the **Options** button, click the **fifth** format, and click **OK** twice.

9. To update the time, position the I-beam over the **Time** field, click the **right** mouse button, and click **Update Field.**

10. Experiment with inserting some of the User Information fields in your document for a few minutes. Be sure to look through the lists of fields in the Field dialog box so you are familiar with the kinds of fields available. When you finish, update the time field again.

11. To save and close the document, click the **Save** tool, type **Exercise 06-07 Inserting Fields,** click **Save** and click the **Close** button at the right side of the menu bar.

❖ ADDING HEADERS AND FOOTERS

A *header* or *footer* is text or graphics that prints at the top or bottom of each page in a document. A header is printed in the top margin and a footer is printed in the bottom margin.

Headers and footers are usually simple document titles and page numbers. You can, however, create headers and footers with graphics, multiple paragraphs, and fields. You can also opt to *not* print a header or footer on the first page of a document. You can specify a different header or footer for odd and even pages in documents that will be printed on both sides of the paper and bound with facing pages. You can divide a document into sections and use different headers and footers in each section.

You can use the Header and Footer command on the View menu to create headers and footers. Word automatically switches to page layout view and displays the Header and Footer toolbar (see Figure 6-13) when you use the Header and Footer command.

Figure 6-13
The Header and Footer toolbar lets you create headers and footers at the top or bottom of your page.

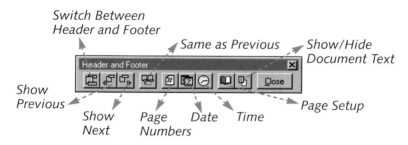

Use the Switch Between Header and Footer tool to switch between viewing the header and the footer.

Use the Page Numbers tool to insert page numbers in the header or footer.

Use the Date tool to insert the current date field.

Use the Time tool to insert the current time field.

Use the Page Setup tool to display the Layout tab in the Page Setup dialog box. That is where you can create different headers and footers for odd and even pages.

Use the Show Next tool (if you are working with different headers or footers on odd and even pages) to move to the next header or footer.

Use the Show Previous tool (if you are working with different headers or footers on odd and even pages) to move to the previous header or footer.

Use the Same as Previous tool when you want to change the header or footer for a particular section. Clicking the Same as Previous tool breaks the connection with the previous section.

Use the Show/Hide Document Text tool to display or hide document text.

The header and footer areas are marked with a nonprinting dashed line. Text and graphics in the document are visible but dimmed. You can type and format text in the header or footer area the same as you do in the document. There are two tabs set in the header and footer areas: a center tab and a right tab.

You can use the Close command on the Header and Footer toolbar, or you can double-click on the document area to return to the document.

Exercise 6-8

1. To open a document, click the **Open** tool and double-click **Exercise 06-08 Headers and Footers.**

2. To see the whole document, click the **Print Preview** tool.

3. To display all three pages if they are not already displayed, click the **Multiple Pages** tool, drag over **three pages** on the top row, and release.

4. To return to the previous document view, click **Close** on the toolbar.

5. To access Header and Footer view, click the **View** menu and then **Header and Footer.**

6. To add the document title at the right margin at the top of each page, press **Tab** twice, and type **Software for the 90s.**

7. To put a border on the header paragraph, click the **Borders** tool, click the **point size** drop-down button, click **1 1/2 pt,** and click the **Bottom Border** button.

8. To hide the Borders toolbar, click the **Borders** tool on the Formatting toolbar.

9. To switch to the footer area, click the **Switch Between Header and Footer** tool.

10. To enter the name of the file, click the **Insert** menu, click **Field,** click the **Document Information** category, click **FileName,** and click **OK.**

11. To enter the page number at the right margin, press **Tab** twice and click the **Page Numbers** tool.

12. To remove the header and footer from the first page, click the **Page Setup** tool, click **Different First Page** on the Layout tab, and click **OK.** When you return to the header and footer for the first page, click **Close,** because you do not want a header or a footer on that page.

13. To see what the header and footer look like, click the **Print Preview** tool.

14. To print the document, click the **Print** tool. After printing, click the **Close** button.

15. To save and close the document, click the **Save** tool and then click the **Close** button at the right side of the menu bar.

❖ INSERTING PAGE NUMBERS

You can also use the Page Numbers command on the Insert menu to insert page numbers in your document (see Figure 6-14).

When you insert a page number with this command, you can specify whether you want it in the header or the footer and whether it should be positioned at the left margin, the center, or the right margin.

The Page Numbers command also offers the option to *not* display the number on the first page of the document.

You can click the Format button in the Page Numbers dialog box to display the Page Number Format dialog box (see Figure 6-15). You can choose from different numbering formats, include chapter numbers and separators, continue page numbering from a previous section, or enter a number other than 1 (one) from which to begin the page numbering.

When you use the Page Numbers command to add page numbers to your document, Word inserts a Page field into the document and encloses it in a frame. (You will learn more about frames in a later lesson.)

Exercise 6-9

1. To open a document, click the **Open** tool and double-click **Exercise 06-09 Inserting Page Numbering.**

2. To preview the document, click the **Print Preview** tool. Notice it is the same three-page document without any headers or footers.

3. To enter the page numbers, click the **Insert** menu, click **Page Numbers,** click **Top of Page (Header)** in the Position box, click **Center** in the Alignment box, be sure Show Number on First Page is not clicked on, and click the **Format** button. Be sure **Page Numbering Starts At 1** is the format, click **OK** to return to the Page Numbers dialog box, and click **OK** again. Notice the page numbers at the top center of pages 2 and 3.

4. To print the document, click the **Print** tool.

5. To close Print Preview, click the **Close** tool.

6. To save and close the document, click the **Save** tool and then click the **Close** button at the right side of the menu bar.

❖ SUMMARY

You have now learned to use the Replace command, record and run a macro, enter breaks, use the Annotation feature, work with fields, and add headers and footers to your documents.

Try the exercises on the following pages to test how well you remember what you learned. Do not be afraid to go back and look up the answers, because that will help to reinforce what you learned.

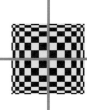

activities

*On the blank line before each sentence, place a **T** if the statement is true or an **F** if it is false.*

_____ 1. The Replace command cannot search for or replace styles.

_____ 2. You can refine searches by using operators and expressions such as *S??rch* in the Find What box.

_____ 3. When you use the find-and-replace feature, you should nearly always use the Replace All option.

_____ 4. You cannot assign a macro to a menu.

_____ 5. When recording a macro, you need to try to anticipate prompts or dialog boxes that might interfere with your macro.

_____ 6. The macro is saved as soon as you finish recording it.

_____ 7. Word's pagination feature can change the position of hard page breaks.

_____ 8. Annotations allow reviewers to make changes to your documents.

_____ 9. When you use the Date and Time command to enter a date as a field, Word updates the field to the current date or time when it prints a document.

_____ 10. A footer is text that prints at the top of every page.

❖ COMPLETION

Fill in the blanks in the following statements.

1. You can turn on the _____ option in the Replace dialog box to find text with the same capitalization as the text in the Find What box.

2. You can use the _____ button in the Replace dialog box to leave a selection unchanged.

3. You can use the _____ tool if you are not satisfied with the results of a find and replace.

4. You can use the _____ tool on the Macro Record toolbar to stop recording until you click the tool again.

5. Before you enter a(n) _____, you should select the text it refers to.

6. Your document's file name is one of the _____ you can enter in your document.

7. You can create different _____ for odd- and even-numbered pages in your document.

8. You can divide a document into _____ when you want to use different headers and footers in different parts of the document.

9. Word inserts a(n) _____ in your document when you use the Page Numbers tool in Headers and Footers.

10. There are _____ tabs set in the header and footer area.

review

Review Exercise 6-1

1. Open **Review 06-01 Macro Practice 1**.
2. Create a macro to print just page 2 of the document.
3. Be sure to assign shortcut keys to the macro.
4. Open **Review 06-01 Macro Practice 2** and run the macro.
5. Save and close both documents.

Review Exercise 6-2

1. Open **Review 06-02 Create Footer**.
2. Use the Date and Time command on the Insert menu to enter the date and time in the header.
3. Use the Field command to insert the file name at the left margin in the footer.
4. Enter the page number at the right in the footer.
5. Print, save, and close the document.

Review Exercise 6-3

1. Open **Review 06-03 Replace Text**.
2. Use the Replace command to replace all occurrences of *PC* with *personal computer*. You may have to turn on some options to get the exercise to work as easily as you might like. Don't give up until you work it out. Remember as long as you close a document *without saving it,* you can open the original as often as you like.
3. Write a paragraph at the end of the document telling your instructor how you finally decided to accomplish the task.
4. Print, save, and close the document.

Review Exercise 6-4

1. Use online Help to find information about what the problems might be if you have trouble printing headers or footers.

2. Read and print the information.

On Your Own

1. Create a macro to enter the file name in the footer for each document.

2. Add the macro to the Insert menu.

3. Test the macro.

4. Use the Customize command on the Tools menu to reset the menu to the original.

lesson 7

Working with Tables

❖ **OBJECTIVES**

When you complete this lesson, you will be able to:

1. Create a table.
2. Move around the table.
3. Edit and format text.
4. Split a table.
5. Use Sort and Formula commands.
6. Convert existing text to a table.
7. Use AutoText and the Table Wizard.
8. Use tables to print text side by side.

Estimated Time: 2 hours

Table
Insert Rows
Delete Rows
Merge Cells
Split Cells...
Select Row
Select Column
Select Table   Alt+Num 5
Table AutoFormat...
Cell Height and Width...
Headings
Convert Text To Table...
Sort...
Formula...
Split Table
✔ Gridlines

❖ **INTRODUCTION**

With Word's Table feature, you can arrange columns of numbers and/or text without using tabs. The Table feature makes it very easy to prepare documents with side-by-side text such as you might find in a resume. You can also use the Table feature to make it easy to arrange text beside graphics.

❖ **CREATING A TABLE**

You can use the Insert Table command on the Table menu or the Insert Table tool to insert a table at the insertion point in a document.

A table can have as many as 31 columns.

❖ GRIDLINES, END-OF-CELL, AND END-OF-ROW MARKS

Word displays dotted gridlines between the cells of a table (see Figure 7-1). The gridlines do not print. You can turn the gridlines off with the Gridlines command on the Table menu, but it is much easier to work in a table when you can see gridlines.

An *end-of-cell mark* identifies the end of text or graphics within a cell. An *end-of-row mark* identifies the end of a row. You can use the Show/Hide tool to display the marks you see in Figure 7-1.

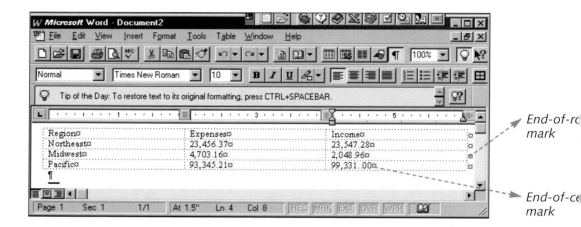

Figure 7-1
The end-of-cell mark, end-of-row mark, and gridlines are nonprinting features that show you the layout of a table.

End-of-row mark

End-of-cell mark

❖ MOVING AROUND THE TABLE

You move from cell to cell from left to right and then down to the next row by pressing (**Tab**).

There is no need to set a number of rows when you insert the table. When you press (**Tab**) in the last cell, Word automatically creates a new row and moves your insertion point into the first cell in the new row. You can move out of the table when you reach the last cell by pressing ⊕ or by clicking the insertion point below the table.

You can hold (**Shift**) and press (**Tab**) to move back a cell. Whenever you use (**Tab**) or (**Shift**)+(**Tab**) to move within the table, Word automatically selects any contents of the cell you move into.

You can use the arrow keys to move one character right or left or one line up or down. You can also use the keystrokes shown in Table 7-1 to move around within a table.

To Move	Press
To the first cell in the row	**Alt**+**Home** or **Alt**+**7** (numeric keypad) with NUM LOCK off
To the last cell in the row	**Alt**+**End** or **Alt**+**1** (numeric keypad) with NUM LOCK off
To the first cell in the column	**Alt**+**Page Up** or **Alt**+**9** (numeric keypad) with NUM LOCK off
To the last cell in the column	**Alt**+**Page Down** or **Alt**+**3** (numeric keypad) with NUM LOCK off

Table 7-1

Exercise 7-1

1. To create a new document based on the Normal template, click the **New** tool.

2. To insert a table with three columns, click the **Insert Table** tool. Then drag over **three columns** in the top row and release. The three columns will fill the entire space between the margins.

3. Enter the information shown in Figure 7-1. Do not worry about any of the formatting. Press **Tab** to move from cell to cell. Word creates a new row each time you press **Tab** at the end of a row. Do not press **Enter** at the end of a row, as that adds a blank line to the cell.

4. To move out of the table when you reach the last cell, click the insertion point below the table or press ↓. If you accidentally create an extra row, don't worry about it for now. (You will learn how to delete rows later in this lesson.)

5. To save and close the file, click the **Save** tool, type **Exercise 07-01 Create Table,** click **OK,** and click the **Close** button at the right side of the menu bar.

❖ USING THE TABLE AUTOFORMAT COMMAND

You can use the Table AutoFormat command on the Table menu to apply one of the table styles provided by Word. As you can see in Figure 7-2, you can select each of the formats and see a preview of what the table looks like with each format.

AutoFormat applies borders, shading, font, color, and AutoFit formats. Word can apply special formats to the heading rows, the last row, the first column, and the last column.

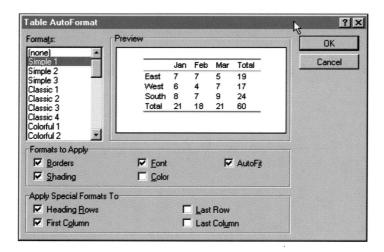

Figure 7-2
Use Table AutoFormat to preview table styles.

In the following exercises, be sure to follow directions carefully. If, however, you do something to your table that you cannot undo, close the file without saving it. Then reopen the file and begin the exercise again.

Exercise 7-2

1. To open a document, click the **Open** tool and double-click **Exercise 07-02 Formatting a Table.**

2. To display end-of-cell and end-of-row marks if they are not already displayed, click the **Show/Hide** tool.

3. To work with table commands, click the I-beam within the table.

4. To turn gridlines off, click the **Table** menu and then **Gridlines.**

5. To toggle gridlines back on (it is easier to work when you can see gridlines), click the **Table** menu and then **Gridlines**.

6. To display the dialog box in Figure 7-2, click the **Table** menu and then the **Table AutoFormat** command.

7. To see the kinds of formats you can apply, click through the various formats and watch the preview.

8. To format your table, click **Simple 3** and click **OK.** Your table should now look like the one shown in Figure 7-3. Notice the numbers in the table are not lined up at decimal points, and the table is not centered between the margins. You will set decimal tabs in columns 2 and 3 in a few minutes. You will also center a table between margins.

9. To save and close the file, click the **Save** tool and click the **Close** button at the right side of the menu bar.

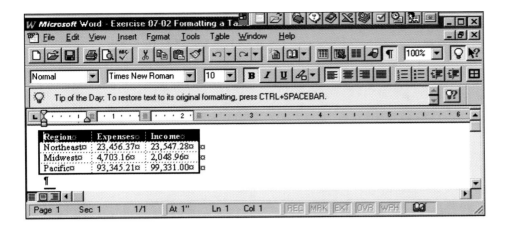

Figure 7-3
This document
shows a table
formatted in
Simple 3 style.

❖ SELECTING ITEMS IN A TABLE

You can use the mouse, menu commands, or keystrokes to select within a table. Once you are comfortable using a mouse, you will probably use the mouse most of the time.

Table 7-2 contains instructions for selecting with the keyboard.

To	Do This
Select the next cell's contents	Press **Tab**
Select the preceding cell's contents	Hold **Shift** and press **Tab**
Select an entire table	Hold **Alt** and press **5** (on the numeric keypad) with NUM LOCK off
Extend a selection to adjacent cells	Hold **Shift** and press an arrow key repeatedly.
Select a column	Position insertion point in top cell of column. Hold **Shift** and press ⬆ or ⬇ until entire column is selected.

Table 7-2

Table 7-3 contains instructions for selecting with the mouse. See the callouts in Figure 7-4 for various parts of the table.

You can also use the Select Row, Select Column, and Select Table commands on the Table menu to select within a table.

note

Remember to use the Undo tool if you get any unexpected results when working in tables.

To Select	Do This
A cell	Click the cell selection bar at the left of the cell before the text.
A row	Click the row selection bar to the left of the row outside the table.
A column	Point to the top cell's top gridline at the left side of the cell and click the filled down arrow (↓).
Multiple cells, rows, or columns	Drag across the cell, row, or column; or select a single cell, row, or column and hold **Shift** while you click in another cell, row, or column.

Table 7-3

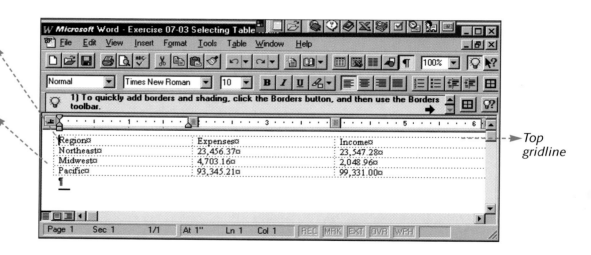

Cell selection bar

Row selection bar

Top gridline

Figure 7-4
The parts of the table you use when selecting.

Exercise 7-3

1. To open a new version of the original table, click the **Open** tool and double-click **Exercise 07-03 Selecting Table Items.** The insertion point is in the first cell of the table.

2. To move to the next cell and select the cell's contents, press **Tab**.

3. To return to the preceding cell and select the contents, hold **Shift** and press **Tab**.

4. To cancel the selection but remain in the cell, press ⊖.

5. To select the second row, click the **row selection bar** outside the table to the left of the second row.

6. To select the first cell in the first row, click the **cell selection bar** to the left of text in that cell.

7. To select the right column, point to the top right cell's top gridline and when you see the filled down arrow (↓), click it.

8. To select the first two cells in the second row, drag across the cells.

9. Press ⏎ to cancel the selection.

10. To select the entire table, click the **Table** menu and then click **Select Table**.

11. To cancel the selection, click anywhere in white space. It may take a little time to get accustomed to selecting within a table. Stay with the exercise and practice selecting until you feel comfortable with it. Use as many as you can of the methods shown here for selecting just the text, the whole cell, and the whole row.

12. To save and close the file, click the **Save** tool and click the **Close** button at the right side of the menu bar.

❖ FORMATTING TEXT IN A TABLE

You can use any of the formatting methods you learned earlier in this book to format text in your table. The Borders and Shading command on the Format menu and the Borders toolbar are particularly useful when working with tables.

Exercise 7-4

1. To open a document, click **Open** and double-click **Exercise 07-04 Formatting Table Text.**

2. To center the headings in the first row of the table, select the first row and click the **Center** alignment tool.

3. To make the headings bold, click the **Bold** tool.

4. To increase the size of the font, click the **Font Size** drop-down button and then click **12.**

5. To select the entire table for borders, click the **Table** menu and then **Select Table.**

6. To add borders, click **Format** and then click **Borders and Shading.** Click **Grid** under **Presets** on the Borders tab. Click **OK.**

7. To add shading on the first row, select the first row, click the **Format** menu, click **Borders and Shading,** click the **Shading** tab, click **20%,** and click **OK.**

❖ SETTING A DECIMAL TAB IN A TABLE

You can set decimal tabs in a table by clicking on the Tab Alignment button on the left of the ruler shown in Figure 7-5 until you see the decimal tab. Then click at the position in the ruler over the column where you want the decimal tab. It may take some moving if your numbers do not seem to fit in the cells. If you select two columns, Word automatically places a decimal tab in the corresponding position in both columns when you set the first.

Tab Alignment button showing decimal tab

Figure 7-5
Use the Tab Alignment button on the ruler to set a decimal tab in a table.

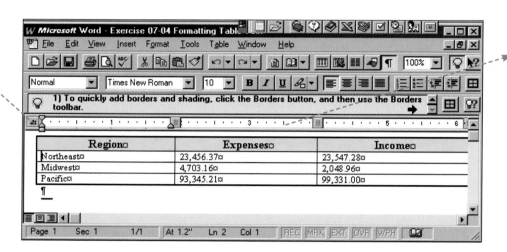

Set decim tab here

As you learned in an earlier lesson, you use a decimal tab when you want to line up columns at the decimal point.

To set a decimal tab in a table:

❖ Click on the Tab Alignment button at the left of the ruler until you see the decimal tab (see Figure 7-5).

❖ Click at the position in the ruler over the column where you want the decimal tab.

You can then drag the tab to move it a bit if your numbers do not seem to fit the cells. If you select two columns, Word automatically places a decimal tab in the corresponding position in the second column when you set the decimal tab in the first.

Exercise 7-5

1. To display the decimal tab at the left of the ruler, click the **Tab Alignment** button until you see the decimal tab.

2. To enter a decimal tab in columns 2 and 3, select the cells in columns 2 and 3 that contain numbers, and click on the ruler over column 2 in a position toward the right side of the column (see Figure 7-5).

3. If your numbers do not fit in the cell, click **Undo.** You might have to move the tab stop around until the numbers are all aligned and fit properly in the cells.

4. To print the document, click the **Print** tool.

5. To save and close the file, click the **Save** tool and click the **Close** button at the right side of the menu bar.

❖ INSERTING AND DELETING CELLS, ROWS, AND COLUMNS

You can insert a new cell, row, or column or delete a cell, row, or column in a table.

INSERTING CELLS

The Insert Table tool changes when you are working in a table. When your insertion point is positioned within a table, the Insert Table tool is the Insert Rows tool. When a column is selected, the Insert Table command becomes the Insert Columns command.

You can use the Insert Rows command on the Table menu to insert a row above the row where you place the insertion point. You can also use the Insert Table tool, which is the Insert Rows tool when your insertion point is placed inside an existing table.

If you want to insert more than one row, select the number of rows in the table you would like to insert. Word will insert that many rows above the selected rows.

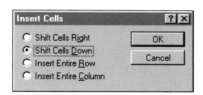

Figure 7-6
The Insert Cells dialog box lets you insert a cell, a row, or a column.

If you select a cell, you can use the Insert Cells command to insert a cell, a row, or a column (see the dialog box shown in Figure 7-6).

You can shift cells right or down or insert an entire row or column.

DELETING CELLS OR THEIR TEXT

You can delete just the text you enter in a cell, or you can delete the cell itself.

To delete text in a cell:

❖ Select as you would anywhere in a document.

❖ Press (Delete).

To delete cells in a table:

❖ Select the cell or cells you want to delete.

❖ Click Table.

❖ Click Delete Cells.

note

Remember, the Delete command on the Table menu differs depending on what is selected when you choose the command.

The Delete Cells dialog box shown in Figure 7-7 appears. You can access the Delete Cells dialog box only when your insertion point is within a table.

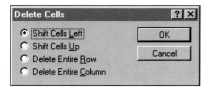

You can choose to shift cells left or up when deleting the selected cells. You can also choose to delete an entire row or column.

When an entire row or column is selected, the Delete Cells command changes to Delete Rows or Delete Columns. When you click the command, Word automatically deletes any rows or columns selected without showing you a dialog box.

❖ MERGING AND SPLITTING CELLS

You can use the Merge Cells command on the Table menu to create a heading that spans several columns. You can also split one or more cells. Word splits cells according to the number of paragraph marks they contain. If there is only one paragraph mark, the contents of the split cell are placed in the cell on the left, and empty cells are inserted to the right.

Exercise 7-6

1. To open a file, click the **Open** tool and then double-click **Exercise 07-06 Inserting Rows and Columns.**

2. To insert a row, click the I-beam (point to text, not blank space, to see the I-beam) anywhere in the last row of the table. *Be sure nothing is selected.* Click the **Table** menu, and then click **Insert Rows.** Notice Word inserted the row and selected it.

3. Press ⏎ to cancel the selection and keep the insertion point in the same row.

4. To delete the row you just inserted, click the **Table** menu, click **Delete Cells,** click **Delete Entire Row,** and click **OK.**

5. To insert a column before the first column, select the **first column** (point to the left side of the top gridline until you see the filled down arrow (↓) and then click), click the **Table** menu, and click **Insert Columns.** Notice a blank column is inserted before the selected column.

6. To remove the column, click **Undo.**

7. If end-of-cell and end-of-row marks are not displayed, click the **Show/Hide** tool.

8. To add one cell to the right of the bottom row, select the **end-of-row** mark on the bottom row (outside the gridlines) by dragging over the mark, click the **Table** menu, click **Insert Cells,** click **Shift Cells Right,** and click **OK.**

9. To cancel the selection and scroll right to see the added cell, press ⊝.

10. To delete the inserted cell, click the **Undo** tool.

11. To return to the beginning of the document and the table, hold **Ctrl** and press **Home**.

12. To insert a new row at the beginning of the table, click the **Insert Rows** tool.

13. To merge the three selected cells, click the **Table** menu and then click **Merge Cells.**

14. Type **1997 Projections** in the merged cell. Notice the new cell uses the formatting in the cell below.

15. Experiment with inserting and deleting until you are comfortable with the procedures.

16. To print the document, click the **Print** tool.

17. To save and close the file, click the **Save** tool and click the **Close** button at the right side of the menu bar.

❖ MOVING AND COPYING TEXT WITHIN A TABLE

You can move or copy text and graphics from one cell to another within a table by using the same cut, copy, and paste or drag-and-drop procedures you learned earlier in this book.

You should keep the following in mind when moving or copying within a table:

- ✦ If you select only the text within a cell and not the end-of-cell mark, the text is inserted at the drop point, and Word does not change the text already in the cell.

- ✦ If you select both the text and the end-of-cell mark, the text you move replaces the existing text and formatting.

- ✦ If you select a whole row, including the end-of-row mark, Word inserts a new row for the row you move and moves all other rows down one.

If you want to use the drag-and-drop feature to *copy* a cell, remember to hold **Ctrl** while dragging and dropping.

Exercise 7-7

1. To open a file, click the **Open** tool and double-click **Exercise 07-07 Modifying a Table.**

2. To see the Tables shortcut menu, position the insertion point in the last row of the table. *Do not select anything.* Be sure the mouse pointer is within the table and pointing at text, and click the **right** mouse button.

3. To insert a row, click **Insert Rows.**

4. To cancel the selection and remain in the first inserted cell, press (Tab). The insertion point should now be in the first cell of the new row.

5. Type **400.00**.

6. To copy the contents of the first cell to the second cell, click in the **cell selection bar** to select the cell's contents, hold (Ctrl), and drag the number to the second cell.

7. To move the contents of the second cell to the third cell, click in the **cell selection bar** to select *400.00* and drag it to the third cell. Notice that the second cell is now empty.

8. Drag to select the number *400.00* in the first cell in the new row. Do *not* select the end-of-cell marker.

9. Use the drag-and-drop feature to drag the number to immediately in front of the *400.00* in the third cell. Notice that Word inserted the number before the original number. Because you did not select the end-of-cell marker, the cell's original contents are unchanged; the new number is simply added to the cell.

10. To undo the drop, click **Undo.**

11. To insert the last row before the third row, select the last row, including the end-of-row mark, by clicking in the **row selection bar** outside the table to the left of the row, drag the selection to the beginning of the third row, and drop it. Notice the other rows moved down to make room for the one you inserted.

12. To delete the last row, position the insertion point in the last row (the one with two cells containing *400.00*), click the Table menu, click **Delete Cells,** click **Delete Entire Row,** and click **OK.**

13. Practice moving and copying information from place to place until you feel comfortable with all of the described methods. It may take a while to get accustomed to selecting within a table.

14. To save and close the file, click the **Save** tool and click the **Close** button at the right side of the menu bar.

❖ SETTING COLUMN WIDTH, SPACING, AND ROW HEIGHT

If the results of using the Table AutoFormat feature to format your tables are not what you want, you can format a table by setting column widths, spacing, and row heights yourself. You can use either the menu command or the mouse to format the table.

CHANGING COLUMN WIDTH

You can change column width by:

❖ Manually dragging the table column markers on the Ruler (see Figure 7-8).

or

❖ Dragging the column boundaries (see Figure 7-8).

or

❖ Using the AutoFit option in the Cell Height and Width dialog box on the Table menu.

or

❖ Using the Cell Height and Width command on the Table menu to set exact measurements for the columns.

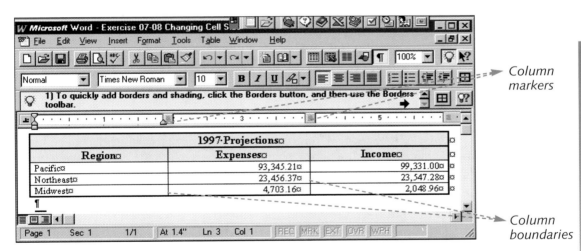

→ *Column markers*

→ *Column boundaries*

Figure 7-8 Dragging table column markers or column boundaries is the easiest way to change column width.

You will probably drag column boundaries more often than you will use any of the other methods.

To change column widths by dragging column boundaries:

❖ Position the mouse pointer on the vertical boundary of the column you want to change.

❖ When the mouse pointer changes, drag the boundary to the right or left (see Table 7-4 for techniques)

Do This	To
Drag	Adjust the current column, and resize all columns to the right in proportion to their original width, with overall table width remaining the same
Hold (Shift) while dragging	Adjust the current column and the column next to it without changing table width
Hold (Ctrl) while dragging	Adjust the current column and make all columns in the direction you are dragging equal in size without changing table width
Hold (Ctrl) and (Shift) while dragging	Adjust the current column without changing other columns (table width changes)

Table 7-4

You can also change the width of columns by pointing to the right boundary of the column and double-clicking. Word resizes the column to fit the cell with the widest line of text. You can use this procedure for more than one column at a time by selecting all of the columns you want to size and then double-clicking the vertical boundary of any one of the selected columns.

USING THE CELL HEIGHT AND WIDTH COMMAND

You can use the Cell Height and Width command on the Table menu to change column widths, row heights, and spacing between columns. You can see the options available in the Cell Height and Width dialog boxes in Figures 7-9 and 7-10.

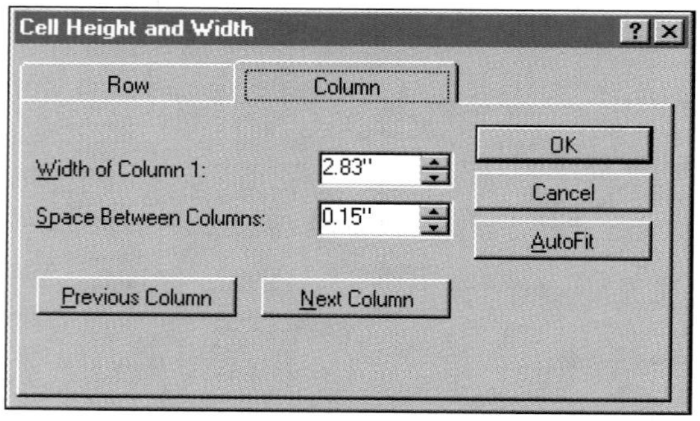

Figure 7-9
To specify an exact column-width measurement, use the Column tab in the Cell Height and Width command.

Click the Column tab in the Cell Height and Width dialog box to see the Width of Column box. You can set an exact measurement for each of your columns. In the Space Between Columns box, you can either accept the default space of 0.15 inch or increase or decrease that measurement. You can use the AutoFit button here to set the column's width to fit the longest entry.

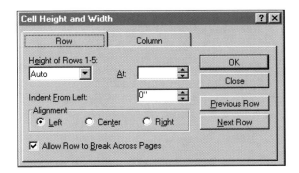

Figure 7-10
The Row tab
displays options
for height and
placement of rows.

Use the Row tab in the Cell Height and Width dialog box to set the height of rows, choose whether the table will be left, center, or right aligned on the page, and decide whether rows can break across pages.

Watch the screen closely while doing the following exercise to see the results of the various instructions.

Exercise 7-8

1. To open a document for this exercise, click the **Open** tool and double-click **Exercise 07-08 Changing Cell Size.**

2. To use Word's AutoFit feature for the column width, select the bottom four rows of the table, click the **Table** menu, and then click **Cell Height and Width.** Click the **Column tab** and click **AutoFit.**

3. To cancel the selection, click anywhere in white space outside the table.

4. To line up the right vertical boundary of the top cell, drag the right vertical boundary and release when it lines up with the boundary of the cell below. It is difficult to line up perfectly, so don't worry if you need to do this a few times to get it right.

5. To add a new row at the end of the table, click the I-beam in the last cell of the table and press (**Tab**).

6. To enter text that wraps to the next line, type **NorthCentral.** Notice some text wraps to the next line because the column is not wide enough.

7. To use the AutoFit feature on the bottom five cells in the first column beginning with **Region,** select the cells, click **Table,** and then click **Cell Height and Width.** Click the **Column tab** if it is not on top. Click **AutoFit.** Notice the text in the column now fits on one line.

8. To return to having the text wrap around within the cell, click **Undo.**

note

By default, Word allows a row to break across pages.

note

Remember to use the Undo tool or command when you get unexpected results.

9. To adjust column width so the text does not wrap, *be sure no cells are selected.* If cells are selected when you drag a column boundary, the boundary is moved for only the selected cells. Drag the boundary to the right of the cell just enough so the text no longer wraps. Notice the first column is wider. Because the table itself does not expand, the other two columns are narrower. Some of the text in the other columns may now be wrapping.

10. To undo the change, click **Undo.**

11. To adjust the column width so the text does not wrap and the other columns hold their size, hold (Shift) while you drag the same column boundary. Notice this time the other two columns remained the size they were before you changed the first column.

12. To undo the change, click **Undo.**

13. To increase the width of the first column again, select the last five cells again, click the **Table** menu, and then click the **Cell Height and Width** command. Use the upward-pointing button to increase the cell size to **1** inch.

14. To change the row height to 15 pts, click the **Row** tab, click **Exactly** under Height of Rows 2-6, change At box to **15 pts,** and click **OK.**

15. To undo the change, click **Undo.**

16. To use the mouse to access the AutoFit feature, *be sure nothing is selected.* Point to the **right boundary** of the *NorthCentral* cell until you see the double-pointing arrow, and double-click.

❖ CREATING TABLE HEADINGS

You can use the Headings command on the Table menu to signal to Word that selected lines are to be considered headings for the table. If the table splits across pages with soft page breaks, Word automatically repeats the table headings on each page. If you insert a hard page break within a table, the heading is not repeated.

When you make changes in heading text, the changes will be updated in all repeated headings.

❖ SPLITTING A TABLE

If you want to insert text between rows in a table, you can split the table.

To do so:

✤ Position the insertion point in the row where you want the second table to begin.

✤ Click Table.

✤ Click the Split Table command.

Word inserts a blank line with a paragraph mark between the two rows as shown in Figure 7-11. To put the table back together, delete the paragraph mark.

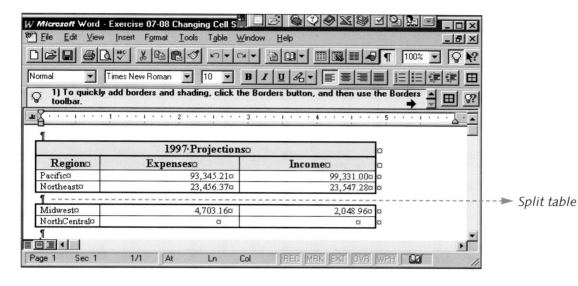

Split table

Figure 7-11
The Split Table
command inserts
a blank line with a
paragraph mark.

To enter text before a table that is at the beginning of a document:

❖ Position the insertion point before any text in the first cell.

❖ Press (**Enter**).

Word inserts a blank line before the table, as shown in Figure 7-11.

Exercise 7-9

1. To split the table, position the insertion point in the fifth row of the table, and *be sure nothing is selected.* Click the **Table** menu and then **Split Table.** Notice the blank line between rows 4 and 5.

2. To rejoin the table, position the insertion point before the paragraph mark on the blank line, and press (**Delete**).

3. To signal that the first two rows are heading rows, select the first two rows, click the **Table** menu, and then click **Headings.**

4. To save and close the file, click the **Save** tool and click the **Close** button at the right side of the menu bar.

❖ CONVERTING TEXT TO A TABLE

You can use the Convert Text to Table command on the Table menu to convert text separated by paragraph marks, commas, or tab characters to cells in a table. If the need ever arises, you can also reverse the process to convert a table to paragraphs.

Exercise 7-10

1. To open a document, click the **Open** tool and then double-click **Exercise 07-10 Text to Table.**

2. To convert the text to a table, click the **Edit** menu, click **Select All**, click **Table**, and then click **Convert Text to Table.** Notice Word recognizes there are three columns of information separated by tabs (see Figure 7-12). Click **OK.** You can now use any of the table features with the converted table.

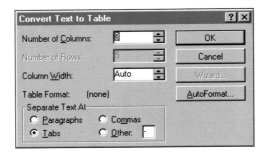

Figure 7-12
You can change text to a table format using the Convert Text to Table command.

3. To print the document, click the **Print** tool.

4. To save and close the file, click the **Save** tool and click the **Close** button at the right side of the menu bar.

❖ SORTING AND NUMBERING CELLS

You can use the Sort command on the Table menu to arrange entries in a table such as that shown in Figure 7-13 in alphabetical or numerical order. You can also use this command to number rows or columns in your tables.

When you close or save the document, be sure to think about whether you want to save the original list or the sorted list. If you want to keep the original list intact, use the Save As command to save the sorted list with a new name.

In the following exercise, you will sort the table by last and then first names. If last names are alike, first names will determine the order.

note

Use the Undo command or tool if you would like to undo the sort.

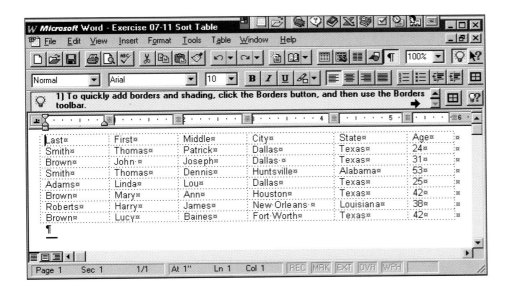

Figure 7-13
Word can sort a table such as this one in alphabetical or numerical order.

Exercise 7-11

1. To open a file, click the **Open** tool and double-click **Exercise 07-11 Sort Table.** Notice the list of last, first, and middle names; cities and states; and ages.

2. To display the Sort dialog box, be sure the insertion point is in the table, click **Table,** and then click the **Sort** command to display the Sort dialog box shown in Figure 7-14. Notice the Sort By box is correctly filled in: you do want to sort by last name (column 1), which is a text field, and you do want ascending order (a to z).

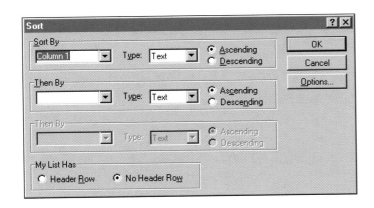

Figure 7-14
The Sort dialog box displays options for sorting your table.

3. To designate column 2, the first name column, as the second column in the sort, click the **Then By** drop-down button, and select **Column 2.** Word automatically suggests text and ascending again.

4. To prevent your headers from being sorted with the list, click the **My List Has Header Row** option.

5. To sort the list, click **OK.** Notice your list has been sorted.

6. To print the document, click the **Print** tool.

7. To save and close the file, click the **Save** tool and click the **Close** button at the right side of the menu bar.

❖ USING THE FORMULA COMMAND IN A TABLE

You can use the Formula command on the Table menu to perform some basic calculations. You can add, subtract, multiply, and divide numbers in the Word table. You can also calculate averages, percentages, and minimum and maximum values.

You must repeat the Formula command if you later change any data in cells you added. Word does not automatically update calculations when data in the table changes.

It is more efficient to use a spreadsheet such as Excel to perform calculations, but the Formula command is easy to use for totaling rows or columns in your tables (see Figure 7-15).

Figure 7-15
The Formula command will total rows or columns of figures.

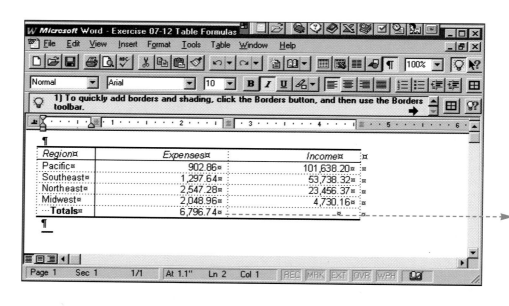

Total entered using Formula command

Exercise 7-12

1. To open a document, click the **Open** tool and double-click **Exercise 07-12 Table Formulas.**

2. To display the Formula dialog box shown in Figure 7-16, click the I-beam in the last row of the second column, click **Table,** and then click the **Formula** command. Notice the Formula box contains the sum function, and Word knows from the layout of the table to sum numbers above.

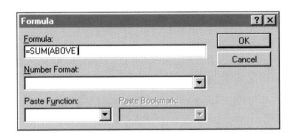

Figure 7-16
Use the Formula
dialog box to
enter totals in
your table.

3. To insert the total, click **OK.**

4. To save and close the file, click the **Save** tool and click the **Close** button at the right side of the menu bar.

❖ USING AUTOTEXT WITH TABLES

If you use a special format for a table often, store it as an AutoText entry. Then you can easily duplicate table formats throughout documents.

To store the entry:

❖ Select the table you want to reuse.

❖ Use the AutoText command on the Edit menu.

Exercise 7-13

1. To open a new document, click the **New** tool.

2. To create a two-column table, click the **Table** tool, drag over the **top two columns**, and release.

3. To make the columns approximately the size you see in Figure 7-17, drag the column boundary between the two columns.

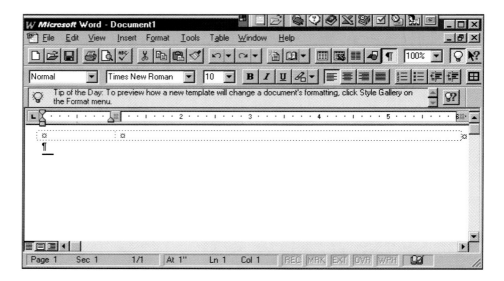

Figure 7-17
These columns
were modified
by dragging the
column boundary.

4. To put a border around the right cell, click in the right cell, click the **Borders** tool, click the **Outside Border** button on the Borders toolbar, and click the **Border** tool again to remove the toolbar.

5. To select the entire table, click the **Table** menu and then click **Select Table.**

6. To store the AutoText entry, click the **Edit** menu, click **AutoText,** type **table1,** and click **Add.** If you are asked if you want to redefine the AutoText entry because someone has already stored the same entry, click **Yes.**

7. To move out of the table, click the I-beam below the table and press ⟨**Enter**⟩ twice.

8. To recall the table, click the **Edit** menu, click **AutoText,** click **table1,** and click **Insert.**

9. To save and close the file, click the **Save** tool, type **Exercise 07-13 Make Table,** make certain that the file will be saved in your personal folder, click **Save,** and click the **Close** button at the right side of the menu bar.

❖ USING A WIZARD TO CREATE A TABLE

You can use a Word wizard to create a table. Wizards take you through the process of creating many common documents as well as tables. You can use a wizard to create, for example, a table with the months of the year in the right-hand column for entering sales data for each of four representatives. Use the New command on the File menu to select and see the different tables the wizard creates for you.

❖ USING A TABLE FOR COLUMNS OF SIDE-BY-SIDE TEXT

Use a table when you need to keep columns of varying amounts of text together as you would for a resume.

❖ PRINTING A TABLE

You print a document containing a table the same way you print any other document. If you want to print one page of your document in landscape mode to accommodate a wide table, use the Break command on the Insert menu to insert a section break. You can use the Page Setup command on the File menu to change the orientation of the section containing the table.

note

Remember, gridlines do not print. You can use borders instead.

Exercise 7-14

1. To open the document, click the **Open** tool and double-click **Exercise 07-14 Side-By-Side Text.**

2. To see how the table is used for side-by-side text, scroll through the document.

3. To close the document, click the **File** menu and then click **Close.** Respond **No** if asked to save changes.

❖ SUMMARY

You have now learned how to create a table, enter text and move around a table, display gridlines and end-of-cell and end-of-row marks, use the Table AutoFormat command, and select in a table. You have also learned to format text within a table, set decimal tabs, insert and delete rows and columns, merge and split cells, move and copy within a table, and change column widths, spacing, and row heights. You've learned to split a table, use the Sort and Formula commands, convert existing text to a table, store a table format with AutoText, and create a table using a wizard.

Try the exercises on the following pages to test how well you remember what you learned. Don't be afraid to go back and look up answers or procedures, because that will help to reinforce what you learned.

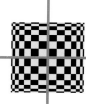

activities

❖ T R U E / F A L S E

On the blank line before each sentence, place a **T** *if the statement is true or an* **F** *if it is false.*

_____ 1. A table can have an unlimited number of columns.

_____ 2. Gridlines do not print.

_____ 3. When you hold (Shift) and press (Tab) to move back a cell, Word automatically selects the cell's contents.

_____ 4. You can only insert whole rows or columns in a Word table.

_____ 5. You cannot use drag-and-drop procedures in a table.

_____ 6. When you create a table, you must know the number of rows you want in the table.

_____ 7. You cannot set table headings to automatically repeat on each page.

_____ 8. To rejoin a table you split, delete the paragraph mark where the table is split.

_____ 9. When you sort a table, you want to include the header row.

_____ 10. The Formula command automatically recalculates totals if you change data in the cells.

Fill in the blanks in the following statements.

1. You can add a new row to a table by pressing _____ in the last cell.

2. You can have a maximum of _____ columns in a table.

3. You can move back a cell in a table by holding the _____ and pressing the _____ key.

4. Click _____ and then _____ to delete a selected row in a table.

5. It is wise to leave _____ turned on so you can see cell boundaries.

6. The _____ command on the Table menu gives you many choices of preset formats.

7. The _____ command or tool is very useful when you get unexpected results during a procedure.

8. You can set _____ in a table to line up columns of numbers.

9. You can use the _____ command on the Table menu to combine cells so you can center a heading over an entire table.

10. When you use the _____ command, be sure to use Save As when you save your document or you will lose the original order of your list.

review

Review Exercise 7-1

1. Use online Help to find out how you create a blank line at the top of a table that is at the beginning of a document.

2. Print the information you find.

Review Exercise 7-2

1. Enter the following table.

	Qtr 1	Qtr 2	Qtr 3	Qtr 4
		1996 Sales		
Jane Collins	38,456	56,934	34,457	36,421
Sue Jenkins	31,213	29,456	37,432	32,534
Joe Wong	25,421	32,365	34,343	33,893
Harry Haig	32,238	28,452	26,476	36,222
Totals				

2. Use AutoFormat to format the table.

3. Center the table between the margins.

4. Add decimal tabs to align numbers.

5. Use the Formula command to total the columns.

6. Print the table in landscape mode.

7. Save and close the document.

On Your Own

1. Use the Table feature to prepare your resume.

2. Print the resume.

3. Save and close the document.

lesson 8

Working with Mail Merge

❖ OBJECTIVES

When you complete this lesson, you will be able to:

1. Use Mail Merge Helper.

2. Work with a main document.

3. Work with a data source.

4. Use the Mail Merge toolbar.

5. Merge a main document with a data source.

6. Print envelopes or labels from a data source.

7. Work with advanced merge capabilities.

Estimated Time: $1\frac{1}{2}$ hours

❖ INTRODUCTION

You can use the Mail Merge command on the Tools menu to personalize form letters, print addresses on envelopes or labels, and produce catalogs or any documents that combine standard text with unique information.

To create any type of mail merge document, you must merge a main document with a data source. The *main document* contains all the items that remain the same in each form letter along with merge fields. *Merge fields* tell Word where to print information from the data source. The *data source* contains the information that changes in each letter.

In this lesson:

❖ You will create a data source document containing information for three registrants in computer classes.

❖ You will create a form letter acknowledging registration for the classes. The letter will contain merge fields for the registrants' names and mailing addresses, for the dates of the classes, and for the class names.

❖ You will then merge the main document and the data source to print the letters.

❖ USING MAIL MERGE HELPER

You begin to create the two documents necessary for the mail merge with the Mail Merge command on the Tools menu.

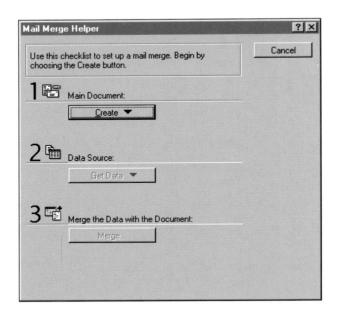

Figure 8-1
The Mail Merge Helper helps you create a main document and a data source for a mail merge.

The Mail Merge Helper displayed in Figure 8-1 prompts you through the steps necessary to create your documents. You must first identify for Word the name of the document you intend to use for the main document and then the name of the data source. If you had existing documents to use with the Mail Merge feature, you could use those instead of creating new ones.

In this first exercise you are setting up the files you will use for the mail merge.

Exercise 8-1

1. To create a new document to use for the main document, click the **New** tool.

2. To see the Mail Merge Helper, click **Tools** and then **Mail Merge.**

3. To begin, follow the directions at the top of the box to click **Create** in the Main Document list box.

4. Because you already created the new document to use for the main document, click **Form Letters** and then **Active Window.** Notice Word entered the unnamed document as the name of the main document.

5. To follow the next prompt, click the **Get Data** button to specify a data source.

6. Because you want to create a new data source file, click **Create Data Source.**

❖ CREATING A DATA SOURCE

When you create the data source document, you actually set up a database. All the information about one person or thing in the database is called a *record*. Each piece of information in a record is called a *field*. Word already has a list of often-used fields.

It is wise to give some thought to the information you will need in a database before you begin. In the data source each record must have the same number of fields. Make sure to plan enough fields to hold even those records that have the most information. The Address2 field is a good example of a field that will be empty for most records but is very important when you have a record that contains a two-line address.

When entering fields for a person's name, be sure to use separate fields for the title (Mr., Mrs., Ms.), first name, and last name. That way, you can address the person either with a title and last name or with a first name.

You should always use the city, state, and postal code fields. If you have separate fields, you can sort by any of them. Then you can send a form letter to everyone in a certain city, state, or postal area.

You can add the POSTNET bar code to speed mail delivery.

In the Create Data Source dialog box shown in Figure 8-2, you can add and remove fields. You can use the Move up and down buttons to rearrange the order of fields. You can also access MS Query to select only certain records in your database for merging.

> **note**
>
> If a field is empty, Word does not leave blank space in the merged documents.

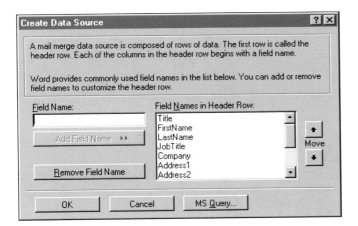

Figure 8-2
Choose fields in the Create Data Source dialog box.

Exercise 8-2

1. Because you will not need the Country field, scroll down to and select **Country** and click **Remove Field Name.**

2. To find and remove **HomePhone** and **WorkPhone** (because you will not need those fields), scroll through the list and select and remove them.

3. Because you are writing a form letter about a computer class and its date, you have to add two fields. Type **Class** in the Field Name box and click **Add Field Name.** Then type **ClassDate** and click **Add Field Name.**

4. To signal you are finished adding and removing field names, click **OK.**

5. To enter a data source file name, enter **Exercise 08-02 Data Source** and click **Save.**

6. To begin adding records to the data source, click **Edit Data Source.**

Now that you have created both the main document and the data source for the merge, Word displays the dialog box in Figure 8-3. Neither of your documents contains any information yet. You can either add new records to your data source or add merge fields to your main document now.

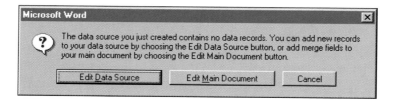

❖ EDITING THE DATA SOURCE DOCUMENT

Word displays the Data Form window shown in Figure 8-4. You will add three records to the data source file by entering information in the Data Form window.

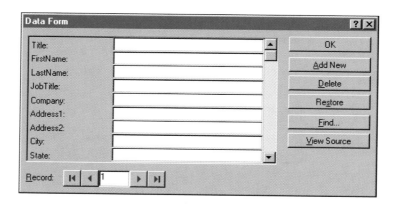

When you finish entering all information for one record, click Add New to display a blank record. Word numbers the records as you enter them.

You can use the Delete button to delete the current record.

You can edit a record by selecting the field you want to change and keying in the new information. If you don't like the changes, you can use the Restore command button to return to the original information in a field. Once you click Add New or Delete for a record, however, you cannot restore the original information.

You can use the View Source button to view your records in table format and to access Word's menu bar to save the document after entering records. You can use the Find button to search records using any of the fields to find a particular record.

To enter the three records shown below, keep the following in mind:

❖ Be sure to enter data in the correct field.

❖ Address2 will always be blank in this exercise.

❖ Press (Tab) or (Enter) to move from field to field.

❖ You can use the scroll bars to move to the fields not displayed.

❖ Hold (Shift) and press (Tab) if you want to move back a field.

❖ When you press (Tab), (Enter), or (Shift)+(Tab) to move to a field with data in it, the data is automatically selected.

❖ After you enter all information for one record, click Add New to display a blank record.

Exercise 8-3

1. Enter the following records.

Ms.	Mr.	Mr.
Mary	Harry	Jim
Smith	Jones	Walker
President	Comptroller	Manager, Central Services
New Company	ABC Company	XYZ Company
124 Main Street	890 Fifth Avenue	412 Central Avenue
Duluth	Smithtown	Orangetown
MN	NY	NJ
67774	87765	07984
Word	Word	Excel
January 25, 1997	February 1, 1997	March 14, 1997

2. To find Mary Smith's record and change the date for her class, click **Find.** Type **Smith** in the Find What dialog box. Click the **Field** drop-down button and click **LastName** to signal the field to search. Click **Find First.** Click **Yes** to continue searching at the beginning of the database.

3. To close the Find dialog box, click **Close.**

4. To enter *March* instead of *January* in Mary Smith's ClassDate field, scroll down to display the field, select **January,** and replace it with **March.**

5. To return to the original date, click **Restore.**

6. To see your data source in table format, as shown in Figure 8-5, click **View Source.** The data may wrap around within a cell but will print properly.

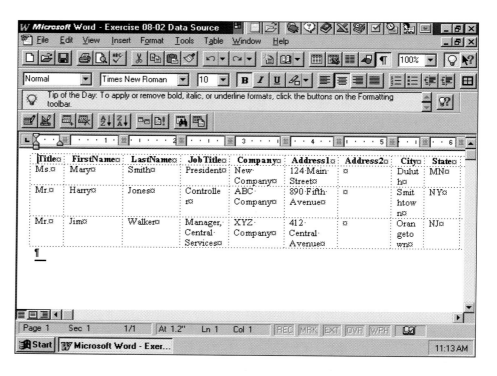

Figure 8-5
Data source records
in table format.

7. To save the records you entered, click the **Save** tool.

8. To return to the Data Form, click the **Data Form** tool on the Mail Merge toolbar (first on left).

9. When you are finished with the Data Form, click **OK.**

 10. To insert merge fields in your main document, click the **Mail Merge Main Document** tool.

❖ PREPARING THE MAIN DOCUMENT

You can now enter the form letter for the three registrants in the main document. You type everything that remains the same for each of the letters in the document, and you insert merge fields for each of the variable pieces of information.

| Insert Merge Field | You cannot enter the merge fields by inserting chevrons (« ») and typing the name of the field, although you might think you could after looking at Figure 8-6. You must enter the fields with the Insert Merge Field tool on the Mail Merge toolbar. When inserting merge fields, you must be careful to enter all spacing and punctuation that will be needed around the merged data.

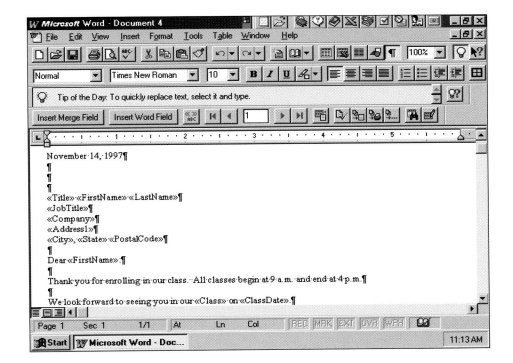

Figure 8-6
Merge fields are
set off by chevrons
in this document.

Exercise 8-4

1. To move the insertion point to 2.5 inches from the top of the page, press **(Enter)** nine times. Watch the status bar as you press **(Enter)** to see the position on the page.

2. To enter today's date, click the **Insert** menu and then click the **Date and Time** command. Click the fourth format on the list showing the *December 7, 1997* format and click **OK.**

3. To move to the position where you begin entering the inside address, press **(Enter)** four times.

4. To enter the first merge field, the recipient's title, click the **Insert Merge Field** tool on the Mail Merge toolbar and click **Title** in the drop-down list. Notice Word displays the field name in chevrons (<< >>).

5. To leave a space between the person's title and first name, type a *space.*

6. To enter the first name, click the **Insert Merge Field** tool again and click **FirstName**. Type a *space.*

7. To enter the last name, click the **Insert Merge Field** tool again and click **LastName.** To move to the next line, press **(Enter)**.

8. To enter the job title, click the **Insert Merge Field** tool and click **JobTitle.** To move to the next line, press **(Enter)**.

9. To insert the company, click the **Insert Merge Field** tool and click **Company.** Press (Enter).

10. To enter the first line of the address, click the **Insert Merge Field** tool and click **Address1.** Press (Enter).

11. To enter the city, click the **Insert Merge Field** tool and click **City.** Type a *comma,* and a *space.*

12. To enter the state, click the **Insert Merge Field** tool and click **State.** Type a *space.*

13. To enter the ZIP code, click the **Insert Merge Field** tool and click **PostalCode.** Press (Enter) twice.

14. Type **Dear** and type a *space.*

15. To enter the first name, click the **Insert Merge Field** and click **FirstName.** Type a *colon (:).*

16. Press (Enter) twice, and type the following: **Thank you for enrolling in our class. All classes begin at 9 a.m. and end at 4 p.m.**

17. To begin a new paragraph, press (Enter) twice. Type **We look forward to seeing you in our** (do not type a period here). Type a *space.* Click the **Insert Merge Field** tool and click **Class.** Type a *space* and the word **on,** followed by a *space.* Click **Insert Merge Field** and click **ClassDate.** Type a *period (.).*

18. To enter the closing for the letter, press (Enter) twice. Type **Sincerely** and a *comma (,).* Press (Enter) four times. Type *your name.*

19. To save the main document, click the **Save** tool and type **Exercise 08-04 Main Document** and click **Save.**

Does your main document look like the one shown in Figure 8-6?

❖ USING THE MERGE AND DATABASE TOOLBARS

When you open a main document that has been identified as a main document, Word displays the Mail Merge toolbar, shown in Figure 8-7.

Figure 8-7
The Mail Merge toolbar.

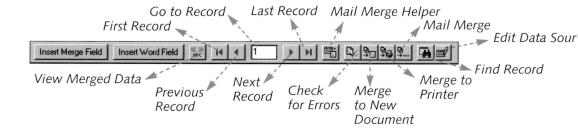

When you view a data source document, Word displays the Database toolbar shown in Figure 8-8.

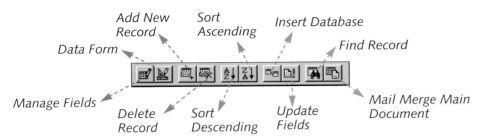

Figure 8-8
The Database toolbar.

 You can use the View Merged Data tool to look at the merged form letters for errors before you send them to the printer. You can also use the Print tool or command to print the merged letter on the screen.

 You can use the First Record, Previous Record, Next Record, and Last Record tools to see the merged form letters for each of the records in your data source.

Exercise 8-5

1. To see the merged form for record 1, click the **View Merged Data** tool.

2. To see the merged form letter for record 2, click the **Next Record** tool. Notice the last sentence needs to have the word *class* after the merged name of the class.

3. To return to the main document, click the **View Merged Data** tool again.

4. To enter the word *class* and a space, click the **I-beam** before the word *on* after the **Class** merge field, and type **class** and a *space.*

5. Click the **Save** tool to save the change.

❖ PRINTING AND SAVING MERGED FORM LETTERS

You can merge to the printer or to a file. It is usually not necessary to keep a copy of each merged form letter you produce, and it would waste a lot of disk space to do so. It is usually enough to merge to the printer and keep a copy of the main document and the data source file.

You can use the Merge to Printer tool on the Mail Merge toolbar to merge the form letters at the printer.

❖ PRODUCING ENVELOPES AND LABELS WITH MAIL MERGE

You can use the Mail Merge command on the Tools menu to produce envelopes or mailing labels for your form letters. You choose either Envelopes or Mailing Labels in the Main Document Create drop-down list in the Mail Merge Helper, shown in Figure 8-1. You can use the same data source you used for the form letters.

Word uses information from your currently selected printer to print envelopes. You will need to know the type of envelope feeder your printer uses. You also have to specify the size of envelope you are using.

Word must know the type of labels you will use to set up for labels. You will do the following exercise using options that may not apply to your printer so you can see how a mailing label merge document looks.

Exercise 8-6

1. To merge the main document with the data source, click the **Merge to Printer** tool on the Mail Merge toolbar.

2. Click **OK.** The documents will be printed.

3. To create mailing labels, click the **Mail Merge Helper** tool. Click **Main Document Create** and click **Mailing Labels.** Click **New Main Document.** Click **Data Source Get Data.** Click **Open Data Source** and double-click the file name you gave your data source **(Exercise 08-02 Data Source).**

4. To display the Label Options dialog box shown in Figure 8-9, click **Set Up Main Document.**

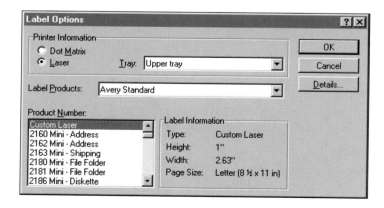

Figure 8-9
The Label Options dialog box offers a number of options.

5. To signal the type of printer, click **Laser.**

6. To set the tray, click **Default Tray (Auto Sheet Feed).** (The exact wording of this option may vary depending on the type of printer being used.)

7. To signal the type of labels to be used, click **Avery Standard.**

8. To signal the product number, click **Custom Laser** and click **OK.**

9. Enter the merge fields for the label so yours looks like the one shown in Figure 8-10:

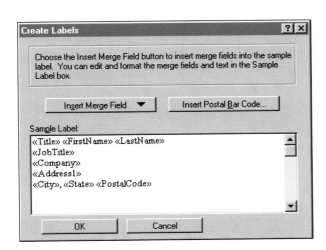

Figure 8-10
The Create Labels
dialog box with
merge fields
entered.

Click **Insert Merge Field,** click **Title,** type a *space*.

Click **Insert Merge Field,** click **FirstName,** type a *space*.

Click **Insert Merge Field,** click **LastName,** press (Enter).

Click **Insert Merge Field,** click **JobTitle,** press (Enter).

Click **Insert Merge Field,** click **Company,** press (Enter).

Click **Insert Merge Field,** click **Address1,** press (Enter).

Click **Insert Merge Field,** click **City,** type a *comma* and a *space*.

Click **Insert Merge Field,** click **State,** type a *space*.

Click **Insert Merge Field,** click **PostalCode**.

Click **OK**.

10. To begin the merge, click **Merge** in the Merge Data with the Document section of the Mail Merge Helper, and click **Merge** in the Merge dialog box shown in Figure 8-11.

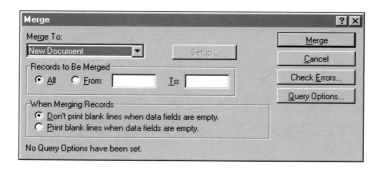

Figure 8-11
Clicking on
Merge starts the
mail merge.

You can see the merged label document in Figure 8-12. Word names the unsaved document Labels to distinguish the merged document from others. You can use whatever file name you want when you save the document.

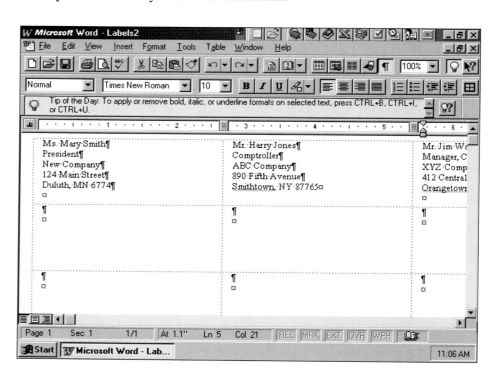

Figure 8-12
The merged label
document showing
three records.

Exercise 8-7

1. To print the labels, click the **Print** tool. (You can print on plain paper to see how labels would print.)

2. To close the open documents, hold (**Shift**) and click **File,** and then click **Close All.** Respond **No** when asked to save changes.

❖ USING A DATA SOURCE FROM ANOTHER APPLICATION

You can use data from another application such as Microsoft Excel, Microsoft Access, Paradox, or WordPerfect when working with Mail Merge. Click the Get Data button and then Open Data Source in the Mail Merge Helper dialog box. Type or select the file name of the data source, and then select the appropriate option in the List Files of Type box. Word provides converters for many types of files.

❖ SELECTING AND SORTING RECORDS

You can use the Query Options button in the Mail Merge Helper dialog box to select a particular set of data records for a merge. On the Filter Records tab in the Query Options dialog box, you can specify what rules Word should use to retrieve (filter) the information you want.

A selection rule is made up of three parts:

1. A field name from your data source.

2. A comparison phrase such as Equal To or Is Not Blank.

3. Text or numbers you want the data field compared with.

You can specify as many as six selection rules to narrow the range of records selected.

You can also use the Sort tab in the Query Options dialog box to sort records in alphabetical or numerical order based on the contents of selected data fields. You could, for instance, put a large mailing in postal code order for the post office.

You created a data source file with three records. Two of those records are for registrants in a Word class; the third is for an Excel class. If you wish, you can send a form letter to just those in the Word class.

Exercise 8-8

1. To open an existing main document, click the **Open** tool and double-click **Exercise 08-08 Main Document.**

2. To display the Mail Merge Helper dialog box, click **Tools** and then **Mail Merge.** Notice the Main Document and Get Data boxes on the Mail Merge Helper contain the proper information because these documents have already been used in a mail merge.

3. To open the dialog box shown in Figure 8-13, click **Query Options.**

4. To see the list of fields in your data source, click the **Field** drop-down arrow.

5. To enter Class as the filter field, scroll to and click **Class.** Notice Equal To is already in the Comparison field and your insertion point is in the Compare To field.

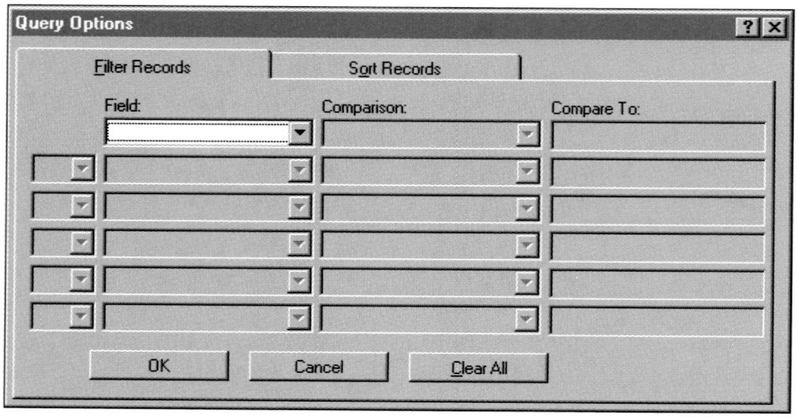

Figure 8-13
In the Query
Options dialog
box you select a
set of data records
for a merge.

6. To select just the records for Word classes, type **Word** and click **OK.**

7. To merge to a new document, click **Merge** in the Mail Merge Helper dialog box. Notice you are merging to a new document. Then click **Merge** in the Merge dialog box. You are now looking at the document Form Letters, like Document1, Document2, and so on, containing the merged form letters. Word gives each form letter's document a name and consecutive number. Scroll through and notice that only two form letters were merged. Notice also the section break between the letters.

❖ ADDING RECORDS TO A DATA SOURCE

You can use the Data Form dialog box to edit, add, and delete data records. To open the Data Form dialog box, click the Edit button under Data Source in the Mail Merge Helper dialog box.

❖ ADDING OR DELETING DATA FIELDS IN A DATA SOURCE

You can add and delete data fields in a data source document. If you remove a field, all information in that field in *any* record is deleted. Use the Edit button under Data Source in the Mail Merge Helper dialog box to display the Data Form. Then use View Form and the Manage Fields tool on the Database toolbar.

The Manage Fields dialog box shown in Figure 8-14 appears. You can use this dialog box to add, remove, or rename fields.

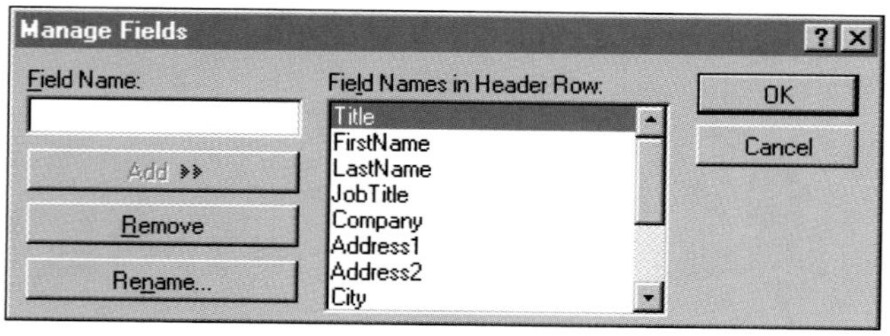

Figure 8-14
Add, remove, or
rename fields in
the Manage Fields
dialog box.

Exercise 8-9

1. To make **Exercise 08-08 Main Document** active, click the **Window** menu and **Exercise 08-08 Main Document.**

2. To display the Mail Merge dialog box, click the **Mail Merge Helper** tool.

3. To edit a data source document, click **Edit** under **Data Source** and click **Exercise 08-09 Merge Data.**

4. To see the source, click **View Source** in the Data Form dialog box.

5. To display the Manage Fields dialog box, click the **Manage Fields** tool (second from left).

6. To add a field for a fee, type **Fee** in the Field Name box and click **Add.**

7. To remove the Address2 field, click **Address2** and click **Remove.**

8. To cancel the deletion, respond **No.**

9. To return to the data document, click **OK.**

10. To save your changes, click the **Save** tool.

11. To close all the open documents, hold **Shift** and click **File,** and then click **Close All.** Respond **No** when asked to save changes.

❖ S U M M A R Y

You have now learned how to use Mail Merge Helper, how to work with a main document and a data source, how to use the Mail Merge and Database toolbars, how to merge to a new document and to the printer, how to print envelopes and labels, and how to use some advanced merge techniques.

Try the exercises on the following pages to test how well you remember what you learned. Don't be afraid to go back and look up answers, because that will help to reinforce what you learned.

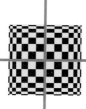

activities

*On the blank line before each sentence, place a **T** if the statement is true or an **F** if it is false.*

_____ 1. The data source contains all items that remain the same in each letter along with merge fields.

_____ 2. The main document contains the database.

_____ 3. You should always separate the city, state, and ZIP code when entering fields in a database so you can sort and select using the individual fields.

_____ 4. There is no need to have a field for a person's title (Mr., Mrs., Ms.).

_____ 5. You can use the Move buttons in the Create Data Source dialog box to change the order of fields.

_____ 6. You can type chevrons (≪ ≫) around the field names in a main document instead of using the Insert Merge Field button.

_____ 7. There is usually no need to save a document with all merged form letters, because you have a copy of the main document and the data source.

_____ 8. When you want to create envelopes or labels, you can use the same data source you used for the form letter.

_____ 9. You cannot use data from other applications with Word's Mail Merge.

_____ 10. You can add or remove fields from your data source after you have been using it for a while.

❖ COMPLETION

Fill in the blanks in the following statements.

1. The _____ document contains the information that remains the same in each form along with merge fields for variable information.

2. You can use the same _____ for many different form letters.

3. You must use the Insert Merge Field button to enter _____ in your main document.

4. You can merge to a(n) _____ or to the _____.

5. You can use the _____ button in the Mail Merge Helper dialog box to select records or to sort records for merging.

review

Review Exercise 8-1

1. Use online Help to get information about sorting merge records.
2. Search the Help index and choose **customizing with fields.**
3. Print the information you find.

Review Exercise 8-2

1. Perform a Mail Merge using **Review 08-02 Main Document** as the main document and **Review 08-02 Merge Data** as the data source.
2. Print the merged memos.
3. When you finish merging the form letters, print labels for the recipients.

Review Exercise 8-3

1. Proofread the merged memos from Review Exercise 8-2.
2. Return to the data file to correct the spacing problems in the class date.
3. Merge and print the memos again.
4. Save and close the document.

On Your Own

You are president of the Northeast Computer Users group. You know from calls you receive from the membership that there is a need to educate some of the members about the Internet.

1. Use Mail Merge to write a letter to six members you know have been using the Internet asking them to share their knowledge with the rest of the group at meetings to be held in the near future.
2. Use Mail Merge to print envelopes for the mailing as well.
3. Save and Close the documents.

lesson 9

Inserting Pictures, Frames, and Objects

❖ OBJECTIVES

When you complete this lesson, you will be able to:

1. Insert a graphic.

2. Size and crop a graphic.

3. Add borders to a graphic.

4. Use a frame to position graphics on the page.

5. Use tables with graphics.

6. Insert objects in a document.

7. Use the Drawing toolbar.

Estimated Time: $1\frac{1}{2}$ hours

❖ INTRODUCTION

Graphics filters installed when you installed the Word program let you import graphics in many different formats. A graphics filter is a software program that enables Word to display a file from another application.

To import a graphic from another application:

❖ Choose Picture from the Insert menu.

or

❖ Copy a graphic in another file to the Clipboard and paste the Clipboard's contents in your document.

Word treats a graphic as a single character. You can size a graphic to make it larger or smaller. You can also crop or trim a graphic to hide parts you do not want to display. You can use the Frame command on the Insert menu to position your graphic so text flows around it.

If you did a complete installation, you also installed graphics files called *clip art* in the **Clipart** folder.

> **note**
>
> If whoever installed Word did not do a complete install-ation, you may have to run the Microsoft Word Setup program again to install the filters.

❖ INSERTING A GRAPHICS FILE

You can use the Picture command on the Insert menu to place a graphics file in a document. Remember, you must have installed the appropriate filters when installing the Word software.

The Insert Picture dialog box displayed in Figure 9-1 lets you preview the picture before you insert it in your document. It also lets you save the picture in the document or store only a link to the picture. When you store only a link, Word finds the picture file and inserts it in your document.

Preview button

Figure 9-1
Use the Insert
Picture dialog
box to preview
a graphic.

You can save both the picture and a link in the document so you will always have the updated version of the graphic. Storing only a link does not increase the file size of your document. However, if you store only the link, Word takes longer to display the graphic.

For more information on importing graphics from various file formats, you can double-click the Help tool, type **readme,** press (**Enter**), and then click Graphics Filters.

Exercise 9-1

1. To open a new document, click the **New** tool.

2. To insert a graphic at the insertion point, click the **Insert** menu and then **Picture.**

3. To preview a picture, click **Clipart**, click the **Books.wmf** file in the Name list, and click the **Preview** button (see Figure 9-1).

4. To insert the picture, click **OK.**

❖ SIZING AND CROPPING GRAPHICS

You can resize a graphic proportionally, or you can stretch the graphic vertically or horizontally. To resize a graphic proportionally, drag a corner handle. To resize a graphic by distorting it horizontally or vertically, drag a middle handle.

You can crop a graphic to hide areas you do not want to display, or you can add white space around a graphic.

You can also use the Picture command on the Format menu to size, crop, and add white space using precise measurements (see Figure 9-2).

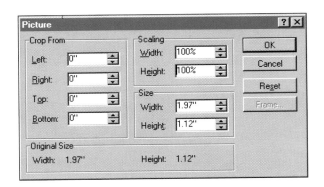

Figure 9-2
You can modify a graphic precisely using the Picture command.

To return to the original graphic, use the Reset button in the Picture dialog box.

You must select the graphic by clicking on it before you can size or crop it. When you select a graphic, Word displays eight sizing handles around it, as you can see in Figure 9-3.

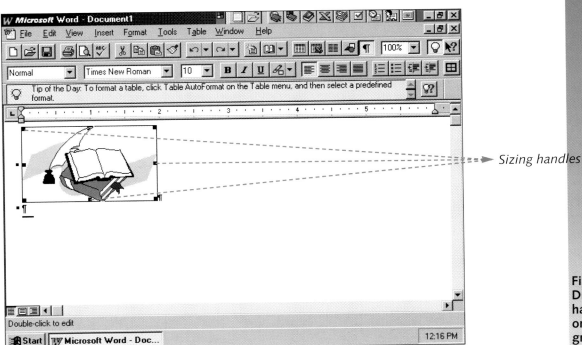

Sizing handles

Figure 9-3
Dragging the sizing handles sizes or crops a selected graphic.

1. To select it, click anywhere on the **Books graphic.**

2. To make the graphic proportionally larger, drag the handle at the **lower-right** corner downward and release.

3. To return to the original size, click the **Undo** tool.

4. To stretch the graphic horizontally, drag the **middle** handle on the **right side** of the graphic to the right and release.

5. To return to the original size, click the **Undo** tool.

6. To stretch the graphic vertically, drag the **middle** handle on the **bottom** of the graphic down and release.

7. To return to the original size, click the **Undo** tool.

8. To crop the graphic so it resembles the one shown in Figure 9-4, hold (Shift) and drag the **middle** handle on the **right** side of the graphic to the left. Word displays the cropping measurements in the status bar.

Figure 9-4
This graphic has been cropped using a sizing handle.

9. To return to the original display, click **Undo.**

10. To add white space to the right and bottom of the graphic, hold (Shift) and drag the **bottom right** handle.

11. To return to the original size, click the **Format** menu and click **Picture.** Click **Reset** and click **OK.**

❖ ADDING BORDERS TO A GRAPHIC

You can add borders to a graphic the same way you add them to paragraphs of text or cells in a table. Use the Borders tool on the Formatting toolbar or the Borders and Shading command on the Format menu to add borders. The Shading tab in the Borders and Shading dialog box is gray because you cannot use shading with graphics.

Exercise 9-3

1. To select the graphic if it is not already selected, click it.

2. To add a border, click the **Format** menu and click **Borders and Shading.** Click the **Shadow** box and click **OK.**

3. To print the graphic, click the **Print** tool.

4. To save and close the file, click the **Save** tool and then click the **Close** button at the right side of the menu bar.

❖ USING A FRAME TO POSITION GRAPHICS

Because Word treats each graphic as a single character, you must use either the Frame command or the Tables feature to help position a graphic in a document.

You can use the Frame command on the Insert menu to position a graphic on the page and to wrap text around it. A *frame* is a box you add to a document. Frames can be moved anywhere on the page, and text can flow around them.

Frames appear at the left margin in the normal view. You must use page layout view to see frames in their correct positions on the page and to move them.

Exercise 9-4

1. To open a document, click the **Open** tool and double-click **Exercise 09-04 Insert Graphic.**

2. If nonprinting marks are not displayed, click the **Show/Hide** tool.

3. To insert a computer graphic into the document, click the **Insert** menu and then **Picture.** Double-click **Computer.wmf.**

4. To select the graphic, click on it.

5. To place a frame around the graphic, click the **Insert** menu and then **Frame.** If you are asked whether you want to switch to page layout view, click **Yes.**

You can see the frame and its shaded border in Figure 9-5. You can also see an anchor next to the title paragraph signaling the frame is anchored to that paragraph. The shaded border and the anchor do not print.

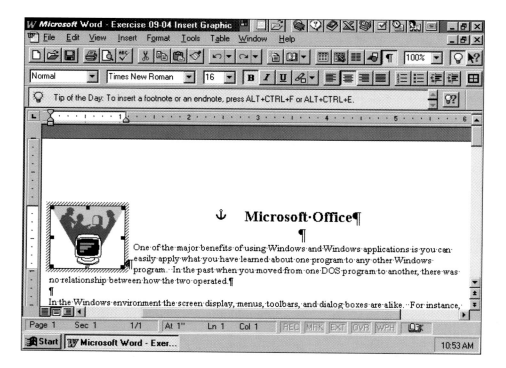

Figure 9-5
Use the Frame
command to frame
and place a graphic.

Exercise 9-5

1. To see the frame in normal view, click the **View** menu and click **Normal.**

2. To return to page layout view, click the **Page Layout View** button on the status bar.

3. To reposition the graphic, drag the graphic to the position shown in Figure 9-6.

4. To add a shadow border to the frame, click the **Format** menu and **Borders and Shading.** Click the **Shadow** option and click **OK.**

5. To deselect the graphic so you can see the effect, click somewhere in white space.

6. Experiment with moving the frame to different places on the document.

7. To print the document, click the **Print** tool.

8. To save and close the file, click the **Save** tool and then click the **Close** button at the right side of the menu bar.

You can also insert a frame for regular text. Use a frame when you want to position text in a specific place on a page or when you want other text to flow around it.

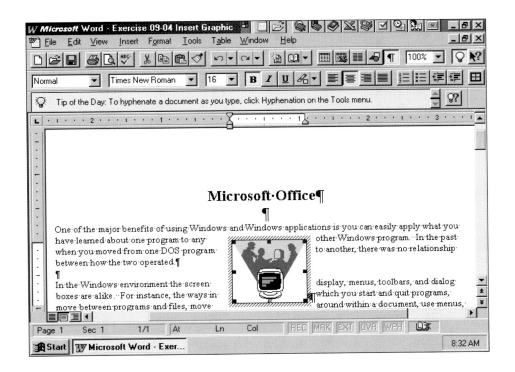

Figure 9-6
Text flows around the repositioned graphic.

❖ USING TABLES WITH GRAPHICS

You can use a table when you want to position text beside a graphic. Create a two-column table, and enter the text in one column and the graphic in the other.

Refer to Figure 9-7 to see how your screen should look when you finish this exercise.

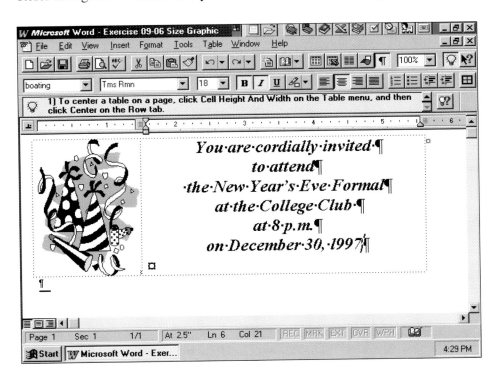

Figure 9-7
This invitation has been created in a two-column table.

Exercise 9-6

1. To open a document, click the **Open** tool and double-click **Exercise 09-06 Size Graphic.**

2. To insert the party graphic, click the **Insert** menu and then **Picture**. Double-click **Party.wmf**.

3. Experiment with sizing the graphic to improve the look of the invitation.

4. To print the document, click the **Print** tool.

5. To save and close the document, click the **Save** tool and then click the **Close** button at the right side of the menu bar.

Remember, you can use paper sizes other than 8½ by 11 inches.

❖ INSERTING OBJECTS

You can use the Object command on the Insert menu to use Word's object linking and embedding feature, known as OLE. Use the Object command to start another application. Use the toolbars, dialog boxes, and menus in that application to create an object, and then exit from the other application and return to Word.

Whenever you want to edit an object, double-click it. Word will restart the application you used to create the object.

You can also insert information from another application by copying a selection to the Clipboard and pasting it in your document.

USING WORDART

You can use the WordArt application to create interesting text effects to enhance documents. You can fit text into a variety of shapes, use unusual alignments, and add 3-D effects.

When you start WordArt, the WordArt menu replaces the Word menu, and a text entry box and toolbar appear in the document window (see Figure 9-8).

You can enclose a WordArt object in a frame and resize it, edit it, and add borders to it. You can return to the WordArt application at any time by double-clicking the object.

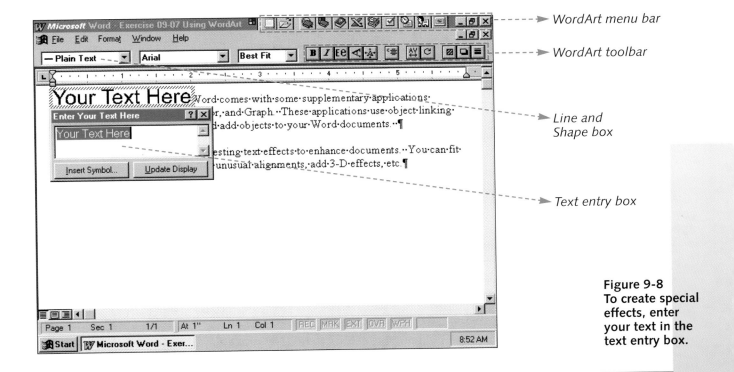

WordArt menu bar

WordArt toolbar

Line and Shape box

Text entry box

Figure 9-8
To create special effects, enter your text in the text entry box.

Exercise 9-7

1. To open a document, click the **Open** tool and double-click **Exercise 09-07 Using WordArt.**

2. To insert a WordArt object at the insertion point, click the **Insert** menu and then **Object.** Scroll through the list of applications and double-click **Microsoft WordArt 2.0.**

3. To enter a heading, type **Fun with WordArt** in the WordArt dialog box.

4. To open the **Line and Shape** box shown in Figure 9-8, click it.

5. To apply a format of your choosing, click it.

6. To return to Word, click in white space outside the WordArt object.

7. To remove the handles, click on white space outside the object.

8. To return to the ClipArt application and its menus, double-click the object.

9. To return to Word, click in white space outside the WordArt object again.

10. To print the document, click the **Print** tool.

11. To save and close the document, click the **Save** tool and then click the **Close** button at the right side of the menu bar.

USING EQUATION EDITOR

You can easily enter fractions, exponents, integrals, and other mathematical elements in a Word document. Use the Object command on the Insert menu to access Microsoft Equation 2.0.

You can see the Equation Editor toolbar in Figure 9-9. When the Equation Editor toolbar and menus appear, you create your equation by typing the variable names and choosing symbols.

Figure 9-9
Equation Editor lets you insert mathematical elements such as fractions and exponents in your document.

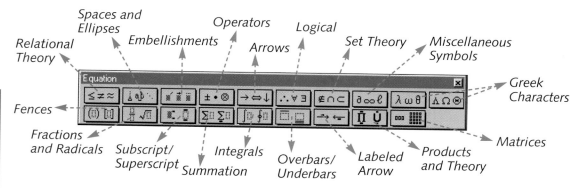

The toolbar is a graphical menu. You click a button to enter an element.

Items on the top row are symbols that you insert in an equation. The items in the bottom row are called templates because they contain fences, radicals, and summation functions.

To add an element:

❖ Click the appropriate button.

❖ Drag the item you want to add.

❖ Release.

The elements you add to an equation fit into slots. Slots expand as you add text.

Equation Editor does most formatting for you. Equation Editor applies superscript format, reduces the font size of exponents, formats variables in italic, and adjusts spacing between elements. When using Equation Editor, you usually should not type spaces or add superscript, subscript, italic, or other formatting.

You will enter the following equation using the Equation Editor:

$$\frac{ab + \sqrt{b^2}}{2b} = x$$

Exercise 9-8

1. To open the document, click the **Open** tool and double-click **Exercise 09-08 Equation Editor.**

2. To move to the end of the document, hold (Ctrl) and press (End).

3. To open the Equation Editor, click the **Insert** menu and click **Object.** Then double-click **Microsoft Equation 2.0.**

4. To enter the fraction line, click the **Fractions and Radicals** button and select the **top left** button on the drop-down list.

5. To begin entering the part of the equation above the line, type **ab+.**

6. To enter the square root symbol, click the **Fractions and Radicals** button and select the **fourth** button on the **left.**

7. Type **b.**

8. To enter the exponent slot, click the **Subscript/Superscript** button and select the **first** button on the **left.**

9. To enter an exponent, type **2** in the exponent slot.

10. To move the insertion point out of the exponent slot, press (→).

11. To move the insertion point into the slot below the bar, press (↓).

12. Type **2b.**

13. To move the insertion point out of the slot, press (→).

14. To enter the rest of the equation, type **=x.**

15. To return to Word, click in white space outside Equation Editor.

16. To remove the handles on the equation, click in white space again.

17. To save and close the document, click the **Save** tool and then click the **Close** button at the right side of the menu bar.

❖ DRAWING

You can use the tools on the Drawing toolbar to create squares, rectangles, polygons, lines, and ellipses. You can also use the Drawing toolbar to add callouts to graphics.

Refer to Figure 9-10 throughout this lesson if you need to check to see which tool to use.

You can combine shapes drawn in Word to create organization charts, flowcharts, maps, and other line drawings.

> **note**
>
> Use the Drawing tools to add a watermark like the one you saw in the memo template.

> **note**
>
> You must be in page layout view or Print Preview to see drawing objects.

When you create an object, it appears in front of text or other drawing objects. You can move objects behind text or behind and in front of other drawing objects. You can also align objects by *snapping* them to a grid.

Figure 9-10
The Drawing toolbar lets you create various shapes and callouts.

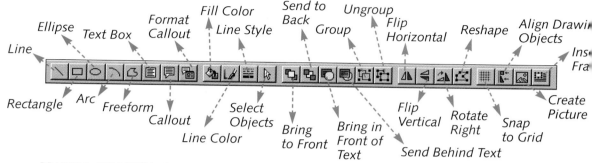

DRAWING, SELECTING, MOVING, AND COPYING WITH TOOLS

To draw an object:

- ✦ Click the appropriate tool on the Drawing toolbar.

- ✦ Position the crosshairs where you want the object to begin.

- ✦ Drag to create the object.

- ✦ Release.

To create a square or a circle while using the Rectangle and Ellipse tools, hold **Shift** while dragging.

To draw rectangles, squares, arcs, ellipses, and circles from the center of the graphic outward, hold **Ctrl** while dragging.

To create a straight line, hold **Shift** while using the Line tool.

To delete a drawing object, click the object to select it and press **Delete**.

To move a drawing object, select it and then position the pointer on the object—but not on a handle—and drag it to a new position.

To make a copy of a drawing object, hold **Ctrl** while dragging the object.

Refer to Figure 9-11 when working on the following exercise. When you finish, your screen should look similar to the one shown. Notice the handles on the square. They signify the square is selected.

Exercise 9-9

1. To open a new document, click the **New** tool.

2. To display the Drawing toolbar, click the **Drawing** tool.

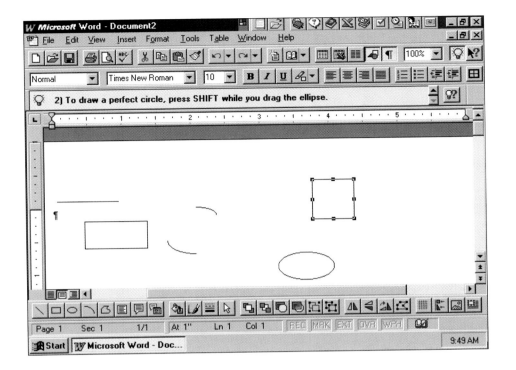

Figure 9-11
You will create these objects in Exercise 9-9 using the Drawing tool.

3. Click the **Line Color** tool and make certain Black is selected. Click the **Fill Color** tool and make certain None is selected.

4. To draw a line similar to the one in Figure 9-11, click the **Line** tool on the Drawing toolbar, position the crosshairs where you want the line to begin, drag until the line is the length you want, and release.

5. To draw a rectangle, click the **Rectangle** tool, position the crosshairs where you want the top-left corner to begin, drag down and right until the rectangle is the size you want, and release.

6. To draw an ellipse, click the **Ellipse** tool, position the crosshairs where you want the ellipse to begin, drag down and right until the ellipse is the size you want, and release.

7. To draw an arc, click the **Arc** tool, position the crosshairs where you want the arc to begin, drag down until the arc is the size you want, and release. (You can drag up to reverse the direction of the arc.)

8. To draw a square, click the **Rectangle** tool, position the crosshairs where you want the top-left corner to begin, hold (Shift), drag the crosshairs down and left until the square is the size you want, and release.

9. To select the rectangle, click on its line.

10. To delete the rectangle, press (Delete).

11. To undo the delete, click the **Undo** tool.

12. To select both the line and the rectangle, click the **Select Drawing Objects** tool, drag the pointer to draw a box around the objects, and release.

13. To move the line and the rectangle up a bit on the page, point to the selection but not to a handle. When you see the arrow with the double-pointing crossed arrows beneath, drag the items up a small distance.

14. To cancel the selection, click in white space.

15. To write your first name with the Freeform tool (not an easy task), click the **Freeform** tool, position the crosshairs where you want to begin, attempt to write your name, and double-click when you are finished.

16. Spend a few minutes experimenting with drawing, deleting, and moving lines, rectangles, ellipses, and arcs, and use the **Freeform** tool as well.

17. To save and close the document, click the **Save** tool, type **Exercise 09-09 Graphic,** click **Save,** and click the **Close** button at the right side of the menu bar.

USING CALLOUTS

You can use the Callout tool on the Drawing toolbar to create callouts, as shown in Figure 9-12, to label parts of your graphic objects.

Refer to Figure 9-12 during the exercise so you can see how to place the callouts.

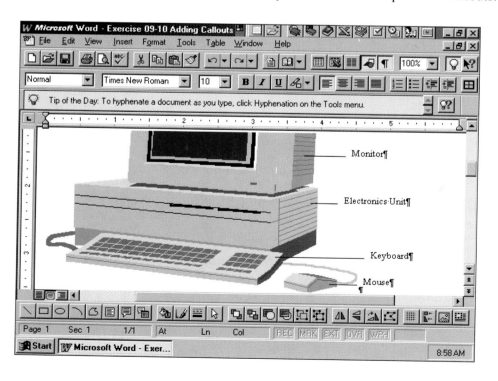

Figure 9-12
Callouts are useful for labeling and explaining your graphics.

Exercise 9-10

1. To open a document, click the **Open** tool and then double-click **Exercise 09-10 Adding Callouts.**

2. To see the entire computer on the screen, scroll down a little.

3. To check to see what callout format is in effect, click the **Format Callout** tool, click **Three** to select that format, and click **OK.**

4. To enter the callout for the monitor, click the **Callout** tool, position the crosshairs where the callout line begins in Figure 9-12, drag to the right, release, type **Monitor,** and click outside the callout.

5. Repeat step 4 for the electronics unit, keyboard, and mouse.

USING TEXT BOXES

You can use a text box to position text on a page. Unlike frames, text boxes do not automatically expand as you add text to them. If you add text that does not fit within the text box, you must make the text box larger.

Refer to Figure 9-13 to see where to place the text box in this exercise.

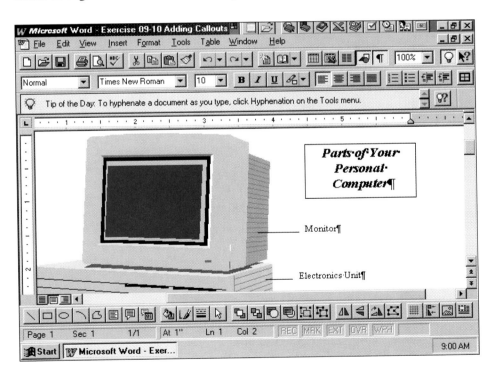

Figure 9-13
Use the Text Box tool to create the text box shown in the upper-right corner of the screen.

Exercise 9-11

1. To enter the text box shown in Figure 9-13, click the **Text Box** tool, position the crosshairs at the top-right corner where you want the text box, drag down and right, and release.

2. To enter the text, type **Parts of Your Personal Computer.**

3. To format the text, select the text in the box, click the **Size** drop-down button on the Formatting toolbar, click **14**, click the **Bold** tool, click the **Italic** tool, and click the **Center** tool.

4. If all of the text is not displayed, click the text box to select it, drag the lower-right handle until all the text fits, and release.

5. To print the document, click the **Print** tool.

6. To save and close the document, click the **Save** tool and then click the **Close** button at the right side of the menu bar.

FORMATTING DRAWING OBJECTS

You can use the Drawing toolbar or the Drawing Object command on the Format menu to format drawing objects. The Drawing Defaults dialog box is displayed in Figure 9-14.

**Figure 9-14
Format drawing objects in various ways in the Drawing Defaults dialog box.**

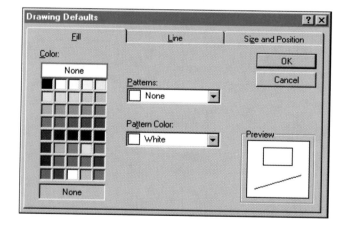

CHANGING LINES AND FILL

You can use the Line Style, Line Color, and Fill Color tools on the Drawing toolbar to change the thickness, style, and color of lines in a drawing object and the color and pattern of the object's fill.

LAYERING DRAWING OBJECTS

Word documents have three layers:

1. The text layer.

2. The layer behind the text.

3. The layer in front of the text.

As you can see in Figure 9-15, when you create a drawing object, the object is placed in the layer in front of the text. You can use Bring to Front, Send to Back, Bring in Front of Text, and Send Behind Text tools to move drawing objects from layer to layer.

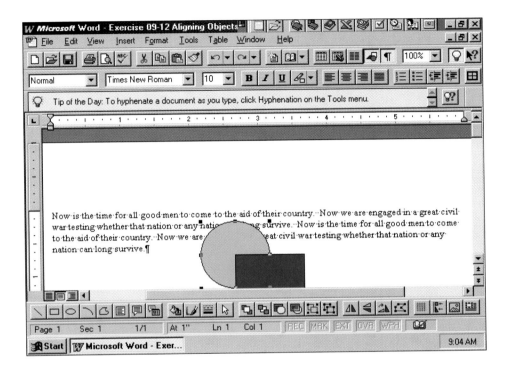

GROUPING DRAWING OBJECTS

You can use the Group tool on the Drawing toolbar to group two or more drawing objects when you want to treat two or more objects as a single unit. If you want to ungroup objects, use the Ungroup tool.

SELECTING MULTIPLE OBJECTS

You can select more than one object at a time by holding **Shift** while you click each of the objects.

ALIGNING DRAWING OBJECTS

You can align drawing objects by selecting the objects you want to align and clicking the Align Drawing Objects tool.

Exercise 9-12

1. To open a document, click the **Open** tool and double-click **Exercise 09-12 Aligning Objects.** Make certain that you are in page layout view.

2. To add a color fill to the circle, click a **border** of the circle to display its handles, click the **Fill Color** tool, and click an **aqua** color.

3. To add a color fill to the square, click a **border** of the square to display its handles, click the **Fill Color** tool, and click a **purple** color.

4.	To move the square behind the circle, click the **Send to Back** tool.

5.	To move the circle behind the text, click anywhere in the **circle** to display its handles, and click the **Send Behind Text** tool.

6.	To change the style of the circle's border, click the **Line Style** tool, and click one of the **broken lines.**

7.	To group the circle and the square as a single unit with one set of handles, click the **Select Drawing Objects** tool, drag the **crosshairs** to draw a box around the objects, and click the **Group** button on the Drawing toolbar.

8.	To ungroup the objects, click the **Ungroup** tool.

9.	To align the square and the circle, click the **Align Drawing Objects** tool, click **Top** in the Vertical box displayed in Figure 9-16, and click **OK.**

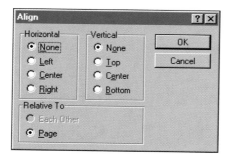

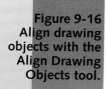

Figure 9-16
Align drawing
objects with the
Align Drawing
Objects tool.

10.	To save and close the document, click the **Save** tool, click the **File** menu, and click **Close**.

RESIZING DRAWING OBJECTS

You can drag a handle to change the size or shape of a drawing object. If you want to maintain the original proportion of the drawing object, hold (Shift) as you drag. You can resize from the center by holding (Ctrl) as you drag a handle.

RESHAPING A FREEFORM DRAWING

A freeform shape consists of connected line segments. When you click a freeform shape, you select the shape as a whole. Click the Reshape tool to select all of the line segments. Then you can drag any handle to change the shape of the object.

You can also add or delete handles when they are selected.

Exercise 9-13

1. To open a file, click the **Open** tool and double-click **Exercise 09-13 Change Shape.** Make certain that you are in page layout view.

2. To increase the size of the rectangle, click a border to select it, drag the **right middle** handle to the right, and release.

3. To return to the original size, click the **Undo** tool.

4. To increase the size of the circle proportionally, click a border to select it, hold (Shift) and drag a **corner** handle.

5. To return to the original size, click the **Undo** tool.

6. To change the shape of the freeform drawing, click to select the drawing, click the **Reshape** button to select all segments, and drag a point on the right side of the drawing so that your drawing looks like the one in Figure 9-17.

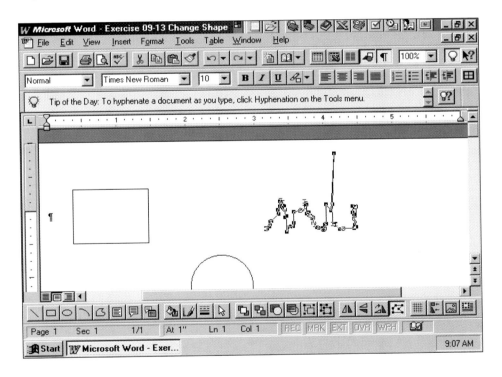

Figure 9-17
You can reshape a freeform drawing by dragging a point.

7. Experiment with sizing and reshaping drawing objects for a few minutes.

8. To save and close the document, click the **Save** tool and then click the **Close** button at the right side of the menu bar.

ROTATING AND FLIPPING DRAWING OBJECTS

You can use the Rotate Right tool to rotate a drawing object or group to the right in 90-degree increments. You cannot rotate patterns, text, or imported graphics.

You can create a mirror image of a drawing object or group by flipping it with the Flip Horizontal or Flip Vertical tool. You cannot flip patterns or text.

USING GRIDLINES

The grid is an invisible network of lines that covers the drawing area. Gridlines do not print, and you cannot see them on the screen. By default, drawing objects *snap* to the grid. In other words, when you drag an object close to a gridline, Word pulls the object into alignment with the gridline. This feature makes it easy to align your objects with one another. If you use the Snap to Grid tool to turn off gridlines, you can position items more freely.

Exercise 9-14

1. To open a file, click the **Open** tool and double-click **Exercise 09-14 Rotate Graphic.**

2. To select the rectangle and the circle, click the **Select Drawing Objects** tool and draw a **box** around the two **drawing objects.** Handles will appear on the object (see Figure 9-18).

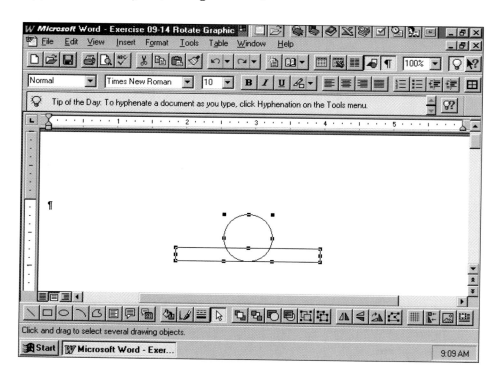

Figure 9-18
These selected drawing objects are ready to be rotated.

3. To flip the drawing objects vertically, click the **Flip Vertical** tool.

4. To return to the original position, click **Undo.**

5. To rotate the drawing objects 90 degrees, click **Rotate Right.**

6. To rotate the drawing objects another 90 degrees, click **Rotate Right.**

7. To rotate the drawing objects another 90 degrees, click **Rotate Right.**

8. Experiment with drawing objects and flipping and rotating them for a few minutes.

9. To hide the Drawing toolbar, click the **Drawing** tool on the Standard toolbar.

10. To save and close the document, click the **Save** tool and then click the **Close** button at the right side of the menu bar.

❖ S U M M A R Y

You have now learned how to insert a picture, size and crop pictures, add borders to a graphic, use a frame to position graphics on the page, insert objects in a document, and use the Drawing toolbar.

Try the exercises on the following pages to test how well you remember what you learned. Don't be afraid to go back and look up answers or procedures, because that will help to reinforce what you learned.

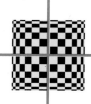

activities

❖ TRUE/FALSE

*On the blank line before each sentence, place a **T** if the statement is true or an **F** if it is false.*

_____ 1. You can use the Picture command on the Insert menu to import a graphic from another application.

_____ 2. When you want to resize a graphic proportionally, drag a middle handle.

_____ 3. You can size a graphic to hide areas you don't want to display.

_____ 4. You can use the Borders tool on the Formatting toolbar to add borders to a graphic.

_____ 5. Word automatically wraps text around a graphic.

_____ 6. Frames appear at the left margin in normal view.

_____ 7. You cannot insert text in a frame.

_____ 8. You can use the ClipArt application to fit text into a variety of shapes, use unusual alignments, and add 3-D effects.

_____ 9. You must be in page layout view or Print Preview to see drawing objects.

_____ 10. When you create a drawing object, it appears in front of text or other drawing objects.

❖ COMPLETION

Fill in the blanks in the following statements.

1. Because Word treats a graphic as a single _____, you must use either a Frame or the Tables feature to position graphics beside text in a document.

2. You can use a(n) _____ when you want to position text in a specific place on a page or when you want other text to flow around it.

3. Hold the _____ key when using the Rectangle and Ellipse tools to create a square or a circle.

4. Hold the _____ key while dragging a drawing object to make a copy of it.

5. Word documents have _____ layers.

6. You can use the _____ tool on the Drawing toolbar to group two or more drawing objects to manipulate them as a single unit.

7. The _____ tool lets you align objects.

8. Hold the _____ key as you drag a drawing object to maintain the original proportion.

9. You can use the _____ tool to rotate a drawing object or group to the right in 90-degree increments.

10. _____ are invisible lines that cover a drawing.

review

Review Exercise 9-1

1. Open file **Review 09-01 Callouts** and add callouts to each of the tools on the Drawing toolbar. Remember, you can use the Drawing tool on the Standard toolbar to display the Drawing toolbar and point to a tool to see the name of the tool.

2. Print the document.

3. Save and close the document.

Review Exercise 9-2

1. Create an invitation to a party to be held at your house at 8 p.m. on Saturday, September 23, 1997.

2. Use the Page Setup command to change the size of the page to 6 by $4\frac{1}{2}$ inches.

3. Use some appropriate ClipArt and WordArt.

4. Print the document.

5. Save and close the document.

Review Exercise 9-3

1. Search online Help for information about the Frame command on the Format menu.

2. Read and print the information.

3. Can you think of an application you might have for the command?

On Your Own

1. Open the **On Your Own 09** file.

2. Print a copy.

3. Add callouts for each of the tools and boxes.

4. Print a copy.

5. Save and close the document.

notes

lesson 10

Working with Long Documents

❖ OBJECTIVES

When you complete this lesson, you will be able to:

1. Use the outline view.

2. Create a cross-reference.

3. Insert a caption.

4. Create footnotes and endnotes.

5. Create an index and a table of contents.

6. Use a master document.

Estimated Time: $1\frac{1}{2}$ hours

❖ INTRODUCTION

Word has many features that you can use to generate quite sophisticated documents and reports. In this lesson you will learn about several of them. Each of these features has many options that are not covered in this book, however. If you see a feature that you think will be helpful to you with your applications, be sure to use the documentation or the online Help program to get information about all of the options available.

You can use Word's outline view (see Figure 10-1) to speed up scrolling, moving text, and changing the order and ranking of topics in a long document.

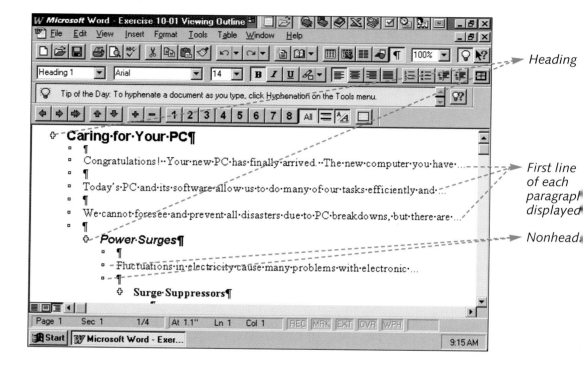

Heading

First line of each paragraph displayed

Nonhead...

**Figure 10-1
Outline view
with headings and
first line of each
paragraph showing.**

When you are in outline view, the Outlining toolbar shown in Figure 10-2 appears at the top of the document. You can refer to Figure 10-2 while doing the outline exercises.

**Figure 10-2
The Outlining
toolbar that
appears at the top
of the document.**

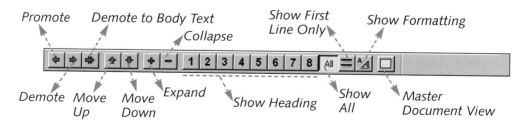

Promote   Demote to Body Text   Show First Line Only   Show Formatting

Collapse

Demote   Move Up   Move Down   Expand   Show Heading   Show All   Master Document View

DISPLAYING A DOCUMENT IN OUTLINE VIEW

When you display a document in outline view, text formatted with a heading style is displayed with a plus sign at its left. Each level of heading is indented under the level above. A heading with no subheadings or text below is displayed with a minus sign. Text that is not formatted with a heading style appears with a small square next to it (see Figure 10-1).

You can use the Show Heading 1 through Show Heading 8 tools to display or hide as many subheadings as you like. The All tool displays all headings and text. You can use the Show First Line Only tool to show only the first line of body text in each paragraph under a heading.

The Collapse tool collapses a heading or hides its subheadings and associated text. The Expand tool expands a heading or displays its subheadings and associated text.

You can use the Show Formatting tool to toggle formatting on and off.

PRINTING A DOCUMENT IN OUTLINE VIEW

When you print a document in outline view, Word prints the headings and body text that are displayed on your screen.

In the following exercise you will display a document in outline view and use tools to view your documents many different ways.

Exercise 10-1

1. To open a document, click the **Open** tool and double-click **Exercise 10-01 Viewing Outline.**

2. To see the layout of the document, click the **Print Preview** tool.

3. To display four pages, click the **Multiple Pages** tool and drag across four pages on the top row. (If four pages do not display on the icon, drag beyond the last page displayed and the box will expand.)

4. To return to the original view, click **Close** on the **Print Preview** toolbar.

5. To display the document in outline view, click the **View** menu and click **Outline.** You now see the entire document. Notice the plus signs to the left of headings and the small squares to the left of body text.

6. To display only the three levels of headings in the document, click the **Show Heading 3** tool.

7. To display all of the document again, click the **All** tool.

8. To display just the first line of body text in each paragraph beneath each heading, click the **Show First Line Only** tool.

9. To display all of the document again, click the **Show First Line Only** tool to toggle it off.

10. To display just two levels of headings, click the **Show Heading 2** tool.

11. To display three levels of headings again, click the **Show Heading 3** tool.

12. To print the outline displaying three levels of headings, click the **Print** tool on the Standard toolbar.

13. To display the text associated with the *Surge Suppressors* heading, select **Surge Supressors** and click the **Expand** tool.

14. To hide the text associated with the *Surge Suppressors* heading, click the **Collapse** tool while *Surge Suppressor* is still selected.

15. To display the outline without formatting, click the **Show Formatting** tool to toggle formatting off.

16. To return to the original formatting, click the **Show Formatting** tool again.

17. To save and close the document, click the **Save** tool and then click the **Close** button at the right side of the menu bar.

MOVING SEGMENTS OF YOUR DOCUMENT

Very often when you are working with a long document, you will want to move large segments of the document from one place to another. Outline view makes that task very easy for you.

❖ Display headings to the level of the heading you want to move.

❖ Select the heading.

❖ Use the Move Up or Move Down tool or drag to move.

The associated subheadings and text move with the heading automatically.

PROMOTING AND DEMOTING HEADINGS

You can use the Promote, Demote, and Demote to Body Text tools to promote headings and their subheadings and body text to higher levels, to demote them to lower heading levels, or to demote them to body text. *Body text* refers to paragraphs of text beneath the headings and subheadings in a document.

In this exercise you will display three levels of headings (see Figure 10-3) and move segments of the document from place to place. You will then promote and demote headings.

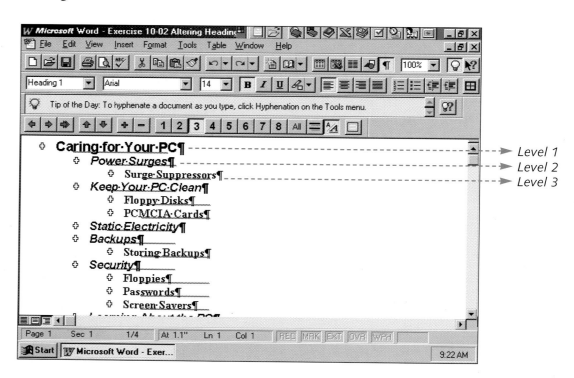

Figure 10-3
Outline view showing three levels of headings.

Exercise 10-2

1. To open a document, click the **Open** tool and double-click **Exercise 10-02 Altering Heading Levels.**

2. To switch to outline view, click the **Outline View** button on the left side of the horizontal scroll bar.

3. To display three levels of headings, click the **Show Level 3** tool.

4. To move the *Passwords* heading and its associated text ahead of the *Floppies* segment, select **Passwords** and click the **Move Up** tool.

5. To move *Security* and all of its subheadings and associated text ahead of *Power Surges*, click the **Show Heading 2** tool, point to the plus sign to the left of *Security* until you see the crossed arrows, drag to *Power Surges*, and release.

6. To deselect *Security*, click the insertion point in white space.

7. To see the result of the move, click the **Normal View** button on the horizontal scroll bar.

8. To see that the *Security* heading with all of its subheadings and associated text did move up before *Power Surges*, scroll through the document.

9. To return to outline view, click the **Outline View** tool on the horizontal scroll bar.

10. To display all the heading levels in the document, click the **Show Heading 3** tool.

11. To move the *Passwords* heading below *Screen Savers*, select **Passwords** (you may have to scroll up through the document to see *Passwords*) and click the **Move Down** tool twice.

12. To promote *Passwords* to a level 2 heading, click the **Promote** tool.

13. To demote *Passwords* to a level 3 heading, click the **Demote** tool.

14. Experiment for a few minutes with displaying different heading levels and moving heading segments from place to place in the document.

15. To save and close the document, click the **Save** tool and then click the **Close** button at the right side of the menu bar.

❖ CREATING CROSS-REFERENCES

A cross-reference tells the reader where additional information on a topic is located either in the same document or in another document. You can also create cross-references to footnotes, endnotes, and captions created by Word or to items marked with bookmarks.

To create a cross-reference:

✤ Type the introductory text for the cross-reference direction in the document, including the opening quotation mark (for example, See ").

✤ Use the Cross-reference command on the Insert menu to display the dialog box where you designate the reference (see Figure 10-4).

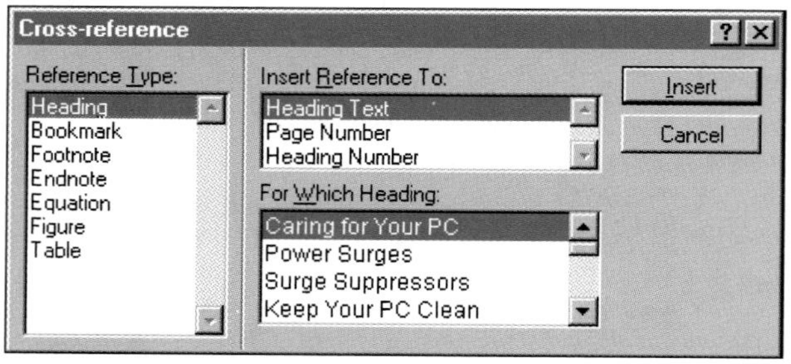

Figure 10-4
The Cross-reference dialog box where you designate the references.

In this exercise you will create a cross-reference from the sentence in the first paragraph of body text about using PC applications to a heading in the same document, *Learning About the PC*. You will then add another cross-reference to display the page number for the heading.

Exercise 10-3

1. To open a document, click the **Open** tool and double-click **Exercise 10-03 Creating Cross References.**

2. To begin entering the cross-reference, position the insertion point in the first paragraph of body text just before the word *You* at the beginning of the last sentence. Type (**See** and a *space,* click the **Insert** menu, and click **Cross-reference.** Click **Heading** in the Reference Type box, click **Heading Text** in the Insert Reference To box, scroll down and click **Learning About the PC** in the For Which Heading box, and click the **Insert** command button.

3. To add the page number to the cross-reference, click the insertion point after the words ***Learning About the PC*** that Word just entered, type a *space* followed by **on page** and then another *space.* In the Cross-reference dialog box, click **Page Number** in the Insert Reference To box, click **Learning About the PC** in the For Which Heading box, and click **Insert.**

4. To close the dialog box, click **Close.**

5. To finish the text for the reference, type **.)** and **two spaces.**

6. To display the field codes Word entered for the cross-references, hold **Alt** and press **F9**. Notice the codes Word entered so the heading name and page number could be added to the document automatically.

7. To turn field codes off, hold **Alt** and press **F9** again.

8. To save and close the document, click the **Save** tool and then click the **Close** button at the right side of the menu bar.

❖ INSERTING CAPTIONS

You can use the Caption command on the Insert menu to add numbered captions to figures, tables, and other items as you insert them. The figure number you see with each of the screen captures in this book is a caption. You can use the AutoCaption feature in the Caption dialog box shown in Figure 10-5 to automatically add a label and a number to each item as you insert it.

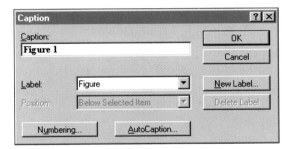

Figure 10-5
Use the Caption dialog box to automatically add a label and a number to figures.

In this exercise you will make copies of Word windows and place them in a document. (You can copy a window to the Clipboard by pressing **Print Screen** at the upper right on your keyboard. You can copy just the active Word window to the Clipboard by holding **Alt** and pressing **Print Screen**.) You will use the Caption command to have Word automatically add the captions.

Exercise 10-4

1. To create a new document, click the **New** tool.

2. To set up for the AutoCaption, click the **Insert** menu and **Caption.** Click **AutoCaption** and then click **Microsoft Word Picture,** click **Figure** in the Use Label box, click **Below Item** in the Position box, and click **OK.**

3. To capture the entire Word window and put it in the Clipboard, press **Print Screen**.

4. To enter the picture in your document, click the **Edit** menu and click **Paste.** Scroll to the end of the graphic and notice the Figure 1 caption at the bottom of the screen capture.

5. To move down on the page, hold **Ctrl** and press **End** and then **Enter** twice.

6. To capture a dialog box (the active window), click the **Insert** menu, click **Caption,** and hold **Alt** and press **Print Screen**.

7. To close the dialog box, click **Cancel.**

8. To enter the picture in your document, click the **Edit** menu and click **Paste.** Notice once again your picture is labeled with a consecutive number.

9. To print the document, click the **Print** tool.

10. To save and close the document, click the **Save** tool and then click the **Close** button at the right side of the menu bar.

❖ INSERTING FOOTNOTES AND ENDNOTES

You can use the Footnote command on the Insert menu to include both footnotes and endnotes in the same document. Footnotes and endnotes allow you to provide references for, comment on, or explain text in your document. Footnotes print at the bottom of the page. Endnotes print at the end of the document.

Word numbers your footnotes or endnotes for you and renumbers them when you insert or delete notes. You can also change the position of notes on the page, change the numbering format, and set other options.

To insert a footnote:

❖ Position the insertion point where you want the reference mark number.

❖ Choose the Footnote command from the Insert menu.

❖ Make your selections in the Footnote and Endnote dialog box shown in Figure 10-6.

note

Word will automatically renumber the notes if you insert, delete, or move one.

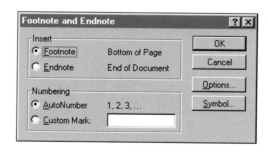

Figure 10-6
The Footnote and Endnote dialog box is used to add footnotes to the bottom of the page and endnotes to the end of the document.

In normal view, a pane opens for you to type the note. In page layout view, you can type the note in its location on the page.

When you want to see a footnote you have entered, double-click the reference mark. In normal view, the notes appear in a pane, as shown in Figure 10-7. In page layout view, the insertion point jumps to the note.

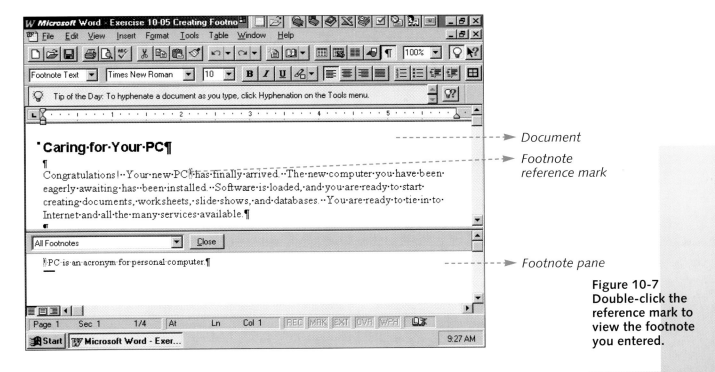

Document

Footnote
reference mark

Footnote pane

Figure 10-7
Double-click the
reference mark to
view the footnote
you entered.

To delete a note:

❖ Select its reference mark.

❖ Press **Delete** or **Backspace**.

To move a note:

❖ Select its reference mark.

❖ Drag it to a new location.

To access the shortcut menu for notes:

❖ Position the insertion point in the note text.

❖ Click the right mouse button.

Exercise 10-5

1. To open a document, click the **Open** tool and double-click **Exercise 10-05 Creating Footnotes.**

2. To be sure you are in the normal view, click the **View** menu and click **Normal.**

3. To enter a footnote to explain *PC* in the first paragraph of body text, position the insertion point after the **C** in *PC*, click the **Insert** menu, click **Footnote,** click **Footnote** and **AutoNumber** if they are not already selected, and click **OK.** At the insertion point in the footnote pane, type **PC is an acronym for personal computer.**

4. To return to the document without closing the Footnotes pane, click anywhere in white space in the Document pane.

5. To enter another footnote, position the insertion point immediately after the last letter in the word *Software* on the second line of body text, click the **Insert** menu, click **Footnote,** and click **OK.** Type **Software consists of application programs that contain instructions for the computer.**

6. To close the Footnote pane, click the **Close** button on the pane.

7. To see the Footnotes in page layout view, click the **View** menu and click **Page Layout.** Scroll to the bottom of the page to see the footnotes.

8. To delete the first footnote, select its reference mark at the beginning of the document (the number **1**) and press (**Delete**). Notice the footnote reference is deleted and notice also the software reference mark is now number 1.

9. Experiment on your own with adding and deleting footnotes and endnotes for a few minutes.

10. To print the document, click the **Print** tool.

11. To save and close the document, click the **Save** tool and then click the **Close** button at the right side of the menu bar.

❖ CREATING AN INDEX

You can use the Index and Tables command on the Insert menu to include an index that gives users page numbers for items they might want to look up in a document.

To mark the text you want as an index entry:

❖ Select the text.

❖ Choose Index and Tables on the Insert menu.

❖ Choose the Mark Index Entry button to display the dialog box shown in Figure 10-8.

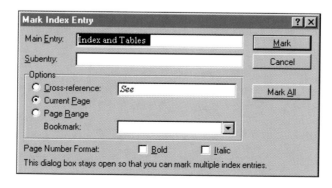

Figure 10-8
The Mark Index Entry dialog box is used to mark text you want as an index entry.

❖ Edit the selected text if necessary.

❖ Choose the Mark command button.

To compile an index from the marked entries:

❖ Position the insertion point where you want the index to begin.

❖ Choose the Index and Tables command from the Insert menu to display the dialog box shown in Figure 10-9.

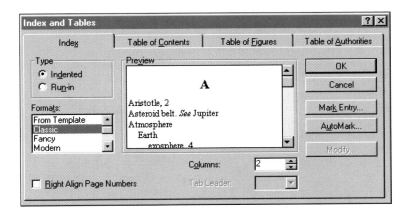

Figure 10-9
The Index and Tables dialog box is used to compile an index from the marked entries.

❖ Choose the type of index and format for the index, the number of columns, and the alignment for the numbers.

❖ Choose OK to enter the index.

To update an index:

❖ Choose Index and Tables on the Insert menu.

❖ Select the Index tab.

❖ Click OK.

❖ Confirm that you want to replace the existing index.

In the following exercise you will mark some entries for an index and compile an index.

Exercise 10-6

1. To open a document, click the **Open** tool and double-click **Exercise 10-06 Indexing.**

2. To display codes if they are not already displayed, click the **Show/Hide** tool.

3. To mark *PC* in the first heading, select **PC** by double-clicking on the word, hold **Alt** and **Shift** and press **X** to access the Mark Index Entry dialog box, and click **Mark All** to mark all occurrences of *PC* throughout the document. Notice the field codes Word enters. You can leave the dialog box open until you finish marking index entries.

4. To mark *Software* (with a capital *S*) in the first text paragraph, double-click the word, click in blank space in the dialog box to activate it, edit *Software* to make the *S* lowercase for the Index, and click **Mark All.** You can use the scroll bars or the arrow keys to move through your document while the dialog box is displayed.

5. To mark the word *software* (it does not begin with a capital letter and therefore was not selected in step 4) on the top line of the next paragraph, select it and click **Mark All.**

6. To mark the word *problems* in the same paragraph, select it and click **Mark All.**

7. To mark the word *files* in the next paragraph, select it and click **Mark All.**

8. To close the dialog box, click its **Close** button.

9. To create an index with those few entries, hold (Ctrl) and press (End) to move to the end of the document, hold (Ctrl) and press (Enter) to insert a page break, click the **Insert** menu, and click **Index and Tables.**

10. To see what the formats look like, click on each and notice the example in the Preview box. Be sure **Indented** is selected in the Type box, **Classic** in the Formats box, and **2** in the Columns box, and click **OK.** Word inserts section breaks and displays the index shown in Figure 10-10.

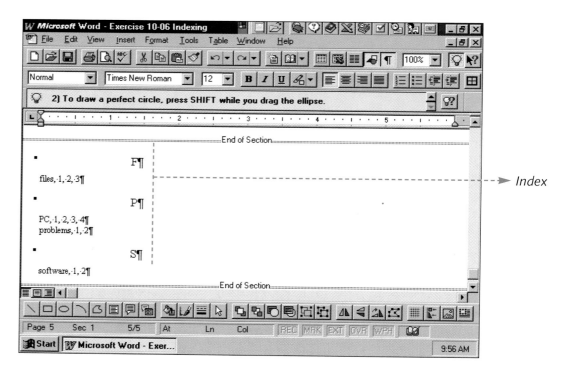

Index

Figure 10-10
The index you
compiled in
Exercise 10-6.

❖ CREATING A TABLE OF CONTENTS

You can use the Index and Tables command on the Insert menu to have Word insert a table of contents, table of figures, or table of authorities (see Figure 10-11). A table of authorities is used in legal documents.

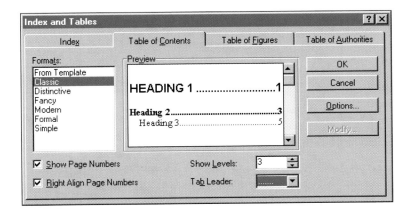

Figure 10-11
Use the Index and Tables dialog box to insert a table of contents, table of figures, or table of authorities.

The easiest way to create a table of contents is to format headings in your document with the Heading 1 through Heading 9 styles and compile the table of contents directly from the styles.

To create a table of contents like the one displayed in Figure 10-12 using built-in headings:

❖ Position the insertion point where you want the table of contents to begin.

❖ Select Index and Tables on the Insert menu.

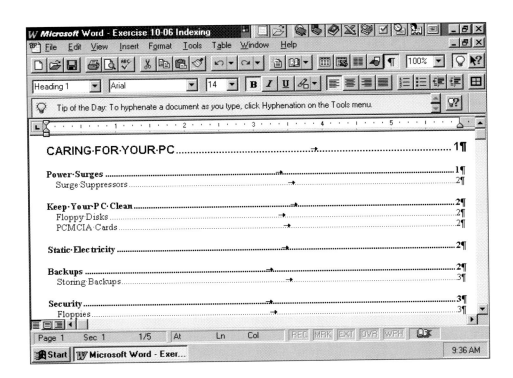

Figure 10-12
A sample table of contents.

note

If you are planning to create an index and other tables in your document, you should create all of those before the table of contents so that they can be included in it.

✦ Make selections about the format for the table.

✦ Click OK.

To update a table of contents:

✦ Position the insertion point in the table of contents.

✦ Press **F9**.

✦ Select Update Page Numbers Only or Update Entire Table.

✦ Click OK.

Exercise 10-7

1. To create the table of contents at the beginning of the document, hold **Ctrl** and press **Home**, click the **Insert** menu, click **Index and Tables,** and click the **Table of Contents** tab.

2. To be sure your table looks like the one shown, be sure **Classic** is selected and that **Show Page Numbers, Right Align Page Numbers,** and **Show Levels 3** are the settings. Also click the drop-down button to open the **Tab Leader** list and select the **dotted line.** Click **OK.**

3. To enter a section break before the first heading in the document, click the **Insert** menu, click **Break,** click **Next Page,** and click **OK.**

4. To hide nonprinting marks, click the **Show/Hide** tool.

5. To preview the document, click the **Print Preview** tool, click the **Multiple Pages** tool, drag over **six pages,** and release.

6. To print the document, click the **Print** tool.

7. To save and close the document, click the **Save** tool and then click the **Close** button at the right side of the menu bar.

✦ USING A MASTER DOCUMENT

Long documents are often awkward and slow to work with, especially when the auto-save and pagination features are at work. You can use a master document to make it easier to work with long documents. A *master document* is a Word document that takes some or all of its contents from one or more documents.

By working with a series of smaller documents and organizing them in a master document, you can save a lot of time. A master document also allows you to create cross-references between subdocuments and to generate tables of contents and indexes for long documents.

With a master document, you can work either with the entire group of subdocuments or with any individual subdocument.

Any Word document can be either a master document or a subdocument.

note

A master document is helpful if several people are working on different parts of a document. Put all the parts together in a master document when it comes time to move parts of one document into another or to print the document.

You use the Master Document command on the View menu or the Master Document tool on the Outline toolbar to access the master document. You can move between master document view, shown in Figure 10-13, and normal or page layout view at will.

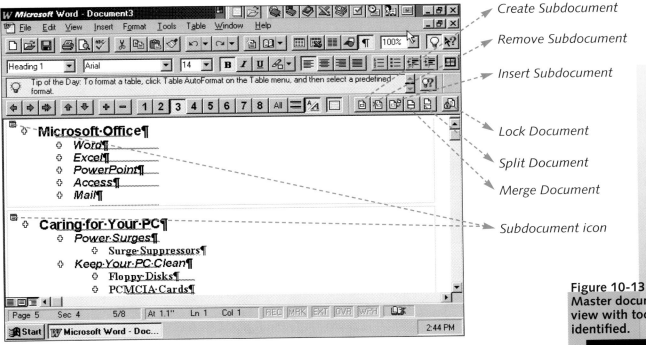

Create Subdocument

Remove Subdocument

Insert Subdocument

Lock Document

Split Document

Merge Document

Subdocument icon

Figure 10-13
Master document view with tools identified.

You can create a master document in one of three ways:

❖ You can set up a new master document by typing an outline in master document view.

or

❖ You can convert an existing long document into a master document and create subdocuments.

or

❖ You can combine several Word documents to make a new master document.

To work with a subdocument:

❖ Open a subdocument from within a master document by double-clicking its subdocument icon.

❖ Edit the subdocument in its own document window while the master document remains open.

❖ Save and close the subdocument the same way you would any other document.

As with the outline view, you can print the document from the master document view with as many levels of headings and body text as you have displayed on the screen.

In this exercise you will combine two Word documents to make a new master document.

note

A master document is limited to 80 subdocuments, and the total size of a master document cannot exceed 32 MB (excluding graphics).

note

Be sure you do not rename subdocuments or change their drives or directories unless you do so from wihin the master document.

Exercise 10-8

1. To create a new file, click the **New** tool.

2. To display master document view, click the **View** menu and **Master Document.**

3. To add the first subdocument to the master document, click the **Insert Subdocument** tool and double-click **Exercise 10-08 Master Document 1.** Notice Word entered the document and put a section break before and after the subdocument.

4. To add the second document, hold (**Ctrl**) and press (**End**) to move to the end of the document, click the **Insert Subdocument** tool, and double-click **Exercise 10-08 Master Document 2.**

5. To display three levels of headings, click the **Show Level 3** tool.

6. To display the document in normal view, click the **View** menu and **Normal.**

7. To see the section breaks Word inserted on each side of a subdocument, scroll through the document.

8. To return to master document view, click the **View** menu and **Master Document.**

9. To open a subdocument in its own window while the master document remains open, double-click the subdocument icon for the second document.

10. To close the subdocument, click the **File** menu and **Close.**

11. To print the outline that appears on the screen, click the **Print** tool on the Standard toolbar.

12. To save and close the master document, click the **Save** tool, type **Exercise 10-08 Combined Document,** click **Save,** and click the **Close** button at the right side of the menu bar.

❖ SUMMARY

You have now learned how to use the outline view, create a cross-reference, insert a caption, create footnotes or endnotes, create an index, create a table of contents, and use a master document.

Try the exercises on the following pages to test how well you remember what you learned. Don't be afraid to go back and look up the answers, because that will help to reinforce what you learned.

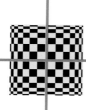

activities

❖ TRUE/FALSE

*On the blank line before each sentence, place a **T** if the statement is true or an **F** if it is false.*

_____ 1. When you are in outline view, you can see only the headings in a document.

_____ 2. When you print a document in outline view, it prints exactly as it would in normal view.

_____ 3. You cannot create cross-references to another document in normal view.

_____ 4. Word can automatically add numbered captions to pictures you insert in your documents.

_____ 5. You can copy a Windows screen to the Clipboard by pressing (Print Screen).

_____ 6. You can have both footnotes and endnotes in the same document.

_____ 7. In page layout view, Word displays footnotes in a separate pane.

_____ 8. The easiest way to create a table of contents is to format your document with Heading 1 through Heading 9 styles and compile the table of contents directly from the styles.

_____ 9. A master document is limited to 32 files.

_____ 10. A master document lets you create cross-references between subdocuments.

❖ COMPLETION

Fill in the blanks in the following statements.

1. When you are in outline view, text formatted with a(n) _____ style is displayed with either a plus or a minus sign.

2. In outline view, you can use the _____ tool to toggle formatting on and off.

3. You can use the _____ tool in outline view to move headings to higher levels.

4. You can create a(n) _____ to another document if you are using a master document.

5. You can add numbered _____ to Word tables you insert in your document.

6. When you want to see a footnote in normal view, _____ its reference mark.

7. You can delete a footnote by selecting its _____ and pressing (Delete).

8. Before you create a(n) _____, you should create the index and all other tables for your document.

9. You can use a(n) _____ to work with a group of documents and print them as one document.

10. You can open a(n) _____ from within a master document while the master document remains open.

review

Review Exercise 10-1

1. Open **Review 10-01 Print Outline**.

2. Print the document in outline format with three heading levels displayed.

3. Save and close the document.

Review Exercise 10-2

1. Open **Review 10-02 Index**.

2. Compile an index and a table of contents. Be sure the index and table of contents are on separate pages.

3. Add a title to the table of contents page (Table of Contents) and to the index page (Index).

4. Print, save, and close the document.

Review Exercise 10-3

1. Use online Help to find information about using outline view from the beginning to type a document.

2. Read the information and print it.

Review Exercise 10-4

1. Use online Help to find information about changing the format of footnotes.

2. Read the information and print it.

On Your Own

You are the secretary of a homeowners' association in a resort area. You need to keep homeowners informed about the island and their neighborhood.

1. Open the **On Your Own 10** file and print it.

2. Use the Newsletter Wizard to create a modern, three-column, one-page newsletter. The name for the newsletter is *River Club News*. Use Fancy First Letters and the Date.

3. When Word displays the newsletter, replace the date with *December 1997*. Replace the graphic with the **Summer** file in the **Clipart** folder.

4. Paste the headings and text from the **On Your Own 10** file one subject at a time until the newsletter has a professional look.

5. Delete the caption box below the graphic. Also delete the topic boxes.

6. Save the newsletter.

Remember to use the Undo tool if things go awry.

Have fun! Good luck!

lesson 11

Working with Forms

❖ OBJECTIVES

When you complete this lesson, you will be able to:

1. Use form fields.

2. Create a form template.

3. Protect a form.

4. Modify a form.

5. Fill in an online form.

6. Share a form template with other users.

Estimated Time: 1 hour

❖ INTRODUCTION

Forms used to be very difficult to produce using word processing programs. Now, however, you can combine many of Word's features (tables, borders and shading, and graphic objects) with form fields to produce professional online forms.

You can use the Form Field command on the Insert menu or the Forms toolbar to create the fields that users fill in on forms. Online forms can include form fields for text, check boxes, and even drop-down lists.

When you create a form, you use a template. The template contains the standard text, graphics, and fields that need to be filled in. You can put a form field in the middle of text, in a table cell, or in a frame. You can edit or modify the templates.

When you protect the form, the user can enter information only in form fields or sections from which you have removed protection.

❖ USING FORM FIELDS

With form fields, you can control the data entered in a specific field, specify macros that run when the insertion point enters a field, or create help messages that are displayed for each form field.

As you can see in the Form Field dialog box shown in Figure 11-1, there are three different kinds of form fields:

1. Text form fields

2. Check box form fields

3. Drop-down form fields

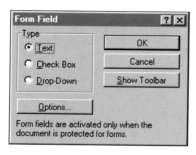

Figure 11-1
The Form Field dialog box showing the three kinds of fields: text, check box, and drop-down.

In the Text Form Field Options dialog box shown in Figure 11-2, there are six kinds of text form fields from which to choose:

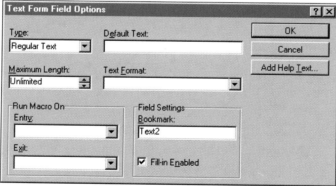

Figure 11-2
In the Text Form Field Options dialog box, you can choose the type of field.

You can click the drop-down arrow in the Type box on the Text Form Field Options dialog box to display the six text form fields.

❖ *Regular Text* form fields can be text, numbers, or symbols.

❖ *Number* form fields are for fields that require a numeric entry.

❖ *Date* form fields are for fields that require a date entry.

❖ *Current Date* form fields supply the current date.

❖ *Current Time* form fields supply the current time.

❖ *Calculation* form fields perform a calculation.

You can also specify the length of what can be entered in a field, default text to be displayed in the field, text formatting, macros, and help text.

You can use the Toolbars command on the View menu or the Form Fields command on the Insert menu to display the Forms toolbar, shown in Figure 11-3.

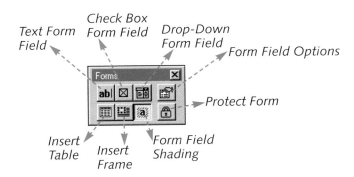

Text Form Field

Check Box Form Field

Drop-Down Form Field

Form Field Options

Protect Form

Insert Table

Insert Frame

Form Field Shading

Figure 11-3
Use the Toolbars command on the View menu or the Form Field command on the Insert menu to display the Forms toolbar.

In this lesson you will enter form fields in a document that has been set up for a form. The form you will work with was created as a regular document rather than a template. When you finish entering the form fields, you will save the document as a template.

Exercise 11-1

1. To open a document, click the **Open** tool and double-click **Exercise 11-01 Using Form Fields.**

2. To turn off nonprinting marks if they are on, click the **Show/Hide** tool.

3. To display the Forms toolbar, click the **View** menu, click **Toolbars,** click **Forms,** and click **OK.**

4. To begin entering the first form field, position the insertion point in the cell to the right of the *Name* cell.

5. To enter a text form field, click the **Insert** menu, click **Form Field,** click **Text,** and click **Options.** Select **Regular Text** in the Type box, **Unlimited** in the Maximum Length box, and **Fill-In Enabled.** Click **OK**. Notice the shading in the cell to signal the field.

6. To enter a drop-down form field for the *Division,* press ⬇, and click the **Drop-Down Form Field** tool.

7. To enter options in the drop-down form field, click the **Form Field Options** tool, type **Marketing,** click **Add,** type **Research & Development,** click **Add,** type **Central Services,** click **Add,** and click **OK.** The first option is displayed. The drop-down button is not displayed until the user clicks the field when filling in a form.

8. To add a text field for *Purpose,* press ⬇, click the **Text Form Field** tool, click the **Form Field Options** tool, change the maximum length to **50,**

click the **Add Help Text** button, click the **Status Bar** tab, click **Type Your Own,** type **You are limited to 50 characters,** and click **OK** twice.

9. To enter a form field for the *Date Needed,* press ⊕, click **Text Form Field** tool, click the **Form Field Options** tool, click **Date** in the Type drop-down list, and click **OK.**

10. To enter a form field for the *No. of Days,* press ⊕, click the **Text Form Field** tool, click the **Form Field Options** tool, click **Number** in the Type drop-down list, change Maximum Length to **2,** and click **OK.**

11. To enter a form field for the car *Size,* press ⊕, click the **Drop-Down Form Field** tool, click the **Form Field Options** tool, type **SubCompact,** click **Add,** type **Compact,** click **Add,** type **MidSize,** click **Add,** and click **OK.**

12. To enter a form field for the telephone *Extension,* press ⊕, click the **Text Form Field** tool, click the **Form Field Options** tool, click **Number** in the Type box, change the Maximum Length box to **4,** and click **OK.**

13. To enter a check box form field for *Others In Car,* press ⊕ and click the **Check Box Form Field** tool.

14. To turn off the toolbar, click the **View** menu, click **Toolbars,** click **Forms Toolbar,** click **OK.**

❖ SAVING AN ONLINE FORM AS A TEMPLATE

You must save an online form as a template. When users need to use the form, they base a document on the template. When you are creating a form from scratch, you can create a new template using the New command on the File menu. Word automatically saves the form as a template. You can also create the form in a document and then use the Save As command to save the document as a template.

❖ PROTECTING A FORM

Use the Protect Document command on the Tools menu to protect your form (see Figure 11-4). Once you protect the document, only fields or sections you authorize can be accessed by a user.

Figure 11-4 The Protect Document dialog box protects documents, fields, or sections of a document.

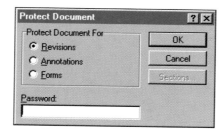

You can enter a password when you protect your form so only those who know the password can change the template. If you want to leave areas of the document unprotected, use the Sections feature.

When the document is protected,

- ✧ Word activates Form Fields.

- ✧ Word displays field results instead of field codes.

- ✧ The insertion point moves only into form fields and unprotected sections.

- ✧ You cannot select the entire document.

- ✧ You cannot alter table column width.

- ✧ Some menu commands are not available.

- ✧ Some commands can be used only in form fields and unprotected sections.

- ✧ Entry macros, exit macros, and form field Help are activated.

❖ MODIFYING A FORM

To edit a form after it has been created and protected, you must first use the Unprotect command on the Tools menu.

USING THE TEMPLATE TO PRODUCE A FORM

Whenever you want to fill in a form using the template, use the New command on the File menu to create a new document based on the template you created and saved. Your template is stored with the other Word templates and appears on the list of templates.

If you use preprinted forms, you can choose to print the data only.

SHARING THE FORM TEMPLATE WITH OTHER USERS

If the form is distributed to other users, make sure any macros or AutoText entries you used are stored in the form template.

Exercise 11-2

1. To protect the form, click the **Tools** menu, click **Protect Document,** click **Forms,** and click **OK.**

2. To test how the protection works, try to click the I-beam in the cells on the left side of the table. To move from field to field, either click the new field or press (Tab).

3. To save the form as a template, click the **File** menu, click **Save As,** click the **Save File as Type** drop-down arrow, click **Document Template** (the Template Directory is automatically selected), enter *your initials* in the Document name box, and click **Save.**

4. To close the template, click the **File** menu and **Close.**

5. To create a document based on your template, click the **File** menu and **New,** click the template with *(your initials)* in the Template list, and click **OK.**

6. To fill in the various fields, press ⟨Tab⟩ to reach each one. Try to enter alphabetic characters or more than four digits in the Extension field to see what happens.

7. To print the form, click the **Print** tool when you have entered all information.

8. To close the document, click the **File** menu and click **Close.** Respond **No** when asked to save changes.

❖ SUMMARY

You have now learned how to use form fields, create a template, protect a template, and fill in an online form.

Try the exercises on the following pages to test how well you remember what you learned. Don't be afraid to go back and look up the answers, because that will help to reinforce what you learned.

activities

❖ TRUE/FALSE

On the blank line before each sentence, place a **T** *if the statement is true or an* **F** *if it is false.*

_____ 1. You cannot put a form field in the middle of a text paragraph.

_____ 2. When you protect a form, users cannot make the table columns wider.

_____ 3. When you set up a drop-down form field, the user can add different information in that field if he or she needs to.

_____ 4. Each time a user creates a form based on the protected template, a new, untitled document is created.

_____ 5. You protect the template from change by adding a password from the Options dialog box in the Save As command.

❖ COMPLETION

Fill in the blanks in the following statements.

1. You can create a(n) _____ form field where the user can choose among several options.

2. You can use a(n) _____ form field for a yes or no response.

3. You can use a(n) _____ form field for a response requiring a number.

4. You can use the _____ command on the _____ menu to prevent users from changing the form.

5. You must save your form as a(n) _____.

review

Review Exercise 11-1

1. Open the document **Review Exercise 11-01 Create Form.**

2. Create form fields for all of the fill-in entries.

3. Add WordArt to display the company name.

4. Protect and save the document as a template named **Balloons and Beyond** and then close the template file.

5. Create a document using the form, fill in the fields, and print the document.

6. Save and close the document.

Review Exercise 11-2

1. Search online Help to find information about removing an item from a drop-down form field.

2. Read and print the information.

Review Exercise 11-3

1. Open the template you saved in Review Exercise 11-1 *(Balloons and Beyond)*.

2. Change the name *Balloons and Beyond* to *Let's Party*.

3. Fill in a form using the revised name, and print the form.

4. Save and close the document and template.

On Your Own

1. Reopen the template you created in Review Exercise 11-1.

2. Use frames, graphics, WordArt, Tables, or any other Word feature you can think of to make the form a work of art and a marketing tool.

3. Save the revised template as **Balloons and Beyond 2.**

4. Create a document using the form, fill in the fields, and print the document.

5. Save and close the document.

Good luck! Have fun! Enjoy Word!

index

index

index

index

index

quick reference card
Microsoft® Word for Windows 95 QuickTorial
Patricia Murphy

getting help

Access Online Help	F1

moving the insertion point

Right, Left, Down, or Up	→ ← ↓ ↑
One Screen Down	Page Down
One Screen Up	Page Up
Beginning of Line	Home
End of Line	End
Beginning of Document	Ctrl + Home
End of Document	Ctrl + End
Beginning of Current Paragraph	Ctrl + ↑
Beginning of Next Paragraph	Ctrl + ↓
Top of Screen	Ctrl + Page Up
Bottom of Screen	Ctrl + Page Down

editing

Delete One Character to Left	Backspace
Delete One Character to Right	Delete
Delete One Word to Left	Ctrl + Backspace
Delete One Word to the Right	Ctrl + Delete
Undo	Ctrl + Z
Repeat	Ctrl + Y

formatting

character

Bold	Ctrl + B
Italic	Ctrl + I
Underline	Ctrl + U
Plain Text	Ctrl + Shift + Z

paragraph

Single-Space Lines	Ctrl + 1
Set 1.5-Line Spacing	Ctrl + 5
Double-Space Lines	Ctrl + 2
Left Align	Ctrl + L
Center	Ctrl + E
Right Align	Ctrl + R
Justify	Ctrl + J
Indent Paragraph from Left	Ctrl + M
Make Hanging Indent	Ctrl + T
Remove Paragraph Formatting	Ctrl + Q
Show Nonprinting Characters	Ctrl + Shift + *

SOUTH-WESTERN EDUCATIONAL PUBLISHING

menu shortcut keys

file

New	Ctrl + N
Open	Ctrl + O *or* Ctrl + F12
Close	Ctrl + W
Save	Ctrl + S *or* Shift + F2
Save As	F12
Print Preview	Ctrl + F2
Print	Ctrl + P *or* Ctrl + Shift + F12
Exit	Alt + F4

edit

Clear	Delete
Cut	Ctrl + X
Copy	Ctrl + C
Paste	Ctrl + V
Select All	Ctrl + A
Find	Ctrl + F
Replace	Ctrl + H
Go To	Ctrl + G *or* F5
Repeat Last Action	F4

view

Normal	Alt + Ctrl + N
Outline	Alt + Ctrl + O
Page Layout	Alt + Ctrl + P

insert

Page Numbers	Alt + Shift + P
Date and Time	Alt + Shift + D
Footnote	Alt + Ctrl + F
Endnote	Alt + Ctrl + E

format

Font	Ctrl + D
Change Case	Shift + F3
AutoFormat	Ctrl + K

tools

Spelling	F7
Thesaurus	Shift + F7

table

Select Table	Alt + 5 (on number pad)

window

Close Active Window	Ctrl + F4
New Window	Ctrl + N
Split Window	Alt + Ctrl + S
Go to Next Pane	F6
Go to Previous Pane	Shift + F6
Go to Next Window	Ctrl + F6
Go to Previous Window	Ctrl + Shift + F6